D0405971

WHEN THE LAMPS WENT OUT

WHEN THE LAMPS WENT OUT

From Home Front to Battle Front:
Reporting the Great War 1914–1918

Compiled and edited by Nigel Fountain
With a foreword by Kate Adie

First published in 2014
by Guardian Books,
Kings Place, 90 York Way, London N1 9GU
and Faber and Faber Ltd,
Bloomsbury House, 74–77 Great Russell Street, London WC1B 3DA

A CIP record for this book is available from the British Library

ISBN 978-1783-35041-4

Design and set by seagulls.net
Printed in England by CPI Group (UK) Ltd, Croydon CR0 4YY

FSC
www.fsc.org
MIX
Paper from
responsible sources
FSC® C008047

2 4 6 8 10 9 7 5 3 1

CONTENTS

'The lamps are going out all over Europe; we shall not see them lit again in our life-time.'

Sir Edward Grey, British foreign secretary, 3 August 1914

FOREWORD

Why read a newspaper in wartime? Everyone knows there is censorship; few believe that the whole truth is to be found in any paper.

Nevertheless, during the first world war, newspapers were grabbed from the paperboys' hands, shared during breaks in 12-hour shifts, ironed flat and crisp in the grandest households, and read by millions who felt the 'need to know' during a war that was consuming the nation. This desire to know, however grim the news might be, meant national and local papers were eagerly devoured in the era before radio and television.

There was a wide range of print media available during the war, from the stately prose of *The Times* to the shouting headlines of the popular press. The *Manchester Guardian*, as the paper was then known, steered its own course among them.

Why should we return to contemporary reports of a war which has now been analysed, and criticised so often and at such great length? Because the voice of the witness is the most compelling. It may not be the entire story – the vantage point may be obscure, the emotions of hope or patriotism may colour the words – but it is a human eye in the storm. What is immediately written down carries a strength that hindsight and reflection might challenge, but that is still potent and sincere.

Perhaps one might add that the style of the era, the measured sentences, add punch to the despatches, alongside the restrained touches of emotion from the correspondent.

And a newspaper also covers the world in which the readers lived. These extracts give us glimpses of the music hall, the countryside in winter, the grumpy response to women taxi drivers in London, the anti-German riots, the nationwide fascination with Charlie Chaplin at 'the kinema'. It connects the readers to huge world events, plucking local names and units out of the fog of battle: 'the Yorkshire lads', 'the Highlanders of the 51st'.

Inevitably, the whole truth is not there, especially where the battlefield is concerned. There can only be glimpses of combat, and generalisations about the numberless attacks and the months of bombardments. Rigorous censorship and correspondents' reticence – often to spare the people at home more horror – combined to deliver what is now seen by many as a limited narrative of the war.

That it was actually reported at all was something of a victory, with many of the military initially despising the very idea of operations being witnessed by the press. 'After all,' as one commander remarked, 'you are only writing for Mary Ann in the kitchen.' But even with a handful of men to cover the vast battle zone in Europe, and a sprinkling of correspondents trying to report the action from Mesopotamia to east Africa, something special was achieved, especially for today's reader. From the paper's pages, the gargantuan war machine emerges, full of ordinary men propelled into an unfamiliar world. They are at times relentlessly cheerful and patriotic, occasionally downhearted – but they always leave the correspondent wondering at their doggedness. The chirpy quotes of soldiers, quoted by the almost disbelieving reporter who can see only mud and mangled bodies, show a determined devotion to the cause amidst a landscape from hell. And they can result in a reporter's dilemma. Then, as now, the issue is the same. Is it your duty to report only the horror – or would that be cruelty to readers desperate for any scrap of information which might console them?

The other universal issue all war reporters face is the accompanying 'minder' at one's elbow. Today's media conduct a never-ending battle with military minders, public relations-mad ministers and obstructive officials. Technology may have brought about the notion of 'live' reporting, but in actuality it is often far from the action. Risk-aversion and insurance worries have added to the diffidence of many editors at home. But nothing is new. A hundred years ago there was constant surveillance of the press on the battlefield – and many attempts to keep them away from it. Statistics were hard to come by and the scale of the conflict ruled out instant accuracy. Editors were assailed by politicians and hemmed in by government demands.

Compared with the multinational horde which heads for conflict these days, the British wartime press of 1915 had to be content with precisely five officially accredited 'scribblers'. Even so, the stories read vividly, and the reality of the situation can be discovered in and between the lines. The eyewitness account, fresh and forthright, mattered then – and still matters now.

The confidence and convictions of the paper itself also mattered and stories about conscientious objectors, women's rights and political dissent prove to us that the nation was no single mass of sheep-brained citizens. Reports on pacifism and radical politics dispel the lazy notion that everyone was riding the warhorse. It was difficult to be the voice that did not join in the marching song – a difficulty that is true of many conflicts still today.

We read these stories with a myriad of other sources now available to us. The private diaries, the scholars' discoveries, and many opinions as to why the war was fought and to what end. But the wartime newspaper brings us closer. The people who wrote for it were not detached. The editorials reflected hopes as well as considered opinion – and were sometimes proved hopelessly adrift in their predictions. But they are key to what was on the minds of many, and what preoccupied quiet people as they wondered where and when it would all end.

The newspaper reminds us that life went on, that there were other momentous events in the wider world: the Easter Rising in Ireland, the end of the tsarist monarchy in Russia. Meanwhile, at home, women were causing social disquiet by assuming the post of 'lady chauffeur' and theatre-goers were vexed about whether they should wear full evening dress.

The wartime *Guardian* reminds us that nearly five years of life were not a monotone picture of conflict. Nor were they a unanimous cheer for victory. The eyewitnesses reported what they saw – and the reality they conveyed matters to us today.

Kate Adie
February 2014

INTRODUCTION

As a child I was taken to Winchester Cathedral, where I contemplated the great West Window. I was told that during the English civil war, Roundheads had shattered the glass, which had once depicted order and majesty, captured in light. When, during the Restoration, the window was reassembled, no attempt was made to recreate its content. Instead, the shards of stained glass were collected into a random mosaic. The Roundheads, it was suggested to me, were a pretty bad lot. On reflection, I thought that they had to have been pretty serious about religion, in their way, to have done such a thing. There was method, and meaning, in their apparent madness.

This is a book about fragments from another time; from an era seen by many, then, as well established in its order and majesty, but which was to conclude with the shattering of everything. It is about reading a great newspaper, based in one of the world's most famous industrial cities, during an inexplicable global cataclysm. It is about how a world which thought of itself as 'modern', within which optimists believed humanity could be liberated, became instead a killing machine. Up until the very moment that war broke out, people – from the Kaiser to working men and women writing angry letters to the *Manchester Guardian* – had difficulty conceiving what was happening around them. As horror followed horror, the difficulty persisted. We are still sifting those fragments a hundred years later.

To read the *Manchester Guardian* from a century ago is to be intrigued by resonances. Then, as now, it was just one voice on the news-stands where other parts of the chorus offered bellicosity, tub-thumping, jingoism, measured conservatism, lofty conservatism, batty ideas and, maybe, still small voices of calm. But the *Manchester Guardian* was different: it was proudly provincial and yet, then as now, renowned throughout the world, with an editor, CP Scott, who had already been in his chair for 42 years (he was to remain there for another 15). Its readers were the liberal upper and middle classes, non-conformists, radicals, socialists, working men and women, suffragists and suffragettes, pacifists. Despite the various serious crises of pre-war times, these were people who – like the newspaper – were committed to the idea of progress. To revisit what they were reading then is humbling, and on occasions uplifting. It is also curious to find all those years ago – alongside an almost unchanged 'Country Diary' – that distinctive *Guardian* tone: amused, exasperated, slightly detached (or smug and exasperating, as some suggest).

This is not a history of the first world war; indeed, entire theatres of the conflict do not feature. What it attempts to do is to provide an insight into what a part of British society was reading about, and thinking, during those times. It does not deal with the vast war efforts of the other combatant nations, save in passing, and because journalism catches the moment at the moment, the coverage can sometimes seem skewed and even wrong – the heavy hand of the censor was, after all, almost ever present. There is boundless – if short-lived – enthusiasm for the Russian revolution, annual optimism for the year ahead, news of devastated villages wrested from the enemy, which never translate into final victory – until, in the summer of 1918, they begin to do so. And to read often superbly written stories from the western front and Mesopotamia, from railway terminals and meeting halls, from the mountains of Italy and the hills of Sussex, is to receive signals from a lost world.

I do not subscribe to the flaccid, smug, 'lions-and-donkeys' vision of the warriors as noble tommies and reckless, stupid generals with silly moustaches. I am sure there were plenty of both, as there are in all wars, but what emerged from the pages of the *Manchester Guardian* was a picture of a process that – like the mud of the Somme, a creation of nature plus high explosive – trapped everybody from Herbert Asquith, Prince Lichnowsky, Mrs Pankhurst, David Lloyd George, Countess Markievicz, Woodrow Wilson and Vladimir Lenin to the most humble common soldier.

And then there is the rest of humanity. One item in the newspaper's 'Our London Correspondence' will not leave me. It concerns a youth seen in 1915 on London's Euston Road who, 'out of sheer love of art' performed his own Charlie Chaplin routine 'before a large and critical audience'. Then, as always, some people had their priorities right.

Nigel Fountain

CHAPTER 1

BEFORE

From 1911 onwards, relations between the great powers were fraught, and were accompanied by an arms race that pitted the dominant Royal Navy against the growing German navy, and the armies of the German and Austro-Hungarian empires against those of the French Republic and the despotic Russian empire. But there were few indications in January 1914 of worsening tensions – if anything, there were signs of the reverse. Wars in the Balkans had ended; internationally, it was a period of calm. But within the United Kingdom, three domestic crises confronted Prime Minister Herbert Asquith's Liberal government: Irish home rule, working class militancy and votes for women.

But in Manchester on New Year's Day 1914 many people were more interested in ice skating, or watching United beat West Bromwich Albion one-nil.

'SIGNS OF A SHARP FROST'

2 January

Manchester, New Year's Day 1914: There were many people in the city, but several thousands of them were swallowed up in the theatres, music halls, picture palaces, and other houses of entertainment. About 18,000 went to Old Trafford to see the football match between Manchester United and West Bromwich Albion ... Another large section of the community found excellent sport in skating on fields and ponds on the outskirts of the city; while many others went to see the flying feats at Belle Vue. In the early part of the day there were all the signs of a sharp frost. This and the fog which overspread the low-lying lands caused the authorities of the Manchester Racecourse to abandon the idea of having the usual New Year's Day races at Castle Irwell ... All the places of entertainment did well. At the Theatre Royal there was the pantomime *Humpty Dumpty*. *The Marriage Market*, with a London company, was played at the Prince's Theatre. At the Gaiety Theatre there was *Fifinella* ('a fairy frolic') in the afternoon and *School for Scandal* at night. The patriotic drama *Drake* was given at the New Theatre ... The music-halls had their crowds, and the picture theatres also.

William Byles was Liberal MP for Salford North. Written on New Year's Day, his letter to the editor was about the Anglo-German naval arms race.

3 January
The Reduction of Armaments

Men have come to see – or are fast coming to see – that it is the experts, and the services, and the armament makers themselves, the men who think (as I don't) that there is 'nothing like leather,' who are pushing the nation into this huge and ever-growing expenditure. They see, secondly, the danger to their social programme if in times of peace the taxation for war must be so heavy. And, thirdly, they are at last realising that relations of friendship and co-operation with our potential enemies is a far surer defence than all the Dreadnoughts in the world. I am full of hope for the new year, and if I were a shareholder in any of the great armament firms I would sell out, for I am convinced the movement for reduction is *en marche*.

'A RATHER UGLY SCENE'

The women's movement was divided between non-militant suffragists and proponents of direct action such as the Women's Social and Political Union (WSPU), Mrs Emmeline Pankhurst and her daughters Christabel, Sylvia and Adela. By 1914, Sylvia, a socialist estranged from her mother and sisters, had set up the East London Federation of Suffragettes (ELFS).

Mrs Pankhurst had been in and out of prison since 1908, and on Thursday 21 May 1914, with a three-year prison sentence hanging over her, she led a WSPU deputation.

22 May
Suffragette 'Raid' on Buckingham Palace

The attempt today of the militant suffragists to force a deputation on the King at Buckingham Palace ended, as must have been expected, in complete failure. One woman of the many who tried to get beyond the police cordon managed to come so near the Palace as the pavement in front of the main entrance, where of course she was at once arrested. [...]

About fifteen hundred policemen were disposed in lines across the roadways debouching on the open place in front of the railings in such a way as to keep the whole of the wide space between the Victoria Memorial and the Palace absolutely clear ... A crowd some thousands strong, crushed between the railings of the Green Park and police barriers, had a good view of all that happened.

The worst of the conflict with the police outside the Palace, such as it was, was over within half-an-hour or so. Women ran past the police into the open space, and were pushed back or taken into custody if they persisted. I was standing within a few feet of the point of disturbance, and it appeared to me that the police acted with good humour and used no unnecessary violence. It was said that at the top of the hill there had been a rather ugly scene, the women trying to pull the police off the horses and striking at them with cudgels, and that the police had struck back with their truncheons, but that I did not see.

The only exciting incident outside the Palace was the arrest of Mrs. Pankhurst. Closely surrounded by her followers she pushed past the policeman, but the constables gathered round and began pushing the women back into the crowd. Mrs. Pankhurst's bodyguard resisted vigorously. The policeman apparently did not realise that they were dealing with Mrs. Pankhurst, and were making no attempt to arrest her, until Superintendent Quinn and some inspectors ran up. A huge inspector plucked Mrs. Pankhurst out of the struggling group and ran away with her in his arms into the clear space in front of the Palace. A taxi-cab was summoned, and Mrs. Pankhurst was quickly bundled into it and driven away. As she was carried past the group of reporters she called out, 'Arrested at the gates of the Palace – tell the King that.' She was pale, but perfectly self-collected.

11 June
Militants Chased by Portsmouth Mob

Scenes of great disorder took place in Portsmouth last night, and but for the action of the police would probably have culminated in serious injury to several suffragettes. Two parties of suffragettes, including, it is said, several well-known militants, arrived in the town yesterday. Last night two of the women, who pitched their stand just outside of the Royal Counties Agricultural Show ground, were chased by a mob numbering several hundreds of people for a considerable distance. Bricks and other missiles were hurled at the women. Eventually they were rescued by the police and removed to a place of safety. Other women attempted to hold a meeting in the centre of the town near the Town Hall, but an angry crowd, whose attitude was distinctly dangerous, broke up their platform, tore down their flags, and made repeated efforts to attack them. The police had considerable difficulty in getting the militants away.

Prime Minister Herbert Asquith met an ELFS delegation at the time when Sylvia Pankhurst was imprisoned.

22 June
Mr. Asquith and Working Women

The Prime Minister received at 10 Downing Street this morning a deputation from the East London Federation of Suffragists. This organisation, of which Miss Sylvia Pankhurst is the head … concerns itself chiefly with the importance of the vote to working women as a weapon in the fight against bad conditions of life and labour.

Of all the many talks on the suffrage which Mr. Asquith has had with suffragists, to-day's was the most intimate and probably the most interesting … In rough and simple language the women told the Prime Minister the actual experience of their lives. 'As I have to work so hard to support my home,' one said simply, 'I feel it is very wrong that I cannot have a voice in the making of the laws.'

Mr. Asquith listened with the greatest sympathy and attention, and made a kindly speech in reply. The part of it which most pleased the women was his promise to consult with the Home Secretary about the request that Miss Pankhurst should be unconditionally released. [...]

Mrs. Scurr read a long statement on the position of the working women under the law … She asked for the unconditional release of Miss Sylvia Pankhurst and Mrs. Walker [a docker's wife arrested for giving an 'inciting speech']. 'Their crime,' she said, 'is only that of speaking, and as you know, men like James Larkin, George

Lansbury and Sir Edward Carson have all made seditious speeches, and Sir Edward Carson has committed seditious acts, and yet these men are free.'

Mrs. Hughes, an elderly brushmaker, handed the Prime Minister a hairbrush and told him, 'I work from eight in the morning to six at night and get twopence for each brush. That brush is sold for half a guinea. I think,' she went on, 'I have a right to a vote the same as my husband, who hardly does any work, while I have to do the housework as well.' Mrs. Hughes told the Prime Minister that her husband was a brushmaker also, but the work he used to do was now done by machinery.

Mr. Asquith handled the brush and asked the woman: 'How many hours does it take to make it?' 'About two hours,' she replied. 'There are 200 holes for five farthings.'

The wife of a transport worker, a woman earning 25s. a week, spoke next ... 'I have six young children, and my husband is one of the best of men. He is a teetotaller, but yet I have a great struggle to bring up a family on the wages he earns, for I have to pay 6s. 6d. a week rent, and then there is the insurance and club money to pay before we can buy anything for ourselves. I am not fighting for the vote for myself because I am one of the best off in the East End. There are thousands worse off than me, with husbands earning only 18s. a week and with far larger families.'

Another life-story given the Premier was that of a worker in a trousers factory who spoke of the ill-treatment of women by foremen. 'Women who have to work under these conditions should have a voice in making the laws to reform the factories,' she said, and she spoke touchingly and at first hand of the hardships of deserted wives and unmarried mothers ... Lastly a thin woman in black described how her mentally defective child was taken away from her and put in a padded room in the workhouse. 'I asked the doctor why it was, and he replied it had nothing to do with me.

It was the father's place. I think we ought to have a voice in the different laws for women.'

'WANTON AND RECKLESS CHATTER'

Early in 1914, the third Irish Home Rule Bill (HRB) was making another passage through the Houses of Parliament, highlighting a crisis that threatened the stability of the United Kingdom. Opposition to the HRB was led by Sir Edward Carson MP, a Dubliner and leader of the Protestant Ulster Unionists of northern Ireland, bolstered by the paramilitary Ulster Volunteers Force (UVF). Carson and his allies were supported by the Unionists (Conservatives) at Westminster. Their demand was for the exclusion of the north from the HRB's provisions for an Irish parliament, a demand that Herbert Asquith's Liberal government effectively offered to concede, but not to the satisfaction of Carson and his intransigent supporters.

The first lord of the admiralty under the Liberal government was Winston Churchill. On Saturday 14 March 1914, Churchill, having sent warships into Irish ports, told a Bradford audience that a 'fair and full offer' had been made to the Unionists. The speech challenged Carson and his allies not to threaten force against parliament.

16 March
Mr. Churchill and the Ulster Problem

That offer has been made. It was made last Monday by the Prime Minister. God forbid that I should ever stand in the path of conciliation, but it seems to me that in principle this is the last offer which His Majesty's Government can make or ought to make. How has it been received? ... A fair offer has been made, and up to the present – and only up to the present we can view it – it has not only been spurned, but taken advantage of. If there is no wish for peace … if all the wanton and reckless chatter we have been forced to listen to all these months is in the end to disclose a sinister and revolutionary purpose then I can only say to you: Let us go forward together, and put these grave matters to the proof.

That Monday, 16 March, what Asquith described as a 'regular rough and tumble' ensued at Question Time. By Thursday, Carson, having denounced Churchill in the Commons, walked out amid a storm of Tory cheers and departed for Belfast.

The commander-in-chief for Ireland was General Arthur Paget, whose alarmism exacerbated the crisis. Thirty-five miles south-west of Dublin at the Curragh camp, British officers mutinied en masse for the first time in more than two centuries, resigning their commissions rather than countenancing a move against the UVF. The British government surrendered, as the Manchester Guardian *reported.*

25 March
Curragh Officers Exulting Over Their 'Victory'

Scenes which have been enacted at the Curragh Camp to-day make it impossible to avoid the conclusion that far-reaching effects of the most serious kind must inevitably result from what is here unquestioningly regarded as the capitulation of the Government to the threats of the cavalry officers … Young officers, exultant in what they look upon as the hour of victory, spoke without restraint of their release from any obligation to take up arms to suppress organised resistance to Home Rule in Ulster. A written undertaking was given at the War Office to General Gough, and its terms are too explicit to leave any doubt as to its import. It is to the effect that the General and the officers under his command shall not be called on to take up arms to force Home Rule upon Ulster. The officers concerned have not moved from the position they took up four days ago and they are applauded as heroes by all who share their political views. General Gough … made it quite clear that if what he regards as civil war breaks out, neither he nor the officers under him will support the Government and the Crown in putting it down.

On 6 April the HRB passed its second reading – with special concessions to the north – but 'loyalists' were not appeased. On 24 April rifles and ammunition were smuggled into Larne to arm the UVF.

27 April
First Overt Act of Rebellion

Belfast, Sunday Night: The Ulster Volunteers, whose activities have been shown hitherto in the making of kinema [cinema] films, have done a real and serious stroke of business. It has been accompanied by a quite unnecessary amount of advertisement fully in keeping with the traditions of the corps, but even without the aid of the limelight, which has been one of the Volunteers' chief helps so far, two facts are startlingly clear.

One is that in the late hours of Friday night and in the early hours of Saturday morning, according to an estimate accepted by the police themselves, thirty-five thousand German Mauser magazine rifles, with three and a half million rounds of cartridges, being a hundred for each rifle, all directed to rebellion and all embarked in defiance of a proclamation of the Privy Council – one fancies, of the common law of the realm besides – were landed on the coast of Ulster. The other is that in the course of their landing, three Irish towns where the King's writ normally runs were 'held up' in the full sense which the term has in a South American Republic. In Larne, in county Antrim, and in Donaghadee and Bangor in county Down, those of the King's lieges who were traversing his highway between the hours of ten o'clock on Friday night and three o'clock Saturday morning, and who had not provided themselves with a pass signed by the president of the Orangemen, who is commandant by virtue of his office, were turned back by the patrols of the commando.

On 22 May, with the HRB back in the Commons for its third reading, the Unionist opposition attempted to shout it down. On 23 May Chancellor of the Exchequer David Lloyd George was speaking in support of Charles Masterman, Liberal candidate for Ipswich, in the last by-election before the outbreak of war. The tone of the speech underlines the febrile atmosphere that the Ireland issue had generated within British politics. Lloyd George told the 7,000-strong audience that the election was critical 'in the history of this country'.

24 May
Representative Government at Stake

'Why? Just you read the story of the scene in the House of Commons yesterday. (Cries of "Shame.") What do you think it means? I will tell you. It was not an outburst of temper. It was not people suddenly losing their heads. If that had been the case I would not have said a word about it. We are all liable to it, especially in this hot weather. (Laughter.) It was deliberate. It was a part of a plan for destroying the House that represents this country (Cheers.) Do you know what that means? ... The liberties of the people are at stake (cheers) and unless they stand by the flag of freedom I shall despair – but only then. Ipswich town delivers a verdict which will resound throughout the ages as a great blow for freedom if it returns my friend Charles Masterman. (Cheers.)'

Masterman lost. And the Ireland issue dragged on, finally colliding with the aftermath of the Sarajevo assassinations. Home rule, it was resolved, was to be suspended until the end of the war. But no allowance had been made for the events of Easter 1916.

'A RATHER REMARKABLE THING'

The pre-war years were turbulent ones for British workers and the nascent trade unions. In 1911 British railway unions went on strike – and in the aftermath members were victimised. In 1912 a 37-day miners' strike polarised society and led to the enactment of a national minimum miners' wage. In 1913 the worst disaster in British mining history – the explosion at the Senghenydd colliery – killed 439 miners. Strikes among dockers, transport workers and firemen erupted from 1910 onwards. In January 1914 a five-month lockout by Dublin employers, who were opposed to the right to unionise, ended in defeat for the workers. Syndicalism and socialism were growing influences within the trade unions of the British Isles, and their aim was a 'triple alliance' of three great unions.

14 March
Labour's Triple Alliance

The Executive of the National Union of Railwaymen … has decided to accept the invitation of the Miners' Federation of Great Britain to a joint conference with the object of promoting a working alliance between the Miners' Federation, the Transport Workers' Federation and the Railwaymen's Union in order to facilitate joint action in support of common demands. The Transport Workers' Federation has already approved of the proposal, and it now rests with the miners to fix the date of the conference. The combined membership affected is close to 1,700,000 with funds estimated at £2,500,000.

5 June
Miners, Railway and Transport Men

The closer federation of the organisations of the miners, the railwayman and the transport workers of this country was advanced another stage yesterday … The result will be an alliance for offensive and defensive purposes, for the first time, of about a million and a half trade unionists engaged on what may be termed the main arteries of industry.

Robert Smillie was president of the Miners' Federation of Great Britain and chaired the committee preparing for the triple alliance. On 2 July he addressed Cleveland miners.

3 July
When a General Strike May Be Called

Mr. Smillie, referring to the new combination between the miners, railwaymen and transport workers, said: '… one line we mean to take is to lay down the principle of a decent minimum wage for all grades of workers connected with this particular combination. We shall require to make sure that if employers in any part of the country begin evicting workmen from their homes during a strike or lock-out there shall be a general stoppage in order to move the wheels of Government. We shall require to be close enough together to see that if workers in any part of Great Britain are out fighting for their rights along trade union lines and the local authorities or the Government bring out soldiers or police to baton or shoot them, we shall be in a position to say, "We will not go on working while you are shooting down our fellow-men." (Applause.)' Mr. Smillie said that the new movement had been designated by certain sections of the press as rank Syndicalism and a threat against the stability of a so-called civilised State. He added that it was a rather remarkable thing that when the shipbuilding and engineering industry on the east coast of England and the Clyde threatened to lock out their workers because of a dispute which might have taken place in some remote corner of the shipbuilding industry, it was not called Syndicalism but intelligent organisation on the part of the employers. This was exactly what was aimed at by the three bodies.

Later that month, Scottish mine owners announced a proposal to cut the minimum wage. The stage was set for the triple alliance to move into action that autumn.

'HURRAH FOR LIGHTNING!'

Italian Futurism was an arts movement born in 1909. Focused around Filippo Marinetti, it celebrated speed, violence, technology and the liberating effects of war. British Futurists included Christopher Nevinson, who achieved fame as a war artist, but some Futurists, such as Wyndham Lewis, redefined themselves as Vorticists.

13 July
Vorticism

Our London Correspondence: From the point of view of noise the Futurist lecture at the Doré Galleries this evening was a little disappointing ... The new seceders from the Marinetti group, Messrs. Wyndham Lewis and Co. – who now call themselves Vorticists – ... dwindled into silence very early in the evening. However, Mr. CRW Nevinson, the faithful disciple of Futurism, addressed us in a lecture which, though delivered in a manner far removed from Marinetti's passionate declamation, had not a little of the master's epigrammatic style. He explained the Futurists – the real primitives – aimed at such things as the emotional expression of a smell or a state of mind in forms and colours, as when we speak of seeing red, having the blues, or feeling green. This is a mechanical age, and therein lies its whole beauty. Only bad work goes on for ever. No one would take the *Mona Lisa* as a gift. Nobody wants a singer to go on singing all day ('I don't agree' from a Vorticist). There have never been any eternal truths – and so on. He then read the manifesto. It enumerated the things against which the Futurists 'give the signal for battle.' Among them were the worship of tradition, garden cities and morris dances, the preference for foreign artists as against English, 'the same revolutionary New English Art Club.' The manifesto ended with '*Hurrah* for motors! *Hurrah* for speed! *Hurrah* for lightning!' Bang! A firework was exploded in the centre doorway! Then came 'What we want,' with a list of 'Vanguard' painters, which included the names of all the seceding Vorticists, at which one of these protested. Signor Marinetti himself followed with an attack on the elegant *Passéist*, *The Times*, and on all the 'isms except Futurism. 'Immortality is an infamous thing, a crime.' He finished with an attack on those rich people who refused to buy Futurist pictures.

'UPPISH IN BRITISH AFRICA'

When, in 1908, the African-American Jack Johnson became the first black world heavyweight-boxing champion, race riots ensued. In 1914 Johnson was in England and the Manchester Guardian'*s editorial, a response to popular controversy, captured the white (liberal and racist) outlook and imperial fears of the time. Billy 'Bombardier' Wells was a white British boxing champion, Sam Langford a black Canadian boxer and Mrs Humphry Ward (Mary Ward) was a novelist, social reformer and leading anti-women's suffrage campaigner of the era.*

22 January
The Negro Boxing Champion

We do not say that *The Times* and others are not right in crying out against prize-fights and boxing shows in which Jack Johnson, the negro pugilist, takes part. But they have rather odd ways of putting it. It all reads as if there were something more which they do not quite like to say. What they most dread is that Johnson should be matched against an Englishman. In that case, as they feel, the Englishman might be beaten; indeed he almost certainly would; and they fear that this would make negroes uppish in British Africa. It has always been a sacred tradition among us that the negro, on the whole, is no good with his fists, and the tradition has the support of numberless cases which British colonials have related in British bars and smoking-rooms that with one well-placed blow they sent some contumacious nigger spinning, and that the nigger then curled up at once and was permanently improved. This tradition the negro race has been pretty widely asked to imbibe, and it is feared that the good work thus done might be partly undone if it were known the best negro boxer had beaten the best Englishman. The negro might then begin to extract from *The Times* and adapt to his own case the great anti-suffragist argument that the only proper basis of the right to a vote, and to political power generally, is personal physical strength. Bombardier Wells, the anti-suffragists argue, ought to have a vote, and Mrs. Humphry Ward ought not, because – to put it briefly – Bombardier Wells could knock out Mrs. Humphry Ward when it came to fisticuffs. It is feared the Kaffir might adopt this philosophic doctrine and begin to argue that if Jack Johnson or Sam Langford were to knock out Bombardier Wells the negro's superior title to political power would be similarly established.

But objections are also brought against any big boxing match between the negroes themselves. We do not refer to any general objections to the modern form of veiled prize-fighting, for the objectors we speak of have none of these. They object to a Johnson–Langford match in London that it would be 'sensational,' that 'highly coloured pen-pictures of Englishmen flocking to see it would be published far and wide,' and that 'their effect, in parts of the British Dominions which are inhabited by native races, would be wholly bad.' ... And, of course, such descriptions would circulate from Cairo to the Cape. We cannot confine the whole negro race to the study of the *Church Guardian* or supply the Zulus with special copies of *The Times* from which the sporting intelligence has been blacked out ... The fact is that these semi-objectors, or occasional objectors, to the new prize ring are muddled. They are up against the fact that 'flocking to see' prize-fights is not a thing for an 'Imperial race' to do. But they want to keep up this delectable subject for pen-pictures and source of robust vicarious emotions. And also they want to keep it dark from the natives. And so they are driven into the somewhat inglorious expedient of keeping negroes out of the ring when negroes are the best boxers, though they never raised any sort of difficulty about the admission of negroes to the ring when they were second-rate. One would think that this fact, too, might be 'published far and wide' and that 'its effect, in parts of the British Empire which are inhabited by native races, would be wholly bad.' There is no middle course, whether logical or creditable, between the alternatives of letting all come and the best man win, and of surrendering the joys of looking on in a dress coat while two expensively hired persons show strength, skill, and courage for your amusement.

'A CERTAIN MAGNETIC POWER'

Imperial Russia was an anomaly. Other European states might be autocratic, but at least they had parliamentarianism and the trappings of enlightenment. In Russia the concessions that had followed the 1905 revolution were being whittled away. If there was one land that symbolised the heart of darkness, it was Russia. And one man embodied that darkness.

22 January
Rasputin

About three years ago a new and ominous figure made his appearance in the confused world of Russian politics ... the appearance of Grigory Rasputin was something wholly unprecedented ... He was simply a Siberian peasant, with a peasant's dress, a peasant's speech. Yet by some strange means he secured such a position at Court and exercised such an influence over the Tsar and Tsaritsa that he became an important factor in politics, and Ministers had to reckon with him. The dangers arising from the presence of such an irresponsible adviser were immediately apparent. The press discussed Rasputin at great length until the multiplication of fines put a check on overt attack, and in the Duma both Opposition speakers and the Octobrist leader Guchkov protested in hardly veiled language against the interference of this ignorant peasant in the most important affairs of the State. Naturally, these protests had no effect, and Rasputin continues to occupy at Court the position of trusted adviser and friend ... His real name is Novykh, and Grigory Rasputin, which may be translated as 'Gregory the Rake,' seems to be a nickname given him by the peasants, in mocking allusion to his personal habits. In his native village ... he gained a reputation for sanctity, and peasants, more particularly women, came to him for advice ... Rasputin is a charlatan, who uses a certain magnetic power he does seem undoubtedly to possess, for purposes the reverse of religious.

The substance of Rasputin's teaching is that 'to live is to love,' that every evil deed is immediately punished in this world, that unless a man sins there is nothing to pardon him for, and that therefore sin is the path to grace. His fellow-villagers long since gave him the cold shoulder ... But ... a new career opened up for him in St. Petersburg … Once installed at Court, he became popular in fashionable society, and was welcomed as a useful instrument by certain reactionary cliques. Since then … he has constantly inspired important decisions on questions of internal policy. The influence he formerly exerted on ignorant peasant women he now exerts on fashionable women … He is received in the homes of various aristocratic families, and here he is permitted a freedom of speech that would cause the immediate ejection of any less highly favoured member of society. […]

Rasputin is a man of medium height; broad-shouldered, well-built, vigorous and erect with a full reddish beard and straight hair parted in the middle and hanging as far as the shoulders. He is a little over forty. He wears a long kaftan of blue serge, a Russian blouse and patent leather top-boots. None of his reported utterances displays force or originality, and the fact that a crude imposter of this kind has attained the position he has is one of the worst symptoms of the moral anarchy prevailing in the higher ranks of Russian society.

15 July

Miscellany: A correspondent who knows Russia well declared that the explanation of Rasputin's constant visits to the Tsar's palace is domestic and not political. He has a soothing effect on the Empress, who is in a very nervous condition, and when somebody diplomatically suggested to the Tsar that the prophet should be told to keep away from the Palace his Majesty remarked, 'Better a dozen Rasputins than family rows.' … She is always fearing that her husband, her son or she herself will be assassinated, and in consequence she is often seized by fits of hysterics. Rasputin (adds our correspondent) is the only person who can manage her. She has absolute confidence in him, and he can do what he likes with her. An intimation that, if she does do something or if she doesn't do something, disaster will befall the Tsar and Tsarevitch is always listened to and acted on when it comes to Rasputin.

'HORROR THROUGHOUT THE WORLD'

Sunday 28 June 1914 was a sunny day in Sarajevo, capital of Bosnia-Herzegovina, part of the Austro-Hungarian empire. The day was the wedding anniversary of Franz Ferdinand – heir to the empire – and the 525th anniversary of the battle of Kosovo, when the defeated Serbs had, nonetheless, seen one of their number assassinate the Ottoman sultan. On the morning of that day in 1914, a Serb student group, funded and armed by the military intelligence of Serbia (Servia), made a first failed attempt to assassinate Franz Ferdinand. But then the archduke's chauffeur took a wrong turning. For the first time in its history, the Manchester Guardian *ran a double-column headline.*

29 June
Assassination of the Austrian Royal Heir and Wife, Shot by Student in Bosnian Capital

The Archduke Francis Ferdinand of Austria, nephew of the aged Emperor and heir to the throne, was assassinated in the streets of Sarayevo, the Bosnian capital, yesterday afternoon. His wife, the Duchess of Hohenberg, was killed by the same assassin ... Two attempts were made on the Archduke's life during the day ... During the morning a bomb was thrown at the Imperial motor-car, but its occupants escaped unhurt. In the afternoon in another part of the town a Serb student fired a revolver at the car, killing both the Archduke and the Duchess. [...]

The assassin of the Archduke and his wife is a student named Gavrilo Prinzip. He is 19 years of age and was born in Grahovo, in the district of Livno. He studied for some time in Belgrade.

On being interrogated, Prinzip declared that he had intended for a long time to kill some eminent personage from nationalist motives. He was waiting to-day for the Archduke to pass by, and made his attempt at a point where the motor-car had to slacken speed when turning into Francis Joseph Strasse. As the Duchess was in the car he hesitated for a moment, but afterwards he quickly fired two shots. Prinzip denies having any accomplices.

The twenty-one-year-old compositor Nideljko Gabrinovic, whose attempt with a bomb failed, declares that he received the bomb from 'anarchists' in Belgrade whose names he does not know. He, too, denies having any accomplices. Gabrinovic behaved very cynically during the examination. After his attempt he sprang into the river to evade the police, but several persons from the crowd jumped in after him and seized him.

A few yards from the scene of the second and fatal attempt, an unexploded bomb was found. It is thought to have been thrown by a third assassin after he had seen the success of Prinzip's attack.

30 June
World's Sympathy with Aged Emperor

The news of the Austrian murders has been heard with horror throughout the world. Messages of sympathy have poured into Vienna, whither the aged Emperor Francis Joseph returned yesterday.

Comments on the crime, all expressing friendly feelings for the Emperor, are made by all the European papers, most of them, as is natural while the shock is still fresh, attaching an over-importance to the political consequences. In Germany the journalistic view is coloured by the belief the Empire has lost a good friend; in Russia the dead Archduke's hostility is remembered. The comments from other countries are of less interest, save those from Servia, which swell the chorus of sympathetic regrets.

At the funeral Prince Arthur of Connaught will represent King George; the Kaiser will be present in person. Because the Duchess of Hohenberg was not a member of the Imperial family the lying-in-state cannot take place in the Vienna Court Chapel, nor can she be buried in the Imperial vault in the Church of Capuchins. The Archduke, knowing this, had expressed a wish to rest elsewhere himself, and in accordance with his desires he and his wife will find a tomb at Artstetten, in Lower Austria.

In Sarayevo, where the murders were committed, the belief is common that a wide-spread Servian plot was made against the Archduke's life. This has led to serious disorders, in the course of which Servians have been attacked and their shops and houses stoned and sometimes looted. Both Vienna and Berlin take a like view, but for the moment at least the evidence is still to seek.

Martial Law

Sarayevo, Monday: Martial law has been proclaimed over the town and district of Sarayevo.

Anti-Servian demonstrations were renewed to-day on a larger scale. Young Catholics and Moslems, followed by a large crowd, paraded through the street bearing a portrait of the Emperor at their head, singing the National Anthem, cheering the Monarchy and dynasty, and raising cries of hostility towards the Servians.

The demonstrators smashed windows at the Hotel de l'Europe, the offices of the Servian Social Club, the Servian school, and several business houses. Finally, patrols of police and troops restored order.

After being dispersed this morning by the police and troops, the demonstrators reassembled at other points of the town. On an undesirable element joining in the demonstrations these assumed a more and more menacing character. Servian shops were stormed and looted.

In consequence of the character the demonstrations had assumed and as excitement continued to grow, the town was placed under martial law, which at the present moment, three o'clock, is being proclaimed by drum and placard. All the chief points of the town are occupied by troops.

A boy this morning threw a bomb at a street corner. The bomb exploded, but only slightly injured a Moslem passer-by. The boy was arrested. No further details at present available.

Royal Mourners

The King paid a visit to the Austrian Embassy in London yesterday and personally expressed sympathy with the Emperor …

The King and the officers attending the investiture at St. James's Palace yesterday wore crêpe bands as a token of mourning for the Archduke and his wife.

Prince Arthur of Connaught has been appointed to represent the King at the funeral. The Emperor Francis Joseph is a British Field Marshal, and the Archduke was a colonel of a British regiment. It is probable, therefore, that Prince Arthur will be accompanied by a military officer of high rank and a small deputation from the regiment.

'NATURAL AND UNAFFECTED'

Despite the developments abroad, the pleasures and preoccupations of high society in Britain continued. In July 1914 the 19-year-old Prince of Wales (briefly, later, King Edward VIII, and subsequently Duke of Windsor) was enrolled at Magdalen College, Oxford.

13 July
The Prince's First Ball

Our London Correspondence: The ball Lady Salisbury gave at her town house in Arlington Street was, apart from two small dinner dances, the first dance the Prince of Wales has been to in general society. It has all along been hoped the Prince would be present, for he and Lord Cranbourne, Lord Salisbury's eldest son, are close friends at Oxford. The Prince, however, is no dancer – he does not inherit the Queen's talent for waltzing. At Lady Salisbury's dance he did not waltz at all, but confined himself to one-steps, three of which he danced with Lady Mary Cecil, the daughter of the house. It was something of an ordeal for so young a boy and of so retiring a disposition as the Prince of Wales, for no one was allowed to dance until he began and for a Prince who described himself as a bad dancer this must have been a trial indeed. The Prince, however, is so natural and unaffected that he had the respectful sympathy of everyone. The Salisbury town house is magnificent in an austere and elevated style, with a grand staircase, a fine corridor leading to the ballroom, and a general air of being a palace rather than a house in a row of other houses.

'A MOMENT'S WEAKNESS'

Meanwhile in Paris, as war loomed, newspapers were dominated by Henriette Caillaux's trial for murder. Four months earlier she had shot dead the editor of Le Figaro, *complaining that the paper had impugned the honour of her husband Joseph, a former French prime minister. In the fetid atmosphere of 1918, Joseph Caillaux would be imprisoned for high treason for seeking a negotiated peace. His wife fared better.*

29 July
Madame Caillaux Acquitted
The trials of Mme. Caillaux in Paris for murder ended late last night in an acquittal. Remarkable scenes followed ... Mme. Caillaux, the

wife of the former Radical leader in the Chamber, was charged with the wilful and premeditated murder of M. Gaston Calmette, editor of the *Figaro*, following on from the publication of a letter written to her by M. Caillaux at a time when she was Mme. Rainouard and he was married to another woman ... On the evening of 16 March Mme. Caillaux called at the *Figaro* office, and after a long wait obtained an interview with M. Calmette. She shot him in his room with a Browning revolver. M. Calmette died within a few hours.

The case had two sides. On the one hand it was a political trial and on the other an ordinary *crime passionel*. The verdict is quite in accordance with the traditions of Parisian juries ... Whatever opinion may be held about M. Caillaux personally or politically, it is impossible to deny that he made a superb defence of his wife and himself, which won over even opponents. [...]

Maître Chenu, addressing the jury, said that Mme. Caillaux was a clever and self-collected woman who did not seem to show much feeling. He thought M. and Mme. Caillaux were one with each other in their happiness and hopes, and this unity extended even to the homicide. He described to the jury the uncontrolled ambition of M. Caillaux. At this moment Mme. Caillaux, who had been greatly agitated by this searching indictment by Maître Chenu, fainted and had to be carried from court.

On the resumption of the sitting Maître Chenu reproached Mme. Caillaux, who he pointed out fainted so often in court, with not having experienced a moment's weakness in the presence of the body of the man she had just shot down. Continuing, he said, that the case was certainly one of premeditated murder, carried out without any sign of weakness before, during, or after the crime. [...]

Maître Labori began his speech for the defence ... 'Let us,' he said, 'keep our anger for our enemies outside the gates. Let us leave here all determined to march as one man against the danger which threatens us.' Tremendous applause greeted this peroration, and the jury retired to consider their verdict. [...]

As soon as the verdict of acquittal was given the crowded court broke out into loud cheers. Mme. Caillaux was then led into court. She looked perfectly composed. Maître Labori communicated the news to her, and she fell fainting in the dock into the arms of her counsel, who embraced her. A paroxysm of weeping followed on the part of the accused. Some of the counsel came to blows. Me. Chenu and Me. Labori embraced each other. The President ordered that Mme. Caillaux should immediately be set at liberty. She was then escorted by guards between a line of people to the door. As she went out Mme. Caillaux covered her face with her hands. Some of the barristers present raised cries of 'Assassin, assassin,' waving their robes.

'THAT MIGHTY VOICE'

If Rasputin represented darkness in Europe, then the great socialist Jean Jaurès represented light. At the turn of the 20th century Jaurès had been a defender of Captain Alfred Dreyfus, the target of a notorious anti-semitic French army conspiracy. An anti-colonialist, in 1904 Jaurès co-founded the newspaper L'Humanité. A decade later, as war loomed, he would plead for Franco-German reconciliation. Thus it was that, on 31 July 1914, Jaurès was assassinated in Paris, by a French nationalist. By the time this piece appeared, France and Britain were at war with Germany. 'The following tribute to the great French Socialist' announced the paper, '... has been specially contributed to the Manchester Guardian *by the famous novelist and philosopher M. Anatole France.'*

5 August
Jean-Leon Jaurès

I say it with mingled pride and sorrow – he was my friend. I knew him in his most intimate moments. Great man as he was, he was simple and warm-hearted in his private relations. He was the very embodiment of sweetness and kindness; of all the gifts with which nature has endowed this superman, that of loving was perhaps the one that he used in the fullest measure. I have heard that mighty voice, whose clear and terrible echoes resounded through the world, become, in speaking to a friend, tender and caressing.

His learning was sure and profound. It extended beyond the limits, wide as they are, of social questions to the whole field of the intellect … Less than a month ago I went to see him at his house at Passy, so modest, ay, so poor, and yet so glorious. I found him reading a tragedy of Euripides in the original. His mighty intellect found relaxation in turning from one study to another, and rested from one task only to take up a new one. Serene in the possession of a pure conscience, pursued by a terrible hatred and made the target of murderous calumnies, he hated none. My heart is too full for speech, I can but stammer. My grief chokes my utterance. Never to see him again – that great heart, that mighty genius, that noble personality.

I offer with respectful tenderness my profound sympathy to his widow, his children, his friends, his colleagues, and to the great Socialist party for whom he still lives.

CHAPTER 2

1914

It took 37 days for Europe to move from the assassinations in Sarajevo, through the 'July Crisis', to war. The deaths of Franz Ferdinand and his wife were followed by an Austrian ultimatum to Serbia. On 5 July, the government of the German empire, the most powerful industrial state in Europe and home of the world's mightiest army, had offered its support to the enfeebled empire of Austria-Hungary. France, allied to Russia, had encouraged the tsar's government to mobilise in support of its fellow Slavs in Belgrade. Two blocs were forming. Vienna, dissatisfied with Serbia's response to its ultimatum, declared war on 28 July, thus turning the Balkan crisis into a European one. Yet many British citizens were slow to react.

'WHERE THEY SLAM THEIR DESKS ALL THE TIME'

28 July
The Crisis and the Man in the Street
Our London Correspondence: The imminence of a European war, despite the wildness of the news bills today and the slump in the Stock Exchange, seemed by all signs to affect the ordinary Londoner very little ... The ordinary man has heard too much about European conflagrations to believe in one till he sees the flames as well as the smoke, and he certainly cannot get his

household to take it seriously. Even the false announcement in one of the Sunday papers yesterday, that war had been declared, roused little excitement ... Austria – 'that's where they slam their desks all the time in Parliament and where they don't know what their right language is, and didn't they steal somebody's country the other year without a word?' Then Servia is still the country that murdered its King and Queen and had a half-mad Crown Prince that killed his servant. Servia and Austria are very remote from the thoughts of the man on the street and he hopes generally that Germany and Russia won't be such fools as to chip in. But the Dublin crisis – that is quite different: everywhere you go, once a bold man has started the subject, the talk is hot and angry ...

One by one, the lamps went out over Europe – but not, yet, in Whitehall.

3 August
The Great War Begins

Russian messages announce the declaration of war by Germany on Saturday evening. Already border troops are said to have invaded France and attacked the defending forces. On the Russo-German border Russian cavalry parties are active, and in several places soldiers have crossed into Prussia.

London, Sunday Night: There was a great gathering in St. Paul's this morning, and though it is holiday time, the season when the services are sparsely attended, the vast Cathedral was filled right to the western doors ... The sermon might have been written for the day, so appropriate was the passions of its prayer for peace.

'A TRULY HELLISH THING'

'What a monstrous and truly hellish thing this war will be,' the editor of the Manchester Guardian, *CP Scott, wrote on Wednesday 29 July,*

'if it really brings the rest of Europe into it.' At the moment war began, opposition flickered into life.

2 August
The First Anti-War Meeting

London, Sunday Night: The peace demonstration in Trafalgar Square this afternoon was evidence of the amazingly sudden way in which our own crisis has flared into being. Although a possible British participation has been rumoured for several days, the whole thing has come upon us so quickly that there has been no organised public protest. And it was left to the Socialists this afternoon to hold the first anti-war meeting in the country. It was the biggest Trafalgar Square demonstration held for years; far larger, for example, than the most important of the suffragist rallies. The solidarity of which all the leaders spoke was present, too, in this curiously composite crowd, in which Germans and Frenchmen stood peaceably beside their English comrades. The mind of the crowd was full of a quiet indignation and of alarm at the realisation that they had been, as it were, pushed to the edge of a precipice without a word of warning. There were feeble attempts at a war demonstration on the edge of the gathering, but the violent downfall of rain at half-past four was enough to disperse these feeble-hearted Jingoes, while the solid core of the meeting stood gallantly to their umbrellas and cheered for the war against war.

3 August
Suggested Labour Action

Huddersfield trade unionists last night passed the following resolution: 'This meeting of citizens of Huddersfield views with horror the news of the war in which European nations have already engaged, and which threatens to involve the whole Continent of Europe in an orgy of bloodshed, unparalleled in the history of mankind. We protest in the strongest possible terms against this country being embroiled in it in anyway, and we call upon Parliament to refuse sanction to any measures in that direction.'

4 August
Women's Appeal for Peace

Our London Correspondence: The great mass meeting of women at the Kingsway Hall ... is organised by the International Women's Suffrage Alliance, the National Union of Women's Suffrage Societies, and the other leading women's union. Mrs. Fawcett will be in the chair ... and prominent women speakers from Hungary, Russia, France and Finland will speak. The chief resolution ... continues: 'Women find themselves in the position of seeing all they most reverence and treasure, the home, the family, the race, subjected to irreparable injury, which they are powerless to avert ... women are to see their country impoverished and their homes broken up, their children and their friends dying from starvation and disease. Whatever its result, the conflict will leave mankind poorer, will set back civilisation, and will be a powerful check to the amelioration of the condition of the masses ... ' The resolution concludes by calling upon the Governments ... to work unceasingly towards a settlement, not by force, but by reason.

'TO THE EDITOR'

Germany had mobilised against France and Russia, with the aim of speedily defeating France before focusing on the eastern front. Germany's Schlieffen Plan hinged on attacking France through Belgium, whose neutrality had been guaranteed by the Europe's great powers – including Britain. Germany hoped Britain would also remain neutral; while Anglo-French military talks had been going on

for three years, British involvement was not certain. The Manchester
Guardian *announced on 3 August 1914 that 'evidence of the public
demand for British neutrality grows from day to day', and published
'a remarkable series of letters in which this demand is presented from
every point of view'. The correspondence was huge, and anti-war in its
stance. The first of the following extracts was signed by the then leader
of the Labour party, Ramsay MacDonald, as well as by the historian
GM Trevelyan and nine others.*

3 August
Public Opinion and the War

Statements are now being freely made in the press that England is
bound both by her engagements and by her vital interest to give
armed support to France and Russia should they become involved
in war. We desire to protest against these statements and to call
attention to the following assurances given by the Prime Minister
and the Foreign Secretary.

On 10 March 1912, Lord Hugh Cecil stated that there was a
'very general belief that this country is under an obligation arising
out of an assurance given by the Ministry in the course of the
diplomatic negotiations, to send a very large armed force out of
this country to operate in Europe.' Mr. Asquith then said: 'I ought
to say that it is not true.'

On 24 March 1913, Mr. Asquith said in answer to a question:
'This country is not under any obligation not public and known
to Parliament which compels it to take part in any war. In other
words, if war arises between European Powers there are no
unpublished agreements which will restrict or hamper the freedom
of the Government or of Parliament to decide whether or not
Great Britain should participate in a war.'

On 11 June 1914, Sir E Grey said: 'That answer remains as
true to-day as it was a year ago. No negotiations have since been

concluded with any Power that would make the statement less true. No such negotiations are in progress and none are likely to be entered upon so far as I can judge. But if any agreement were to be concluded that made it necessary to withdraw or modify the Prime Minister's statement of last year it ought, in my opinion, to be, and I suppose that it would be, laid before Parliament.'

These Ministerial statements make it clear that no national engagements exist of the kind suggested, and with respect to the arguments from national interest, no fact has been disclosed which would make it otherwise than disastrous, both to the domestic and to the Imperial interest of the United Kingdom, to engage at this crisis in a great Continental war.

'An Insensate Conflict'

Journals which seem to confuse 'ententes,' or good understandings, with 'alliances,' talk glibly of our duty to stand by our 'friends.' I, for one, protest against treating Germany, our best European customer and a country inhabited by a race akin to ourselves, with whom we have no quarrel, otherwise than as a 'friend.'

(Lord) Shuttleworth, Gawthorpe Hall

'The Suffering of Womanhood'

We, the officers of the Manchester and District Federation of Women's Suffrage Societies, a body of upwards of 3,000 women, wish to declare our earnest hope that our statesmen will preserve our nation from the horrors of participation in a European war ... they have the deeper moral obligation of considering the welfare of the majority of the nation, the women whose sanction can never be obtained under present political conditions ... Until we are granted the direct power to shape the destinies of our country, we demand that our fellow men shall especially endeavour to realise their obligation to reserve peace and prevent the destruction of countless homes, both in our own and other countries … in protection of our homes today we ask that they shall not be devastated by wars made in semi-secret conclaves by statesmen for purely diplomatic purposes, that our fellow-men shall to lay upon the women of this country a burden of suffering to which the women have not consented.

Margaret Ashton, Chairman and Julie E Tomlinson, Hon. Sec., Manchester and District Federation of WSS (This letter has been signed on behalf of 28 branches of the Federation.)

'Refusing to Be Fooled'

Everyone one meets is dreading what the next few days may mean to Britain; everyone also seems agreed that a war in which this country becomes involved will be so disastrous that the very thought of it makes one tremble for the consequence. And yet somehow the people most concerned, the people who will have to fight, to suffer, and in the end of all to pay, seem for the moment impotent to do anything to avert disaster we all dread so much … most here and elsewhere have got into the habit of leaving this horrible business of war-making entirely into the hands of the governing classes, who are themselves hopelessly in the grip of the war party. […]

Is it not high time the sane elements in this country took these matters into their own hands and refused to be fooled in this way any longer?

W Mellor, Secretary, Manchester and Salford Trades and Labour Council, 3 Clarence Road, Chorlton-cum-Hardy

'The Industrialism of the North'

We ought to have without delay a statement from the Prime Minister that as long as British interests are not directly attacked, strict neutrality is Britain's policy. And we ought to proclaim to the world that the *Manchester Guardian*, and not *The Times*, represents the industrialism of the north and the wisdom of the north.

Arthur Rowntree, Bootham School, York

'Turmoil of Militarist Insanity'

Though but a mere workman I wish to know in what way I may be of use in this turmoil of militarist insanity. I earnestly hope that all friends of peace will do their utmost by deed and word to strength the movement which will show the world that English men and women are in the right mind and know it. My wages are small, but I would invest my spare earnings in a grand solid peace movement.

John W Dixon, New Bridge Street Institute

'ON THE EDGE'

3 August
Excitement But No War Fever

London, Sunday Night: 'Mobilisation of the British Fleet – official,' was being yelled by newsboys with armfuls of Sunday papers all over the West End ... This shriek of impending war seemed to bring the people running into the streets. By ten o'clock, Piccadilly, Coventry Street and other streets, three parts empty on normal Sundays, were thronged. There was a rush for the papers, the armfuls melted away, and under every lamp in the glare of the café windows there were groups of eager readers. There was plenty of excitement, but none of that furious passion one remembers so well from the early times of the Boer War. The street crowd did not seem to know what the fight, if fight there is to be for us, would be about. Papers were read quietly, with some such colourless remark as, 'Looks as if we are going to do something now.'

You realised the strange nature of this Sunday night best in Trafalgar Square, where people were standing in a solid mass, kept out by a mere scent of excitement. Late at night these watchers for something to turn up were delighted by the appearance of half-a-dozen redcoats and a couple of bluejackets. The soldiers and sailors were surrounded and loudly cheered. There were a few Frenchmen in the crowds, and they cheered loudest of all.

Tears in Soho

One came nearest to the reality of the situation in the French quarter in Soho or in the narrow streets off Tottenham Court Road, where hundreds of the poorer Germans live. In Compton Street one could hardly get along for the groups of young Frenchmen, waiters in restaurants, in their Sunday clothes, talking things over. Friends and relations of these young fellows had left for France only a few hours before. One saw French mothers and wives with red eyes. The little French restaurants were almost deserted; perhaps people were too excited to eat. In the wider streets motors came along occasionally adorned with British and French flags entwined, the occupants singing patriotic songs and waving little flags. Here and there English people were calling for cheers for King George and for the President of the French Republic, and shrill cries of 'Vive Angleterre' were heard.

Helplessness

Last night about eleven o'clock in Piccadilly Circus, in the middle of a crowd pouring out of the theatres and music-halls, a news seller shouted the first tidings of war. He was drunk, rather unsteady, and he flourished his news bill instead of selling his papers. He had not read his bill, but he knew what he hoped. 'War between England and Germany,' he yelled. 'Bloody war! England and Germany! War! Blood–.' The crowd surrounded him, and he was soon in the middle of a quarrel, as he wanted sixpence for a penny paper. Then the crowd engulfed him, but his voice could be heard now and then shouting 'Blood!'

People soon discovered that he had got his story wrong. His paper gave the news of the German proclamation of war against Russia, but he seemed to stand for a symbol for the horror and helplessness of the events that were reaching their fever point. Most people seemed thunderstruck, for all the preparation of the London press. This is the cosmopolitan centre of London, and many were foreigners. To the majority it meant fighting in the next few days. The appearance of the Sunday paper itself which made the announcement was a sign of the new state of things. A morning paper also came out at that time, and papers never seen later than seven o'clock were being rushed through the town at midnight. What seemed almost unanimous was that no one seemed to want war. There were no war songs or war talk except by way of joke or forecast. The 'We don't want war' that one heard so often should be made into a song to counter the old Jingo one.

At Charing Cross

Charing Cross Station was the dramatic reflection of the history of the day. It was there that the reservist hastening to Vienna, St. Petersburg, Berlin or Paris made his way, and it was there that the holidaying Englishman, appalled by the apparition of war that had risen so suddenly before him, or the English business man abroad, suddenly uprooted from the peaceful ground where he had himself been cultivating his fortune, found himself again in familiar London with his brain still reeling from the war scenes through which he had passed. All the boat trains that came in were run in three portions, and the outward trains were scenes of exultation or poignant farewells. Many French people, including large numbers of French women, went away. Many of the men went to join the army. Round the barriers and on the platforms there were affecting farewells. Few of the Frenchmen seemed to go off without someone to regret their going. The expressions of feeling, too, were not confined to words. In some of the carriages there were notices in neat penmanship: 'Ici pas des Prussiens.' I met a French friend at the train looking very sad and said to him, 'This is a sad day. You are all going … ' 'With good countenance!' he said, 'with good countenance. Not only the reservists – the deserters too. They are going back. Everybody is going.' We talked for a little and then he said: 'You will forgive me. I must go to my friends. I may not see them again.'

The German Reservists Go

Then I saw the German reservists going. They left with something like the circumstance, if not the pomp, of war. A special train took them from Charing Cross to Gravesend, where a steamer was chartered to sail direct to Hamburg. For nearly half an hour Charing Cross was like a scene in Germany.

There were about 600 travellers, with several hundreds of friends, and suburban passengers arriving on the other platforms were brought up standing, as they sat, by the roar of 'Die Wacht am Rhein' and the sight of this regiment of young Teutons, very excited and at times noisy, dressed in all varieties of costumes, many with the appearance of hurried dressing and many with their things packed anyhow in hat-boxes and in newspaper. The majority were probably waiters, the men one sees in a mass at great public dinners being drilled by the chief, halting at the buffet and deploying into line down the tables with the duo courses. Now very masculine, almost truculent, they charged through the crowd, carrying the platform at a rush.

King on Palace Balcony

An extraordinary scene – extraordinary at least for the English capital – took place today when a company of young Frenchmen led a crowd of Londoners down to Buckingham Palace to cheer the King. The French youths, waving little French flags or flourishing bunches of tricoloured stuff on the ends of their sticks, marched through Piccadilly Circus and down to Charing Cross singing the 'Marseillaise.' An excited crowd, vague but pursuing, hurried across the end of Northumberland Avenue after them towards Admiralty Arch, gaining hundreds of adherents as it marched.

Afire with the news that Britain's fleet was mobilised, it moved rapidly down the Mall straight to the Palace, a crowd of some 6,000 or 7,000 people scattered over the wide roadway.

Crowd Wild with Excitement

The windows behind the balcony opened, and the crowd went wild with excitement when the King and Queen stepped out. There was a rush to the gates, hats and sticks were waved, and the excitement was so great that at first no one thought of singing the National Anthem. The three Princes appeared at an upper window, and then at another Princess Mary's fair head was seen and the crowd cheered again. More cheers, snatches of the National Anthem, and a verse of 'Rule Britannia,' and then the King, who has stood quite still watching the tumult, bowed, waved his hand in a cheery fashion, and returned with the Queen to the Palace.

The cheering crowd then streamed back to Trafalgar Square and held another meeting there, with more waving of the French flag, before it was dispersed.

All night there were small processions of young men, usually headed by a decorated motor-car and some guardian police, marching from somewhere to the Palace, where they sang 'God Save the King' and 'Soldiers of the King.' The processions consisted largely of very young French waiters, too young for service, newsboys who had had a good day, and a stiffening of men dilated by the day's excitement and unready for bed.

'OVER THE PRECIPICE'

On 3 August, the German army crossed into Belgium. On 4 August, Britain declared war.

5 August
England Declares War on Germany

Great Britain declared war on Germany at 11 o'clock last night. The Cabinet yesterday delivered an ultimatum to Germany. Announcing the fact to the House of Commons, the Prime Minister said: 'We have repeated the request made last week to the German Government that they should give us the same assurance in regard to Belgian neutrality that was given to us and Belgium by France last week. We have asked that it should be given before midnight.'

Last evening a reply was received from Germany. This being unsatisfactory the King held at once a Council which had been called for midnight. The declaration of war was then signed.

The Foreign Office issued the following official statement:

'Owing to the summary rejection by the German Government of the request made by his Majesty's Government for assurance that the neutrality of Belgium will be respected, his Majesty's Ambassador to Berlin has received his passports, and his Majesty's Government declared to the German Government that a state of war exists between Great Britain and Germany as from 11pm on 4 August 1914.'

'HOW IT WILL END ...'

*'The war ought not to have taken place,' CP Scott wrote on Friday
7 August. 'But once in it the whole future of our nation is at stake,
and we have no choice but to do the utmost we can to secure success.'
The following extract from the* Manchester Guardian *editorial of
Wednesday 5 August confronts controversies that persist a century on,
and offers an insight into the reasonable – and faulty – assumptions
made during the opening days of the war.*

5 August
The Declaration of War

England declared war upon Germany at eleven o'clock last night.
All controversy therefore is now at an end. Our front is united.
A little more knowledge, a little more time on this side, more
patience, and a sounder political principle on the other side
would have saved us from the greatest calamity that anyone living
has known. It will be a war in which we risk almost everything of
which we are proud, and in which we stand to gain nothing. Even
those who have worked for the war will enter upon it without
enthusiasm, and amongst the majority of our countrymen the
thought of it has aroused the deepest misgivings and the most
poignant regret. Some day we shall all regret it. We ourselves have
contended for the neutrality of England to the utmost of our
power and with a deep conviction that we were doing a patriotic
duty. The memory of those efforts will not weaken our resolution
now, but rather strengthen it. Some time the responsibility for
one of the greatest errors in our history will have to be fixed, but
that time is not now. Now there is nothing for Englishmen to do
but stand together and help by every means in their power to the
attainment of our common object – an early and decisive victory
over Germany. [...]

The war … will fall into three natural divisions. The first will be the war at sea. The second will be the war between France and Germany, until such time as Russia is able to bring her forces into decisive action. Unless Germany can win crushing victories over France in this time she will have lost the war. In two months or three months at the outside we shall probably know how it will end.

6 August
London and the First Day of War

Pitiless rain thrashed the streets to-day, but it could not sweep away all the signs of the excitement that you breathe in London just now like a thickening atmosphere. In Whitehall at noon, for instance, in the very fury of the downpour there was the sight of an Irishman, angry at being taken for a German, and another man rolling, fighting, on the ground. Quite a row developed, and the mounted police had to come in and suppress the brawl. […]

Mr. Churchill was seen at once when he appeared in Whitehall in a finer interval of the afternoon … He looked, as someone said, 'cock-a-hoop.' The Prime Minister, whose reception in the streets has been remarkably cordial ever since the crisis began, again made his way to the House through a press of people. Men ran alongside his green car.

'TEARS ON HER FACE'

Prince Lichnowsky, the German ambassador (1912–14) born in what is now Poland, was aristocratic, Roman Catholic and an Anglophile. On 29 July 1914 he told his Foreign Office that 'war would be the greatest catastrophe the world has ever seen'. In 1916 he privately published My Mission to London, *which denounced Germany's pre-war diplomacy.*

6 August
The German Ambassador

Those who went to Carlton House Terrace in expectation of seeing Prince Lichnowsky depart for good were disappointed. The Ambassador, his face haggard with care, was sighted in his mourning on the way to his final interview with Sir Edward Grey. The evening papers recorded that the doorkeeper at the Embassy was seen in tears ... A workman removed the brass plate from the Embassy door.

7 August
Our London Correspondence, Thursday Night: The few strollers in St. James's Park at six o'clock saw a handsome lady, bareheaded, taking a walk with her dachshund. This was Princess Lichnowsky, and when she went into the Embassy for the last time there were traces of tears on her face. Prince and Princess Lichnowsky have made themselves to be greatly liked in their short stay among us, and their going is regretted ... when the big house was quite empty the Ambassador and his wife departed last of all in a motor-car. The dachshund travelled with his mistress ... The Government extended the hospitality of a passage on the vessel provided at Harwich to a good many of Prince Lichnowsky's friends, so that the whole party numbered nearly a hundred. Princess Lichnowsky, after leaving the car at the station, turned back to bid farewell to the chauffeur, and that trifling incident seemed, in a way, to be her farewell to London and happy memories.

10 August
The Germans in London

Our London Correspondence: The best instance of the public attitude is perhaps to be seen at the police office in Tottenham Court Road. For the last three days there has been a long queue of

the Germans waiting to be registered … They consist of Germans of all classes, including many quiet-looking old ladies, probably teachers, young German girl students, tourists caught without money, barbers, stockbrokers, shipping clerks, waiters, hawkers and some of much less reputable occupations. They are gathered in a narrow street behind the police office in a district which is one of the very worst in London. I have gone there several times by day and night, and have never seen them abused in any way. It must be said that they put a brave face on their troubles, and no one to look at them would think that they were in a hostile land with the shouts of German defeats ringing in their ears.

12 August
The Scouts at Work

Our London Correspondence: The Chief Scout, who has issued a stirring appeal to the boys of Britain ('Don't go about waving flags because there is a war – any ass can do that,' he says) is at present with a large body of Scouts who are helping the authorities on the east coast. Three thousand boys are watching telephones and telegraph wires in various places, and a hundred more are being used by the War Office as special messengers. Applications for Scouts are pouring into headquarters. Usually the Scouts are wanted to help the charitable works now in full swing. They are acting as patients for bandage work in the Red Cross nursing depots, as cyclist messengers for the Prince of Wales's and other charitable funds, and so on. Between three and four thousand Scouts have gone out on such errands in the last few days, and the same kind of thing is going on all over the country. The especial call for the services of the Scouts is sending up the numbers of the troops everywhere, but the chief need of the moment is for Scoutmasters to take charge of troops. The Scouts are not being wasted by being sent out on indiscriminate spy hunts. All kinds of suggestions reach the head office in Queen Victoria Street, and it is the boast of the organisers that they have been able to supply boys for every useful purpose that has been brought to their notice.

'PANIC-STRICKEN REFUGEES'

When the German army crossed into Belgium on 4 August, its high command uniquely interpreted The Hague conventions on war as implying that civilians could not resist invasion. 'Our advance in Belgium is certainly brutal,' wrote the Chief of General Staff Helmuth von Moltke the following day, 'but we are fighting for our lives and all who get in our way must take the consequences.' There was little civilian resistance, yet more than 5,000 Belgian civilians died, which earned Germany international condemnation. On 5 August 1914 the siege of Liège, and its 12 forts, began.

11 August
Bombardment of Liège by Moonlight

The following letter is … the first narrative of the events of Liège sent by any English correspondent from his own personal observations. Mr. Granville Fortescue was in Liège during the first two days of the German attacks. […]

Liège, Thursday: Last night and early this morning the Germans attacked this city in force. About 11.30pm, on hearing heavy cannonading, I crossed the river by a bridge and took up a position on the heights to the north of the city. It was a full moon … The artillery practice was perfect. Shell after shell was exploded fairly on the ramparts of the forts. The effectiveness of the return fire of the Belgians I could not judge, as the German gun positions were admirably concealed. The rough nature of the country and the night favoured the attackers. In my opinion no siege guns were in action. The Germans used high explosive shell that burst with extraordinary vividness.

About three o'clock in the morning infantry broke out in the woods west of the River Ourthe, between Embourg and Boncelles … The engagement attained its fiercest stage about five o'clock in the morning … The hilly nature of the country to the south favoured the concealment of the Germans. I would not attempt to estimate closely their force at this point. It might have been a division. They were occupying the intervals between the fortresses, and had as their objective the bridges south of the city. The attack was checked all along the line. Battalion after battalion was thrown back by the Belgians, whose 9th Regiment of the Line fought like demons.

Four Times Arrested: My own adventures were many and varied. The most stirring was when I was held up by a lancer, who kept his revolver pointed at the pit of my stomach while I explained that I was not a German. Four times I was arrested and brought before the authorities. When I got back into town the crowd that swarmed on the street would one minute surround me and threaten me as a German and the next loudly acclaim me as the first of the arriving English.

That was the question in every mouth – 'When would the English come?' The whereabouts of the French was another topic eagerly discussed by the mob.

Panic-stricken refugees came hurrying in during the morning and continued throughout the day to flood the city. Wherever they could find listeners, which was easy, they would tell the story of their night's experience. One woman, with her two daughters, had spent the whole night in the cellar of their home. A shell had exploded in the kitchen. Had any of her family been injured? 'Yes monsieur, the poor cat was dead.' A stout gentleman with a pointed grey beard was inconsolable because his 'collection of little birds' has been left behind at the mercy of the Germans. This influx of frightened outsiders had a very bad effect on the people of Liège itself. [...]

Last Train Out: The last train out of the city was crowded with refugees fleeing with such little property as they could gather together. The scenes were pitiful in the extreme when the train pulled out. Never can one forget the expression of those left behind. [...]

The Belgians were greatly helped by the fact that the enemy advanced in close order. Battalion after battalion of Germans was thrown in the fight in solid formation. It is small wonder that they were decimated ... The spirit of the citizens of Liège also merits the highest praise. Fortunately so far the German shells have done little harm to the city proper. But Liège is a fortified town, and under this classification it is liable to artillery attack without notice. And as soon as the Germans can bring up artillery of the necessary range, God help the women and children of Liège.

To overcome the Belgian border forts the Germans deployed vast siege guns, which had been transported from the Krupps and Skoda works in Germany and Austria-Hungary. By 17 August the Germans were advancing through Belgium, and they arrived in Brussels on 20 August. Their progress was accompanied by stories of outrages they had committed. Their sacking, as a 'deterrent', of the medieval city of Louvain (25–30 August) generated global publicity. It was, possibly, sparked by a shooting incident.

4 September
Burning of Louvain

From a Correspondent at The Hague: Terrible stories ... are reaching neutral Holland from Dutch eye-witnesses and others, of the destruction of the city of Louvain by the Germans ... The Maastricht correspondent of the *Handelsblad* visited Louvain with two others, and he tells how, after leaving Thienen, they rode through troops of fugitives; men, women and children, hardly clothed; sometimes the entire household of a convent, with old and sick nuns being pushed along by other sisters in wheelbarrows. In Louvain itself they found it impossible to ride along without now and then shutting their eyes. The car had to search everywhere to find an entrance into the town, which was shut off on all sides by flames, and when in the end they had found a way they had to drive in zigzag fashion in order to avoid the bodies of people and horses lying along the streets. They passed one spot where lay the bodies of four clergymen, all shot down.

Another Dutchman, Mr. W Rutgers, who was himself in Louvain during the terrible affair, and fled to Tiel with his wife and children, tells how, in the beginning of the panic, he took refuge in the cellar with his wife and his children of 2½ years and six weeks.

'About ten o'clock in the evening I ventured to take a look from my garden, when I had a view over the street and town. It was burning fiercely in the neighbourhood of the station and on the Great Market, and there was still a rain of bullets and of fire. What with the fear of the flames and the crackle of continuous rifle-firing, it was enough to drive one to desperation. At two o'clock every window in the house was smashed in, and our house, which, like every other, has on German orders been lighted from top to bottom, was riddled with bullets, evidently with the object of killing or driving out any possible fugitives.'

Yet another Dutchman, who was with others of his nationality and was conducted to the station by the Germans, says: 'The journey through the town was the most terrible it is possible to imagine. It was like walking through hell. The entire town was in flames. Everywhere in the town bodies were lying, whilst we still heard cries from some houses.'

Even a German, writing in the *Kölnische Zeitung*, who of course holds on the German story of how the affair started, says, 'Before our eyes a great number of inhabitants found with weapons were shot down without ceremony … The next morning the drama was frightful. Here lay people who had been shot dead, and there again more. Weeping women and children passed. Despite all the rage over this attack, which, according to a fixed plan, began precisely at eight o'clock, no German heart could remain unmoved at the sight of these innocent victims.'

14 October

Our London Correspondence: When war broke out Miss (Kate) Scott, who is a trained nurse, was about to leave Antwerp, but at the request of the authorities she remained to assist her friend, a Belgian lady … in the organisation of a hospital that had to be rapidly improvised on the unexpected outbreak of war. These two ladies were at that time the only two trained nurses in Antwerp, the nuns who, of course, do the nursing in normal times having left for the field. The hospital was … located in a boys' school, where naturally the sanitary and other requirements were altogether inadequate … It was exceedingly uphill and difficult work at first, as the hospital was staffed with voluntary workers with no training … For the last two or three weeks English nurses have been coming into Antwerp in large numbers … Tetanus was terribly prevalent, and the doctors now are taking the precaution of injecting the serum into the wounds as soon as the men reach hospital.

'THE GREATEST OBLIGATION'

'Our part in the war, for the present at any rate, is intended to be purely naval,' the Manchester Guardian *editorialised on 5 August,*

'and it is greatly desired that it should remain so.' In reality, earlier Anglo-French negotiations had led to a secret plan to place the British Expeditionary Force alongside the much larger French army. On 5 August it was decided to send the 100,000-strong British Expeditionary Force (BEF), then commanded by Sir John French, to France.

18 August
The British Army Lands

The British Expeditionary Force has been landed safely on French soil. Announcement of the fact was made last evening by the London Official Press Bureau. This successful transportation of a considerable army across seas not far from the German ports must humiliate the Kaiser's navy. While an official explanation of how the British army was kept at home through fear of German submarines was being sent out from Berlin, British troops were crossing the Channel without meeting with any interference. Field Marshal Sir John French visited Paris last Saturday. He … has also conferred with General Joffre, the French generalissimo.

The restrictions and censorship imposed on the British press would be an issue throughout the conflict. Now the secretary of state for war, Field Marshal Lord Kitchener, took the opportunity to express his gratitude to the journalists who had helped cover up the BEF's movements.

Keeping a Secret, Lord Kitchener Thanks the Press

The Director of the Press Bureau, Mr. FE Smith, stated: 'Lord Kitchener wishes me to add that he and the country are under the greatest obligation to the press for the loyalty with which all reference to movements of the Expeditionary Force in this country and to their landing have been suppressed.

'Lord Kitchener is well aware that much anxiety must have been caused to the English press by the knowledge that these matters were being freely described and discussed in the Continental press, and he wishes to assure the press in this country that nothing but his conviction of the military importance to this country of suppressing these movements would have led him to issue instruction which placed the press of this country under a temporary disadvantage.'

The Spread of the News

For a number of days past the press have been receiving reports which made it clear that the work of transporting British troops to the Continent was proceeding busily. One report would say that, at a certain point on the coast, bodies of troops who had been seen in their stations in the evening had disappeared altogether by the next morning; another would describe the high spirits of a particular regiment as it left a certain port; another, again, would chronicle the 'indescribable enthusiasm' with which the arrival of the British troops had been received at various places on the Continent. Besides this, a certain number of foreign papers which had reached this country contained reports and even photographs of the arrival of British troops on the Continent, but these, of course, at the request of the military authorities, have not been reproduced in this country.

30 September
The Shutting Out of the War Correspondent

Our London Correspondence: The case of the authorised war correspondents who were accepted by the War Office to represent the press and the news agencies of the country at the front, but who are still detained in England, has entered into a new phase. Twelve correspondents, all men of proved responsibility and knowledge ... and one well-known American correspondent were proposed under an arrangement come to with the authorities.

Their names were submitted to the Army Council and accepted by the War Office. They were instructed to buy houses, engage servants, and get proper equipment and arrange for their mess with the Expeditionary Force. Passes for themselves and servants were prepared, photographs were taken, and everything was done so that these accredited representatives should be ready to record for the nation the events of the greatest war which it had ever undertaken ... After that the correspondents were left to kick their heels at home, and were told that the cause of this was the attitude of the French General Staff. At last, however, this difficulty was understood to be removed. The press officer last week was summoned to the British Headquarters in France, and there learned that all objections were now removed. On his return it was expected that permission would immediately be given, but this time apparently the objection came from the English War Office. Permission has been indefinitely been withheld. Even the German General Staff have permitted several accredited German correspondents to be with the forces. But apart from General French's terse and splendid despatches, England is permitted to hear nothing but the moderately sprightly essays in journalism by 'an eye-witness' with the Headquarters in France ...

'For the first few months of the war we had no status whatever,' wrote the journalist Philip Gibbs in 1923. 'We were outlaws subject to immediate arrest (and often arrested) by any officer, French or British, who found us in the war zone.' For weeks Gibbs and his colleagues, taking advantage of the chaos of the initial period of war, remained on the move. In 1915, despite having been arrested, Gibbs became one of five accredited war correspondents. 'There was no need of censorship of our despatches,' Gibbs added, 'we were our own censors.' Nonetheless, strict censorship was conducted by the military and backed by the ubiquitous catch-all of the Defence of the Realm Act. The publication

of unauthorised news meant the invocation of the act; consequently,
rumour and charlatans flourished.

'AS THICK AS HIELAN HEATHER'

On 23 August the Germans, advancing from Belgium, attacked the
outnumbered BEF in the French town of Mons. In comparison with
what followed, the British fighting retreat at Mons – which went
on into September – was a minor engagement, yet it entered into
British mythology. Soldiers' personal testimonies, meanwhile, were an
additional news source.

5 September
With the Black Watch at Mons

A corporal and two privates of the Black Watch, who have just
arrived in London from the front, were surrounded by a crowd of
admirers and loudly cheered in Leicester Square, London, yesterday
afternoon. Two were wounded in the hands and the third in the
leg. It was at Mons that the Black Watch came into action.

'We travelled 246 miles in five and a half days before we came
to grips,' one of the trio explained, 'and you can guess we were not
feeling fresh when we started our shooting match. We had packs
on our backs weighing 90lb. In these we carried something to eat
as well as bullets. I had a tin of jam in mine, and next day I found
a German bullet in the tin. This must have got in when I ducked
to a volley – there was no time to dig.'

The corporal took up the narrative: 'I want to let the public
know how the Black Watch went through it. Well it was a terrible
bit of work, but our fellows stuck to their ground like men. The
Germans were as thick as the Hielan heather, and by sheer weight
forced us back step by step. But we had our orders, and every man

stuck to them, and until the order came through not a living man flinched. We stuck there popping off the Germans as fast as we could, and all around us the German shells were bursting. And in the thick of it all we were singing Harry Lauder's latest, 'Roamin' in the Gloamin',' and the 'Lass of Killiecrankie.' At times the odds at 300 yards were not three to one, but twenty to one.'

Somebody asked a question about the Jews – what were they doing? The Highlander broke in sharply, 'Doing? Well, their duty. We had three with us, and bonnier lads and braver I don't wish to see. They fought just splendid.'

There was a private of the Berkshire Regiment with the Highlanders, and he also had a good word to say of the Jews at the front. 'We had ten in our company,' he remarked, 'all good fighters, and six won't be seen again. So don't say a word against the Jews.'

The Lad Who Ran Away

The following are extracts from soldiers' letters:

Corporal S Haslett: The other day I stopped to assist a young lad of the West Kents who had been badly hit by a piece of shell. He hadn't long to live, and he knew it, too, but he wasn't at all put out about it. I asked him if there was any message I could take to anyone at home, and the poor lad's eyes filled with tears as he answered: 'I ran away from home and 'listed a year ago, Mother and Dad don't know I'm here, but tell them from me that I'm not sorry I did it.' When I told our boys afterwards about that they cried like babies; but, mind you, that's the spirit that's going to pull England through this war, and there isn't a man of us that doesn't think of that poor boy and his example every time we go into fight ... I am writing to tell his people that they have every right to be proud of their lad. He may have run away from home, but he didn't run from the Germans, anyway.'

Private T MacPherson: The Germans don't give you much peace, but we expect they will reach the end of their tether sooner than you would think, and then when they have tired themselves out our turn will come. It's not pleasant for a British army to have to learn to step backward, but we don't mind it in the least when we know that's the best line to make victory sure later on. You at home have every reason to be proud of your army, for it has fought under conditions that are always trying to the soldiers, and it's a long way off being beaten yet by the Germans. We've had just eight full days of hard, solid fighting, with little or no rest, except what you can get lying in the trenches waiting for the Germans to come on. When it comes to close fighting it has been shown more times than I can count that, man for man, our regiments are equal to anything the Germans can put in the field, and we're certainly not impressed with the fighting finish of the German soldier.

'RIGHT THROUGH THE UHLANS'

The retreat of the BEF ended between 6 and 10 September with the French victory at the battle of the Marne, which shattered the Schlieffen Plan and ended mobile war on the western front, ushering in four years of trench warfare. Earlier forms of warfare persisted. On 8 October 1914, the Manchester Guardian's *London correspondent interviewed a soldier from the Middlesex regiment about a clash between the Scots Greys and Prussian light cavalry.*

8 October
The Scots Greys' Charge

The Greys crouched forward with their arms straight out and swords extended, forming a rigid line like a lance. 'Of course,' he said, 'if they did not get their man then they cut out for all they were worth.' I asked if the engagement split up in groups like the mêlées at the Military Tournament. He said no – they went right through the Uhlans, except in two or three cases where the horses got stuck together and two or three men were slashing away at one another and then bursting free. He saw two men whose horses were killed laying about them like fury. It was a living wonder how they were not trampled to death. 'I don't know how they did it,' he said, 'but they were stark mad. They all go mad at a charge like that. You'd see the queerest thing – like one of the Greys sticking his man and a German sticking him on the other side, and another Grey sticking the German – and the whole thing like a flash.' I asked him if the Germans shouted to them when they were fighting closely. He told me the same story as the other Middlesex man had done. He said that the Germans kept on shouting, 'Stand up, English dogs!'

'WHEN THE INDIANS ARRIVED'

The people of the Raj – modern India and Pakistan – were not consulted about their participation in the war. More than 1 million soldiers served overseas in the Indian army – and 75,000 died. By autumn 1914, Indians were on the western front, facing the threat of projectiles like the 'Black Maria'.

12 November

France, Sunday: It was a curious sight to all of us, French or English, the day when the Indians arrived in a dreary little town of Northern France ... Suddenly the Indian Lancers appeared, and the pavement on both sides of the street was at once filled by a crowd of soldiers and civilians watching the procession, as a London crowd will do in Whitehall on the day of the opening of

Parliament. In fact, those Indians looked all like kings. The Lancers sat proudly in their saddles, with their heads upright under the Oriental crowns; then came a regiment of Sikhs, walking at a brisk pace, all big and strong men, with curled beards and the wide 'pagri' round the ears; the Pathans followed, carrying on their heads that queer pointed bonnet, the 'kullah,' which reminds one of the warriors seen on old Persian tapestries – a more slender type of men, but equally determined, and with faces at the same time smiling and resolute.

... The day after, we heard that during the night one of the Sikh regiment had had to recapture the trench, which the Germans had taken by surprise, and that their bayonet charge was so tremendous that the enemy did not dare counter-attack. Almost immediately after that feat an order came not to allow the Indians uselessly to expose their lives by walking out of the trenches. The fact was that, in order to show their contempt for death, some Sikhs had refused to hide themselves in the trenches and had immediately drawn a fierce fire on their regiment. Fortunately, they did not insist on playing that sort of game; otherwise the Indian Army Corps would have disappeared in one week's time out of sheer bravery. [...]

A 'Black Maria' fell quite near a sapper while he was lying on the ground and steadily firing on the advancing foe. It did not hurt him, but dug a hole six feet deep at his side. The sapper – a Sikh, I believe – waited until the smoke had gone, and then jumped into the hole. He soon found that the position was a comfortable one, and started firing from the cover the Germans had dug for him; according to officers who were standing by, he managed to kill some fifteen or twenty Germans by himself, and would have remained there for ever if he had not been eventually ordered to retreat. He was warmly congratulated afterwards, but did not appear to think he had done anything remarkable.

A major recruiting tool was the establishment of Pals battalions, bringing together volunteers from particular localities, trades or sports. A consequence of this was that, as casualties mounted, neighbourhoods could lose a whole generation of men.

17 November
Second Sportsman's Battalions – A Chance for Footballers

There are many reasons which should induce recruits to join the Sportsman's Battalions, where the recruit will have the best of companionship and as much care and comfort as is consistent with getting fit. The football player ... will have in the Sportsman's Battalions the companionship of other men of similar tastes; and he can still play his favourite game with some of the well-known players of the country. The first battalion has eight football teams; for a second [battalion] a whole football team enlisted in the body of the North. Every effort will be made to keep footballers together who join in company.

'WAR IN THE HEART OF AFRICA'

In 1914 only Ethiopia and Liberia were outside the network of European empires in Africa. Portugal did not join the allies until 1916, but the British, French and Belgian empires were deploying their forces against German colonies in east, west and south-west Africa. Compared with Europe the number of combatants in these theatres of war was minuscule, but the number of casualties among Africans and Europeans was not. The Royal Navy dominated the Indian Ocean, and forces drawn from India, Africa and white South Africa were vastly superior in number to the Kaiser's white and African troops.

> ## THE LAND OF SUNSHINE.
>
> Investigate the possibilities of
> **RHODESIA**
> —its wonderful climate—its unlimited resources for
> Ranching and all kinds of
> profitable Agriculture.
>
> Send Sixpence for Illustrated
> **DESCRIPTIVE HANDBOOK**
> or apply for Free **PAMPHLETS**
> **INFORMATION OFFICES FOR RHODESIA,**
> 138, Strand, W.C.,
> or
> 140, Buchanan Street,
> Glasgow.

Appeared 3 August 1914

15 August
German Steamer Captured on Lake Nyasa

The secretary of State for the Colonies has been informed by the Governor of Nyasaland [a British protectorate in Africa, now part of Malawi] that on Thursday morning the Nyasaland Government-armed steamer *Guendolen* completely surprised the German Government armed steamer *Von Wissman* at Sphinx Haven, on the eastern shore of Lake Nyasa … The waters on which this naval victory was achieved are in Central Africa, some four hundred miles from the sea. The western shore of Lake Nyasa is wholly British, but the other side, at the North end, bounds German East Africa. The eastern shore is half German, half Portuguese. The Nyasaland Protectorate, which had a population last year of 758 Europeans and about a million natives, possesses military, volunteer reserve and civil police forces, and also a Marine Transport Department with a fleet of three vessels.

17 August
Raid on a German Colony

Zanzibar, Sunday: All trade with the German coast has ceased. The British have sunk a German surveying ship and the floating dock at Dar-es-Salaam and have smashed the wireless apparatus. The British authorities have regained possession of the letter mails sent up the coast, and it is expected that the parcel mails will soon be recovered. Dar-es-Salaam has been deserted by the Germans.

Zanzibar is quiet. The natives are loyal, and the Government is encouraging them in every way to continue to work. Prices are normal.

Amsterdam, Saturday: News has been received in Berlin from German South-west Africa that up till now the protectorate has not been molested. There are similar reports from the Cameroons … The port of Lome and part of Togoland have been occupied by a joint British and French force, and in German South-west Africa, according to a report previously published, the Germans had abandoned two ports after blowing up the jetties and dismantling the tugs in the harbours.

'OUT OF THE EAST'

In 1897 Germany acquired Tsingtao (Kia-chau, now Qingdao) on the Chinese mainland, which became its principal overseas naval base and home of its East Asia naval squadron. But in 1902, Great Britain and Japan had made an alliance that was to pay a dividend, of sorts, 12 years later.

17 August
Japan Delivers an Ultimatum

Japan has delivered an ultimatum to Germany demanding the withdrawal from Japanese and Chinese waters or the dismantling of all armed German vessels in the Far East and to deliver to Japan, for eventual restoration to China, the territory of Kia-chau. Germany is given a week in which to signify her unconditional acceptance.

Japan's object is, says her ultimatum, the preservation of peace in Eastern Asia, which is the chief aim of the Anglo-Japanese Alliance.

In Eastern and Australasian waters Great Britain and the British Dominions maintain a naval force overwhelmingly superior to Germany's ... The German garrison in Kia-chau is only 3,000 men, some of whom are Chinese. Japan's intervention, therefore, does not seem necessary in the British interest. Perhaps the Tokio ministers are influenced by the memory of how Germany played a leading part in compelling Japan to leave Port Arthur after she had taken in from China in 1895.

In the United States the news has been received with anxiety. The Washington Government desire to maintain status quo in China; they also would regard with uneasiness the establishment of Japan among the Southern Pacific islands, several groups of which, such as Samoa, now belong to Germany.

Racism played its part in American – and Australasian – attitudes to Japan, but for the British, the Anglo-Japanese alliance relieved pressure on the Royal Navy. On 21 August Japan declared war on Germany. With token British assistance, Tsingtao later fell to the Japanese on 7 November, while Australia would take most of German New Guinea.

When war was first declared, the powerful German East Asia naval squadron – commanded by Admiral Maximilian von Spee – divided. The cruiser Emden *operated as a successful surface raider in the Indian Ocean (it was eventually sunk by an Australian cruiser in November 1914). The rest of the squadron set sail in August for the Marshall Islands – German possessions which would later fall to Japan. In September, von Spee's squadron shelled French possessions in Papeete, Tahiti, and on 1 November, at Coronel off the coast of Chile, his ships heavily defeated Admiral Cradock's Royal Naval squadron.*

In response, the Admiralty assembled a new force under Sir Doveton Sturdee. This was vastly more powerful than the German squadron. On 8 December 1914, off the Falkland Islands in the south Atlantic, Sturdee's ships took their revenge on the Germans.

26 December
German Squadron Falls into a Trap

New York, Monday: I have received from Monte Video, where Admiral Sir Doveton Sturdee paid a brief visit yesterday, the first account by an eye-witness of the brilliant victory won by the British over the German raiding squadron. [...]

The British are reported to be in high glee ... bringing up two powerful battlecruisers to reinforce the remnant of Admiral Cradock's squadron without giving their foes any warning of their presence. These battlecruisers, with the battleship *Canopus* and the armoured cruisers *Carnarvon* and *Cornwall* and the light cruisers *Bristol* and *Glasgow*, arrived at Port Stanley, the seaport of the Falklands, on 7 December to coal. The big battlecruisers ran into the bay, which is almost completely landlocked. Surrounded by the high hills, they were entirely hidden from outside.

On the morning of the 8th the German squadron, consisting of the *Scharnhorst*, *Gneisenau*, *Leipzig*, *Nürnberg* and *Dresden*, appeared in the offing, accompanied by the converted merchantman *Prinz Eitel Friederich*, with the evident intention of taking the Falklands by surprise and seizing Port Stanley as a coaling station for themselves. Finding apparently only a British squadron of five cruisers, none of them equal to the German armoured cruisers in fighting value, and one old battleship on guard, the Germans promptly cleared for action and, closing in, opened fire, the British cruisers replying.

The action was already furious and apparently evenly contested, when out through the narrow harbour entrance came tearing the long grey forms of two great battlecruisers, each with her eight 12in. guns swung out for action. Admiral von Spee realised his terrible mistake and the trap into which he had been lured, and made a signal for his little squadron to scatter.

It was too late, however, the Germans having in their eagerness to finish the supposedly feeble British squadron drawn far within British range. The *Scharnhorst* and *Gneisenau* at once became the targets for the British battlecruisers' salvoes, the light German ships being left to the smaller British cruisers.

The *Invincible* Hit

The *Invincible*, being in the lead of the two battlecruisers, received the brunt of the German fire. Both German armoured cruisers, although seeing at once their hopeless position, fought desperately … with the last of their guns still blazing defiance, first one and then the other of the two cruisers heeled slowly over and went down. Admiral von Spee's flag at the maintop of the *Scharnhorst* was the last seen of the cruiser …

… When the *Gneisenau* sank she was without ammunition, but refused to surrender. Some officers stood at attention and the *Gneisenau*'s glee club formed in line on the after-deck and sang 'Wacht am Rhein.' … A large number of the *Gneisenau*'s crew, including several officers, were rescued. Some of these men died later from wounds or from shock sustained by submersion in the cold water. The *Scharnhorst* was ablaze when she sank with all hands, including Admiral von Spee. The two sons of the Admiral, one aboard the *Gneisenau* and the other aboard the *Leipzig*, were lost.

'A FRIENDLINESS EXCEEDING NEUTRALITY'

In the pre-war era, when the dreadnought was seen as the definitive weapon of mass destruction, the Ottoman empire ordered two of the battleships from Britain – financing them with £7.5 million from a patriotic public subscription. However, with the coming of war, a cancellation of the deal was noted in a throwaway story.

5 August

Our London Correspondence: It has always been known that the building of foreign battleships in the yards of English firms must be an important asset to the naval strength of this country in time of war, and it is therefore not surprising that the Admiralty have exercised the right of purchase which they possess in the case of one Turkish battleship now completed and another nearly completed ... The first of these battleships would appear to be that built by the Armstrong firm at Elswick ... [it] is to be called the *Agincourt* ... The second Turkish battleship, which is being built by the Vickers firm and which was launched last year, is to be called the *Erin*, a well-deserved tribute to the patriotism of the Irish nation at the present moment.

The Turks, who were already negotiating a secret alliance with Germany, were outraged that the British had reneged on the sale. On 4 August, in a deft move by Berlin, the commander of the German battlecruiser-cum-dreadnought Goeben, *which was at sea in the Mediterranean with the light cruiser* Breslau, *was ordered to sail to Constantinople. The British authorities provided the public with a positive spin on the affair.*

17 August
The Navy's Work

The sale to Turkey by Germany of the warships *Goeben* and *Breslau* is no longer doubted. Thus the German navy loses in a humiliating manner a super-Dreadnought more powerful than any British vessel in the Mediterranean, and a fast light cruiser. Report says the Ottoman Government have not observed strictly their international duties, but have treated the Germans with a friendliness exceeding neutrality ... During their flight to the Dardanelles the German cruisers were driven eastwards by British ships. The light cruiser *Gloucester* attempted to take or destroy the *Breslau*, but was compelled to draw odd by the approach of the immensely more powerful *Goeben*.

In fact, the Germans were by no means humiliated and their ships were ineffectively pursued – rather than 'driven eastwards' – by the Royal Navy. On 16 August the two vessels dropped anchor in Constantinople and were 'transferred' to the Turkish navy. By late October the ships were shelling Russia's Black Sea coast. In early November Russia, Britain and France declared war on Turkey.

The Goeben *survived – as the Turkish navy's* Yavuz *– until 1973. By this time, it was the only dreadnought in the world.*

'A LONG WAY TO GO'

British soldiers fighting abroad sung 'Pack Up Your Troubles' and 'Mademoiselle from Armentières'. And then there was 'Tipperary'.

8 October

Our London Correspondence: A word about the song 'Tipperary' ... thousands of soldiers have marched to their fate singing it, just as in the Boer War they went out singing 'Soldiers of the Queen.' Mr. Jack Judge and Mr. Harry Williams are responsible for the words and music. Mr. Judge, who is a music-hall singer, tried several publishers with it before he approached Mr. Feldman, who, I am told, was impressed, and with a few alterations published the song. The result was not at first encouraging, until it was introduced into the Isle of Man by Miss Florrie Forde. Its popularity grew quickly, and when a great war broke out the soldiers found the song waiting for them. They were going 'a long way' and they were saying 'Farewell Leicester Square,' which every reader of the semi-comic press and every music-hall goer knows is the symbol of all that is bright and characteristic in town life. America is just as enthusiastic. One American manager offered $3,000 for the rights for six months. The offer was declined. Over two million copies of the song have been sold, and the words of the song are being printed and used in many directions. Several million boxes of matches which are being sent to the front will bear the words of the chorus. One would like very much to know what the song-writer and what the composer got for their work. It ought to be something tremendously handsome.

It was £5, but later Jack Judge was given a £1 weekly pension.

8 October

Our London Correspondence: Wounded soldiers who are able to go about are now fairly common sights in the town. Officers with an arm in a black silk string are often to be seen about Bond Street, especially about the tobacconist shops – it is the usual thing for a wounded officer, whenever he is able to go out, to go to the shops and order cigars and cigarettes for his regiment at the front. Wounded men getting better can now be seen with their friends at the music-halls or in the Tubes and 'buses. They have usually either got their story pat and ready after many tellings in the family circle, or are men of few words who have only answer for questions, if the questioner takes their fancy ... A private of the Middlesex regiment whom I met to-day gave me his experiences. He had been wounded in six places by a 'Jack Johnson,' and one of the pieces was still in him awaiting a final operation. When a man was hit he usually said, 'That's got me,' and if he was well enough he'd ask for a cigarette. They gave up their last cigarette to the wounded. Then he'd smoke and wait for the stretchers. He himself had seen his pals looked after by Belgian women, who had done everything for them like sisters. If a Belgian wanted anything now, and he was at his last penny, he'd give him it. I asked him what songs the soldiers sang. He said that in the trenches they sang 'Get out or get under' when they saw the shells coming. 'Tipperary' was a favourite on the road, but 'The Germans got my Daddy,' a parody of another song, was popular. The Scotties had their own songs and they made most noise with 'We're the lads from Bonnie Scotland.'

Jack Johnson was the African-American boxer. A 'Jack Johnson' was the explosion of a 15cm German artillery shell.

Back at home, the music halls provided one of the most popular forms of entertainment, with Vesta Tilley one of its biggest stars. At her farewell performance in 1919, the great actress Ellen Terry proclaimed that the music-hall star 'does not know what she has done for England. She made us laugh when, God knows, we needed to laugh.' In those times only the ailing Marie Lloyd was, perhaps, a bigger female star than the 'Great Little Tilley'. Tilley's (lost) art was male impersonation – 'Girls if you'd like to love a soldier, You can all love me!' – and her following was vast.

27 October
Variety Theatres

If these were not days of grim warfare it would be a matter of some importance that Miss Vesta Tilley has at last given her sanction to the wearing, by her adopted sex, of evening clothes in blue cloth. Nearer to the moment, however, is the appearance of the little lady in khaki uniform. Neither in the old nor the new armies could you find the prototype of Miss Tilley's soldier creations, but that is not a point to be scored against her. No soldier could swagger around with the same touch of inoffensiveness that relieves the singer's acting. There is something curiously gentle behind Miss Tilley's assumption of bumptiousness. She pokes light fun for satire, and allows you to laugh at him without bringing him into the zone of the ridiculous. When she slants a cigar at a silly angle, swishes a cane in alarming circles, winks broadly on the march, and claims fictitious acquaintance with those in high places, you can smile without a thought of disloyalty to the men who have answered the call to arms. For a serious patriotic song, given with the feeling and charm which are hers to command, Miss Tilley has promoted herself to the rank of lieutenant. No one is likely to accuse her of audacity. So genuine is her popularity that if the War Office could appoint her colonel, one could imagine her recruiting a battalion in record time.

'HALF THE WORLD IN ARMS'

'In two months or three months at the outside,' the Manchester Guardian *had editorialised in August 1914, 'we shall probably know how it will end.' By early winter such confidence was evaporating. The battle of the Marne in September was followed on 30 October by the first battle of Ypres. In November the BEF thwarted the German offensive – but the victory effectively destroyed that small, highly*

professional army. Earlier, at the end of August, the armies of Paul von Hindenburg and Erich von Ludendorff had inflicted shattering defeat on the Russians at the battle of Tannenberg, and vast, inconclusive battles ensued across the east. On Tuesday 10 November the Lord Mayor's banquet was an occasion for Britain's war leaders to boost morale, flatter allies and promote British war aims. Speakers included Prime Minister Herbert Asquith.

10 November
Ministers at the Guildhall

The Lord Mayor's annual banquet was held tonight at the Guildhall. This historic building has been the scene of great civic ceremonies for more than five hundred years, but rarely if ever has the incoming Chief Magistrate 'bidden his guests to the feast' in circumstances so strongly appealing to the popular imagination. No previous head of the municipality has entered on his year of office with half the world in arms … Even the Lord Mayor's invitation card bore witness to the world-wide conflict which is now raging, for it bore as its chief design the flags and coats of arms of the Allied Nations … Carriages began to set down their occupants shortly after five o'clock, and the seating accommodation … very soon became taxed to its utmost capacity. The London Rifle Brigade detachment, which lined the stairway, had discarded its full dress for a service uniform … The Japanese Ambassador [was] enthusiastically acclaimed, the entire assemblage rising to cheer him. […]

Mr. Asquith, who, on rising to reply to the toast of 'His Majesty's Ministers,' was received with loud cheers, said: 'Never has any Government in modern history more needed the whole-hearted confidence and the unselfish co-operation of the community without distinction of party or class than during the one hundred days which are now nearing their completion

since the commencement of this war ... We shall not sheathe the
sword, which we have not lightly drawn, until Belgium recovers
in full measure – (cheers) – all and more than all that she had
sacrificed – (prolonged cheers), until France is adequately secured
against the menace of aggression, until the rights of the smaller
nationalities of Europe are placed upon an unassailable foundation
– (cheers), until the military domination of Prussia is finally and
fully destroyed. (Loud and prolonged cheers.)'

'MANY IN NEW MOURNING'

17 December
Intercession

At eight o'clock this morning, a day and night watch of intercession
began at St. Paul's Cathedral. The order of service is so arranged
as to fill a full hour with the aim of uniting thought and prayer.
The prayers offered up ask for guidance and protection for those
in command, for courage and endurance for the Allies, gentleness
in victory and patience in reverses. Silent prayers are asked 'for our
soldiers and sailors and those of our Allies, especially those who
serve in submarines and aircraft, for our enemies and that they may
be forgiven, that there may be no spirit of personal hatred in our
hearts towards them, that the causes of bitter misunderstanding
between us may be taken away, that they may be recompensed
for the acts of kindness shown by them to our wounded and
prisoners.' More than a thousand persons took Communion in the
morning, and all day the great church was thronged. There were
many soldiers, policeman, postmen, nurses and clergymen from all
parts of the city and from rural parishes. The majority there were
women, many in new mourning. After five o'clock there was a great
stream of City men and women clerks and typists. A noticeable

thing was the number of old men and the number of working men and women. A great many seemed unfamiliar with the Cathedral and with the Anglican service. It was, in a memorable degree, a national assemble, and the great Cathedral in the dusky afternoon light, with its few lamps overpowered by the mist, and its tall piers and the cloudy hollow of the dome, was a noble setting for it ...

'TEN THOUSAND THUNDERSTORMS'

There was not a massive loss of life – 137 deaths (592 were wounded) – but the German navy's shelling of Hartlepool, Whitby and Scarborough on Wednesday 16 December 1914 undermined any ideas of invulnerability that the British might have harboured.

17 December
German Cruisers Attack Yorkshire and Durham Towns

German cruisers made a raid on the English east coast yesterday. Between eight and ten o'clock in the morning they bombarded Scarborough, Whitby and the Hartlepools, and then disappeared to sea. The three towns all suffered heavily, many buildings, mostly private houses, being destroyed and damaged, while many persons were killed and wounded. At Hartlepool, a father, mother and their six children were killed by one shell; at Scarborough a family of four lost their lives. The immense majority of the victims were civilians. [...]

Hopes that the raiders were trapped persisted until late last night, when the Press Bureau announced that the enemy had escaped. This report, the second issued from the Admiralty during the day, said the German cruiser force, composed of the Kaiser's fastest ships, after remaining about an hour, retired at full speed and in the mist evaded pursuit. A patrolling squadron attempted to cut the Germans off but failed. On both sides the losses were small ... Almost 350 miles due east from Scarborough, the Heligoland rock, Germany's island fortress and advanced naval base, rises from the North Sea before the approaches to the Elbe. [...]

The cruisers first appeared off Scarborough just before eight o'clock. They came far into the South Bay and opened fire. The bombardment continued for half an hour. Two churches, St. Martin's, South Cliff, and All Saints', Falsgrave, were struck. Many shells were plainly aimed at the Admiralty wireless station and the gasworks, but all missed. Several hotels were partly wrecked, and throughout the town private houses suffered much damage ... At Whitby the attack began at nine o'clock and lasted for 15 minutes. Two men were killed, two Boy Scouts wounded, and many houses were damaged; the bombardment was not so severe and the destruction not so general as at Scarborough. [...]

The Hartlepools were the greatest sufferers. An attack on them by a third hostile detachment began at eight o'clock and lasted 35 minutes. Three large warships fired broadsides into West Hartlepool and Hartlepool. Although the first replied the enemy seem to have escaped almost unhurt. In the towns, widespread destruction was effected by the German shells. The gas-works were struck and set on fire, and in the district behind the old fort at Hartlepool the damage was serious.

Schoolgirls and Their Bits of Shell

Throughout the afternoon trains arriving in Manchester from Yorkshire coast towns brought passengers who had graphic stories to tell. The majority of these people were from Scarborough, and ... included a small party of girls who were at school there. They were full of excitement and freely recounted their experiences to their fellow-passengers. Each of them had a small portion of a shell which at an early stage in the bombardment struck a portion of the school. The scholars were immediately ordered to pack up and prepare to go home by the earliest train. The impression conveyed to the mind of one of the girls by the noise of the bombardment was described in a homely sentence. 'It was just like ten thousand thunderstorms all coming at once,' she said.

A business man who passed through Manchester on his way from Scarborough told a *Manchester Guardian* representative that he was just about to dress, shortly before eight o'clock, when he was startled by a deep booming and the rattling of his windows. He rushed to the window and saw volumes of smoke rising from a building a short distance away. Even then the fact that the town was being bombarded did not dawn upon him, but there was soon no room for doubt. Many people had run out of doors in scanty attire and hurried off to places of safety. Horses had taken fright and bolted. [...]

'The firing ceased as suddenly as it has begun,' our informant proceeded, 'and one of the vessels disappeared in the direction of Filey. The shots had followed one another in quick succession – like reports of a rip-rap. In the half light of the early morning the flashes of light seemed to illumine the whole town. People were soon abroad examining the wreckage, assisting in putting out the fires, and collecting pieces of shell as mementoes of their thrilling experience.'

Our London Correspondence, Wednesday Night: The news of the raid on the coast towns reached London early, and ... caused an instant mobilisation of Fleet Street at King's Cross, where the refugees were expected on the Great Northern express. In fact, very few people came to London from the bombarded towns, and the only man found by the journalists who came because of the bombardment was a business man from Scarborough, who was injured by a piece of shell. This man had his head swathed in bandages, and his talk seemed to convey a thrill of excitement and terror into the placid dinginess of the station. He was a big, sturdy man, and a touch of the incongruous was given to the look of him by the fur tippet wrapped around his neck. His language was vivid and detailed, and one got from him a sharp impression of the utter bewilderment and the upheaval of all his notion of settled existence which assailed him when he was struck down by shrapnel on the pavement of his street. It was a moment of fantastic nightmare. Sailormen up on leave elbowed in the group to hear the story, and one shook the bandaged man's hand fervently, and said, 'Trust our boys to see they don't get back.' Alas! There was not even that consolation. The Scarborough man was the journalists' chief prize, but there was a cheerful schoolboy, who told how he woke up and watched the flash of guns from his bedroom windows. He was still bursting with the tremendousness of the experience. He had remembered especially how he saw the front of a house fall out, exposing all the rooms 'like a doll's house.' One saw representatives of enterprising papers shepherding their finds away to taxicabs. A soldier was showing a piece of shell which he had picked up in a Scarborough street. He consented to lend it to a newspaper man for photographic reproduction as the first piece of shrapnel shell ever fired into an English town.

'THE CHRISTMAS TRUCE'

For the Manchester Guardian, *speculation on Thursday 24 December 1914 was realised in an event that became an emblem of dashed hope and the Great War.*

24 December
Miscellany: The English, Irish and German regiments (leaving aside the Jews in each, a very considerable number) will be all for

Christmas. It will be strange if one of those little truces arranged tacitly by the men and winked at by commanders does not occur to-night in order that, if possible, the Germans may find something to take the place of Christmas-trees and the English something to take the place of holly in the trenches. German illustrated Christmas numbers have already reached England showing miniature Christmas-trees lighted with little candles in the trenches.

The paper quoted from a letter written by a British officer at the front:

31 December
A Christmas Truce at the Front

Last night we moved back into our old trenches ... the next day was Christmas Day, and I wanted to see the state of the trenches throughout my our section. Had it not been freezing they would have been awful, but as it was just freezing the top crust was comforting, but in places one sunk nearly up to one's knees in mud. At 11pm on 24 December there was absolute peace, bar a little sniping and a few rounds from a machine gun, and then no more. 'The King' was sung, then you heard 'To-morrow is Christmas; if you don't fight, we won't.' And the answer came 'All right!' One officer met a Bavarian, smoked a cigarette, and had a talk with him about half-way between the lines. Then a few men fraternised in the same way, and really today peace has existed. Men have been talking together, and they had a football match with a bully beef tin, and one man went over and cut a German's hair!

1 January
British and Germans Exchange Presents

Writing on Boxing Day from the trenches to his wife in Lower Broughton, a Manchester soldier gives the following account of the exchange of Christmas greetings and the hospitality between our troops and those of the enemy: 'The Germans had a lot of Christmas trees lit up with candles, and our men wrote on a board 'A Merry Christmas,' and the Germans wrote on another 'Extreme Thanks.' Then they beckoned for one of our men to go for some cigars, and he met the Germans half way between the trenches. This was the Welsh Fusiliers. Then their officer brought a bottle of champagne, which was drunk between them. Then all the men came and shook hands. The Germans, having occupied a brewery, rolled two barrels of beer up to our men.'

4 January
German Urges Our Men to 'Be British'

Sergeant HA Barrs, of the Cyclists Corps, a prominent Reading swimmer, in the course of a letter written from the front on Boxing Day to his parents, says: 'On Christmas morning, after some shouted conversation across the open space between the trenches a German shouted: 'Be British and come half way!' and out goes one of our officers. He shook his hands and exchanged cigars and cigarettes with the German officer. The German man suggested, 'You no shoot, we no shoot.' That started the ball rolling, and they all came out and had a spree, exchanging souvenirs and autographs. After sixteen shells, which the Germans had sent out in the morning, there wasn't a shot fired all day. On Boxing morning (today) I had a topping time, and wouldn't have missed it for pounds … There are loads of warm clothing and plenty of food and rum.' Sergeant Barrs concludes by saying, in respect to the war – 'The general opinion seems to be that scrapping will soon be over.'

Aston Villa Player Who Does Not Know What to Think

Gunner Herbert Smart, an Aston Villa football player, now in France with the 5th Battery Royal Field Artillery, writes home: 'The German I met had been a waiter in London, and could use our language a little. He says they do not want to fight. Fancy a German shaking your flapper as though he was trying to smash your fingers and then a few days later trying to plug you! I hardly know what to think, but I fancy they are working up a big scheme. But our chaps are prepared.'

6 January
More About the Extraordinary Unofficial Armistice

An officer writing to friends says: 'The Germans looked upon Christmas Day as a holiday; and never fired a shot, except a few shells in the early morning to wish us the compliments of the season, after which there was perfect peace, and we could hear the Germans singing in their trenches. Later on in the afternoon my attention was called to a large group of men standing up halfway between our trenches and the enemy's, on the right of my trench. I ... found a large party of Germans and our people hob-nobbing together, although an armistice was strictly against regulations. The men had taken it upon themselves. I went forward and asked in German what it was all about and if they had an officer there, and I was taken up to their officer, who offered me a cigar. I talked for a short time, and then both sides returned to the trenches ... The officer and I saluted each other gravely, shook hands and then went to shoot at each other. He gave me two cigars, one of which I smoked, and the other I sent home as a souvenir.' [...]

Corporal TB Watson, Royal Scots (Territorials), writes: 'On Christmas Day the greatest thing took place here. Somehow or other a friendly feeling got up between the Germans and us, so we both left our trenches, unarmed, and exchanged greetings about 300 yards apart ... This took place in the forenoon. After dinner we were firing and dodging as hard as ever; one could hardly believe such a thing had taken place.'

Private J Higham, of the Stalybridge Territorials, in a letter home, says: 'I was a bit timid at first, but me and a lad called Sterling went up, and I shook hands with about sixteen Germans. They gave us cigars and cigarettes and toffee, and they told us they didn't want to fight, but they had to. Some could speak English as well as we could, and some had worked in Manchester. All the Cheshires and the Germans were now together by this time, and we sang "Tipperary" for them, and they sang a song in German for us.'

Private Bricknell, 60th Rifles, writes to his mother at Wootton (Oxon): 'After dinner on Christmas Day I went over the front of the trench with a few of our chaps and met some Germans half-way between the two lots of trenches. We had a chat as best we could, and I exchanged a few fags for one cigar and also a bit of their Christmas cake; and then we returned to our respective trenches. This kind of thing has been going on all day, proper pals for the time being, but to-morrow I expect we shall be shooting at one another. They told us they would be glad if the war finished that night. Some of them were very young men and some were rather old, wearing spectacles and having long beards. They looked as though a wash would do them good, also a clean shirt. I expect you will think it an extraordinary piece of business, but, as I say, they have been walking about and conversing with different parties of us all day. They say they are not going to shoot again until after the New Year, at the same time asking us when we are going to start again, but I am afraid they will change their minds when we send them a few shots across.'

From a letter received in Birmingham from Private AF Lewis, 1st Battalion King's Royal Rifles: 'We occupied a line of excellent trenches made by miners, and provided with sleeping facilities. The enemy was only 50 yards away. Christmas Eve was a very dark night, and the Germans attempted to take advantage of the fact. Rifle fire, which became very hot, was commenced at five o'clock, and it continued for some time. Then all was quiet … They evidently wanted to catch us unprepared and as Christmas morning dawned the enemy was out of the trenches. Every man of the Royal Rifles was at his loophole, and we got the order to fire as rapidly as possible. We were assisted by the artillery, and the noise was deafening. No wonder the Germans did not pay their projected visit.'

6 January
French and Germans Refuse to Fight Afterwards

Paris, Saturday: I have heard one such story from a wounded French soldier who ... said that on the night of 24 December the French and Germans at a particular place came out of their respective trenches and met halfway between them. They not only talked, exchanged cigarettes, etc., but also danced together in rings ... The French and German soldiers who had thus far fraternised subsequently refused to fire on one another, and had to be removed from the trenches and replaced by other men ... There is more bitterness against the Germans among the French soldiers than among the British, who, as a rule, show no bitterness at all, but the general spirit of the French army is much less bitter and more moderate than that of many civilians, especially Academicians. Among the French civilians the bourgeois are much more violent as a rule than the people, and the 'Intellectuals' are the most violent of all. To that rule M. Romain Rolland is a conspicuous and almost a solitary exception.

Romain Rolland, who won the 1915 Nobel prize for literature, was a dramatist, novelist, and a friend of Albert Einstein and Gandhi. He proclaimed that in the Great War he had stood 'above the fray'.

A British Officer's Letter

A truce had been arranged [on Christmas Day] for the few hours of daylight for the burial of the dead on both sides who had been lying out in the open since the fierce night-fighting of a week earlier. When I got out I found a large crowd of officers and men, English and German, grouped around the bodies, which had already been gathered together and laid out in rows. I went along those dreadful ranks and scanned the faces, fearing at every step in recognise one I knew. It was a ghastly sight. They lay stiffly in contorted attitudes, dirty with frozen mud and powdered with rime. The digging parties were already busy on the two big common graves, but the ground was hard and the work slow and laborious ... we chatted with the Germans, most of whom were quite affable, if one could not exactly call them friendly, which indeed, was neither to be expected nor desired. [...]

They spoke of a bottle of champagne. We raised our wistful eyes in hopeless longing. They expressed astonishment and said how pleased they would have been, had they only known to have sent to Lille for some. 'A charming town, Lille. Do you know it?' 'Not yet,' we assured them. Their laughter was quite frank that time. Meanwhile time drew on, and it was obvious that the burying would not be half finished with the expiration of the armistice agreed upon, so we decided to renew it the following morning.

On Boxing Day ... we turned out again ... The German soldiers seemed a good-tempered amiable lot, mostly peasants from the look of them. One remarkable exception, who wore the Iron Cross and addressed us in slow but faultless English, told us he was Professor of early German and English dialects at a Westphalian university. He had a wonderfully fine head ... The digging completed, the shallow graves were filled in, and the German officers remained to pay their tribute of respect while our chaplain read a short service. It was one of the most impressive things I have ever witnessed. Friend and foe stood side by side, bare-headed, watching the tall, grave figure of the padre outlined against the frosty landscape as he blessed the poor broken bodies at his feet. Then, with more formal salutes, we turned and made our way back to our respective ruts.

CHAPTER 3

1915

In May the last Liberal government in British history gave way to a coalition, still headed by Herbert Asquith. Yet the key question remained: how could Germany, which occupied almost all of Belgium and large swathes of eastern France, be dislodged, and defeated without a large army from the British empire on the western front?

One solution, it had been thought, was an attack through the Dardanelles. Thus, the disaster that has gone down in history as Gallipoli began in April – and cost Winston Churchill his place in government. A Franco-British force arrived in Salonica that autumn in time to observe the crushing of Serbia by Austria, Germany and Bulgaria. On the western front, still the key battlefield, the Germans deployed poison gas; the French, Belgians and British responded in kind while launching a series of abortive offensives, partly to relieve pressure on the Russians. Italy entered the war in the spring. The Germans composed 'Hassgesang' – a 'hymn of hate' directed against the British – while the sinking of the Lusitania *in May exacerbated a wave of anti-German propaganda.*

As 1915 ended, Sir John French, the ineffective commander of the British Expeditionary Force, was ousted. His replacement, Sir Douglas Haig, would lead the largest army the British empire had ever assembled to victory within 36 months, a success accompanied, and followed, by a storm of controversy.

'KEEPING THE SUFFRAGE FLAG FLYING'

For women the war dramatically widened employment opportunities – in factories, on the land, in secretarial work, nursing and military service – despite widespread male resistance. While suffragette Emmeline Pankhurst backed the war ('Could any woman face the possibility of the affairs of the country being settled by conscientious objectors, passive resisters and shirkers?' she asked), others, like Emmeline Pethick-Lawrence, were forthright in opposition.

The war intensified state authoritarianism, including the policing of women's sexuality, at a time when women were winning greater personal, sexual and financial freedom. One weapon deployed was Regulation 40d of the 1914 Defence of the Realm Act (DORA), which made it an offence for any woman suffering from venereal disease to solicit or have sexual intercourse with a member of His Majesty's forces. In Cardiff a curfew was imposed on women, who were also banned from pubs, and in Sheffield women were banned from drinking after 6pm in hotels and restaurants. Nina Boyle was a founder of the first, voluntary, women's police force, which sought to assist women.

28 January
The Soldier's Wife: Suffragists and Unequal Treatment

A meeting was held in the Association Hall, Manchester, last night to protest against 'police surveillance and other indignities and disabilities imposed upon women whose husbands and sons are serving with the colours.' ... Miss Nina Boyle, of the Women's Freedom League, speaking of the restrictions of liberty imposed upon women, said that ... it was a dastardly thing to take away the right and liberties of women ... Women suffragists were doing some of the finest work in the country arising out of the war, and if they were not attacked they would not dream of fighting now ...

Miss Evelyn Sharp, who represented the United Suffragists, said that ... we must be quite sure that our country was not oppressing the weak, or else we could not ask men to make the sacrifice. That was why they were keeping the suffrage flag flying. This country had to be made decent. Atrocities that went on in this country had to be wiped out. In our midst, hidden by a conspiracy of silence, terrible things went on, and the people who fought against them were particularly the suffragists. [...]

A resolution demanding the withdrawal of police surveillance of women and the equal imposition upon men and women alike of any necessary restrictions of liberty was carried. The Government was also asked to ... extend the Parliamentary franchise to women as the only permanent safeguard against the misgovernment of women by men.

Sexual politics were taking many forms. Louisa Garrett Anderson was the daughter of the first British female surgeon and suffragist Elizabeth Garrett Anderson, and she and her fellow doctor Flora Murray had both been members of the Women's Social and Political Union. The army initially rejected their plans for a military hospital in Holborn, London, but its slogan was 'deeds not words' and the deed followed.

25 February

Our London Correspondence: Dr. Garrett Anderson and Dr. Flora Murray, who as heads of the Women's Hospital Corps have done such admirable work in the Paris hospital established in Claridge's Hotel, and the hospital for English soldiers at Wimmereux, near Boulogne, have now closed both those hospitals in order to take up a much larger work – the organisation of a hospital of 500 beds in London. This will of course be staffed entirely by women, and, like the Wimmereux hospital – the first to have that distinction – will be under the War Office, drawing army pay and army rations, and sending in daily reports like every other military hospital. It is not generally known that in addition to their work at Wimmereux two of Dr. Garrett Anderson's staff used to attend every day at the so greatly admired stationary hospital in the Gare Maritime, Boulogne, and take their share of work in the operating theatres there. The officers of the Royal Army Medical Corps told visitors to Boulogne how much they admired the work these women did.

'BETTER THAN LOSIN' TWO LEGS SIR'

18 February
'Gallant Spirit of the Maimed'

On the Steamship, Wednesday: I am coming across from Flushing to Folkestone with the first batch of permanently disabled British prisoners in exchange for Germans … In a cabin nearly opposite mine lies Private Smith, of the King's Royal Rifles. Smith was a football player. Now his right leg has been cut off from the hip. 'Better than losin' two legs, sir,' said Private Smith, 'an' lots better than losin' your 'ead. I'm satisfied if the Government is.' One of the men was a sergeant in the Grenadier Guards. His right leg was gone above the knee. Another had lost his left foot. Stepping out of my cabin I saw the first playing a sort of hopscotch along the passage way. He shouted back to his comrade: 'Come along here, Bill. They got rings to 'op in.' Bill, who followed on his crutches, came up just as I was taking in my boots. Pushing his good foot in front of him he said gaily, 'Cheer, oh! On'y one boot to clean.'

London, Thursday Morning: Those who were on the arrival platform at Charing Cross when the long-delayed ambulance train, almost at midnight, came in with the wounded prisoners released from Germany, said that the scene as the men, maimed and crippled, limped off the train or were carried out by the Red Cross workers was too painful to talk about. The delight of the men at being safe once more in England obscured the tragedy for them, but made it all the more poignant for the onlookers. The crowd outside the barrier, which grew with the waiting hours till it reached the Strand, vociferously welcomed the heroes. It was useless for the police inspector to chasten the crowds with, 'No noise now, if you please; it is bad for the men who are very ill.' Because the next closed ambulance car, filled with the most serious cases, was sending cheers out to the crowd, and, from every succeeding car, heads and hands were thrust to wave exultantly. A silence fell at the sight of the first car, whose windows bristled with white-handled crutches, but the invalids were so gay that the cheering revived and grew all the way down to the Strand, and after that, crutches or no crutches, we knew it was jolly for the men to be back again. A few friends of the men stood near the gates and examined car after car. The police and officials did all in their power to bring the friends together, and one inspector fairly shone with delight when, at last, in the depths of a covered ambulance, he discovered the soldier for whom an elderly lady had eagerly been watching.

Edinburgh-born, sturdy, bandy-legged Harry Lauder, the ultimate stage Scotsman, was an international music-hall star from the early 1900s until his death in 1950. He was knighted for his war work in 1919; his only son was killed in action in 1916.

27 February
Mr. Harry Lauder: A Recruiting Campaign of his Own

Mr. Harry Lauder, who is to be in Manchester next week, has become one of our most fervent recruiting agents … He has organised quite a national campaign of his own by the engagement of a band of pipers and drummers, who have begun an extensive tour through Great Britain. Mr. Lauder, who is appearing at a Birkenhead music-hall … told a representative of the *Manchester Guardian* last night something about his scheme and the feelings which led him to inaugurate it. 'I first thought of it,' he said, 'when I was crossing the States on my return home after my world tour. I felt that I ought to do everything I could to help to stir up martial enthusiasm and induce young men to come forward to defend their country, and when I got back I decided that the best thing I could do was to organise a pipers' band to go through the country.'

… He engaged fifteen pipers and drummers, and three weeks ago they started their tour in the Glasgow district … Manchester people saw for themselves a few weeks ago that the pipes are wonderfully persuasive – that they can fire a modern city as they once fired the glen … He is proud of his campaign, and particularly of his band – 'it's ma ain band,' he said with a bland smile of delight – and he believes firmly that it will accomplish all that he expects it to do … 'It began in the Glasgow district three weeks ago,' he said, 'and it is visiting all the towns of about a thousand inhabitants. It plays national music, and marches are being arranged with detachments of soldiers in the places where men are being trained. Where there are theatres or halls the band takes a turn, in addition to parading the streets, and we are working in conjunction with the recruiting officers.'

8 May

Our London Correspondent: The outbreak of war suspended the animation of dancing, and the recent closing of the night clubs has almost finished it. There is no London season, and therefore no private dances are being given, but while the night clubs were open there was still hope, for it was in these places that most of

the new dances were first tried. The military order only prohibited officers going into night clubs in uniform, but the effect of it was the officers did not care to go to them at all. Quite recently four of the best-known clubs have closed their doors. Dancing people, at any rate, are disposed to question the wisdom of the prohibition. Officers home from the front on leave used to go to a club to enjoy a dance first of all. The London magistrate who the other day dismissed a man charged with dancing in the street with the remark, 'It is refreshing to find a man dancing in these days of trouble,' is a popular person with the dancing profession. Apart from the schools for teaching stage dancing, which are not much affected, the dancing schools throughout the country have been hard hit by the war. Music and dancing were the first things on which war economists cut down expenses. The dancing congresses, which ordinarily attract to London teachers from all over the country to learn the latest invention, will not be held this year. The dancing papers record plucky attempts to introduce a new American diversion, 'the fox trot.' It is said that the next Hippodrome revue will be 'all fox trot.' This weird gymnastic may flourish on the music-hall stage, but hardly anywhere else.

22 May
Returning to the Front

Our London Correspondence: The departure of soldiers from Victoria Station for the front is a scene that stings as few other scenes in London can. There is something profoundly moving in the arrival of the wounded, but in that case the suspense is more or less over; the fact has happened and the worst is known – and it is generally not the worst. But here at the departure platform are men, fit, healthy and strong, in the prime of their life, going to the unknown. There is a tone of sympathetic solicitude on the part of the officials at the barrier as officers and soldiers pass through, their mothers, wives, and friends all obviously in a state of tense feeling. The terse station directions are softened into instructions that are persuasive rather than imperative. For some time before the two o'clock train left for Folkestone to-day, a band was playing outside the station yard and it was remarkable what a sense of relief this military music brought into an atmosphere of silent, anxious waiting. It added a touch of outside excitement which helped to dull the edge of the last few trying moments, and a touch of inspiration – however mediocre the music – that exalted. It is easier to tramp along to the front behind a band and amid cheering crowds than to walk singly and quietly to the train surrounded by friends waiting for the whistle to signal the departure. There were soldiers, and some sailors too, and one big naval man swung along the platform with a little girl in white perched happily on his shoulder. It brought several sympathetic smiles through tears. It is a merciless thrill that is sent through the heart when the porters come along with 'Take your seats, please.' The sting seems acutest just then. It signals the horrid moment, and one feels bound to turn aside from the final farewells. As the train moves out on a journey that leads none dares think to what end, a platform crowded almost exclusively with womenfolk watches and waves until the carriages turn the bend. It is harder to stay behind than to go.

'THE LAST RESORT'

'The government,' wrote CP Scott on 23 May 1915, 'has failed most frightfully and discreditably in the matter of munitions.' The allied landings at Gallipoli in the Dardanelles were proving a disaster, and bloody stalemate in France was exacerbated by ammunition shortages and inadequate artillery. Prime Minister Herbert Asquith responded

with a new coalition government. The last Liberal government in British history had ended.

19 May
A Ministry of All Parties

Our London Correspondence: The Coalition Ministry, or, as its friends would prefer to call it, after the Continental model, the Ministry of National Concentration or National Safety, has not yet been formed, but it is in process of formation. It is unlikely now that any obstacles will arise – though one must always remember that in the last resort the decision rests with the Prime Minister, and it is always possible for him to throw over all negotiations, especially when he holds so strong a personal position as does Mr. Asquith.

'THE DAY WE ALL LIVE FOR'

Throughout 1915, the British army – while still very much the junior partner of the French army – was expanding rapidly. In March, Ellis Ashmead-Bartlett reported on a military force that was in the midst of a transition to mass mobilisation.

13 March
Baths Every Ten Days

Scattered over Northern France and Flanders are many factories for making beet-sugar and beer. These possess enormous vats ... [which] have been utilised for the purpose of washing the British army. This experiment of cleaning every man in an army several hundreds of thousands strong, once every ten days, has never been tried before in war. [...]

A battalion comes off duty and marches to its rest billets, the men and their uniforms covered with mud. Above all, it is necessary to change their shirts and underclothes. Let it not be supposed that the only enemy our men have to face is found in the German trenches. There is another [lice] that takes ten times as much killing as any German … The battalion is paraded and marched to the nearest bath. Often this is under shell fire, and the shrapnel is screaming overhead. But no one heeds such trifles as these. Each man strips and throws his shirts, underclothes, and socks into a heap. His uniform he takes off and ties to it his tin identification disc.

At a word of command groups of 14 nude figures, with a wild howl of joy, rush into each of the steaming tubs. From these arise a chorus of screams and chaff as the men soap or duck each other in the soap suds. Meanwhile the uniforms are placed in another vat and steamed for ten minutes. The heat is so great that no evaporation takes place, and they come out perfectly dry. Each man as he emerges from the bath after his allotted span is handed a towel and a fresh set of underclothing. He then dries himself, puts his new garments on, and claims his uniform, recognising it by the identification disc. The underclothes which he took off are then handed over to the washerwomen, who are employed for this purpose at four francs a day. The clothes are then carefully inspected, and if found perfectly clean and made up into sets and are available for the next battalion which comes to be washed … A young printer's clerk said to me: 'This is the day we all live for. It helps you to get back your self-respect just when you feel you are sinking to the level of brute beasts from mud and dirt.'

'THE CHEMISTRY OF DEATH'

The main focus of Germany's military offensives in 1915 was on the eastern front – with one aim being to bolster the faltering armies of Austria-Hungary. The results were spectacular territorial advances, huge Russian losses and unspeakable horrors visited by both sides on Polish and Lithuanian civilians. In the west there was only one major German offensive. It came at Ypres and a key purpose was to test out a new weapon.

Fritz Haber was a chemist, a patriot and a friend of fellow future Nobel prize winner Albert Einstein – who rejected Haber's politics. Haber worked on the development of poison gas, arguing that it would break the trench warfare deadlock, and even that it was more 'humane' than explosives. On 22 April 1915 Haber witnessed the first well-publicised example of its use, which took place during the Ypres offensive. Haber's horrified wife committed suicide 10 days later. In the 1920s Haber worked on the Zyklon-B gas that the Nazis deployed during the Holocaust. Persecuted as a Jew after Hitler's accession in 1933, Haber died in Switzerland the following year.

26 April
Thick Yellow Smoke from the German Trenches

Paris, Saturday Afternoon: The French War Office makes the following announcement: 'The Germans succeeded in forcing our lines back during the evening of the day before yesterday to the north of Ypres … Thick yellow smoke emitted from the German trenches and driven by a northerly wind produced an effect of complete asphyxiation upon our troops.'

Masks for German Soldiers in the Poison Belt

Paris, Sunday: The special correspondent of the *Patrie* at Hazebrouck wires: 'The gas used is believed to be chlorine. It rolled on in thick clouds of dark vapour. Taking advantage of the first moment of surprise of our troops the Germans left their trenches and attacked, sustained by artillery fire. The first German soldiers were seen to be wearing a curious kind of mask to enable them to cross with impunity the poison belt.'

27 April
The British Defence Scene from a Hill near Ypres

From a Correspondent with the British Army: The fumes were blown against both the French and the Canadian trenches. Their effort was felt a mile and a half behind the trenches. The German soldiers rushed into the fumes unharmed – last week a number of Germans prisoners were captured who had wads of cotton in their pockets, and who said that they had been told to put this cotton in their noses when they charged after the gas guns had been fired. [...]

Ypres was being shelled mercilessly. Both white shrapnel and black 'Jack Johnson' shells broke around the tower of Cloth Hall. The tower and the two church spires stood up in the sunshine from a sea of smoke which filled the city. The fires of six burning Belgian villages were visible. British aeroplanes flew above bedlam.

The poison thrown by the Germans was so great in quantity that the ground is coloured in yellow with it.

28 April
Watching the Battle of the Guns

From a Correspondent with the British Army: The greatest aid of the Germans since they have begun using asphyxiating gas is the north wind. It blew to-day, and they threw huge quantities of the yellow poison into the air. On a hill in Belgium five miles from Ypres an officer called my attention to the fact that there was a sulphurous odour in the air. Whether it was the German gas or the smoke from the hundreds of shells breaking along the sixty miles of Flanders that was stretched out before is, we could not be certain. [...]

The sun shone brightly over the indescribable scene. The wind was so strong that the aeroplanes facing it made no headway. In one place, like kites, British aeroplanes remained stationary, directing, presumably, the British gunfire. From behind our hill two British monoplanes soared so low over us that we could see their guns. Then they climbed into the sky to drive away a Taube biplane which was flying over the hill sidewise in the heavy wind. The Taube took to flight at a height so great that it looked like a dot in the sky, even with our glasses turned on it. Soon the white puffs of the German anti-aircraft guns and the muddier white puffs of the British sky guns were seen in the sky above and below the glimmering dots which were the aeroplanes, gleaming in the sunlight.

Behind our hill were Belgian peasants ploughing; further behind them in a meadow we could see men playing football. I discovered later that some of the men in the match were to march five miles to-night and enter the trenches in the maelstrom of fire which we were beholding.

Tonight the glares of the battle illuminate the sky of Belgium for many miles. The tower of the Cloth Hall at Ypres and two church steeples were visible in the rays of the evening sunset, but many fires were burning in the town, and my glimpse of the ruins of the beautiful Cloth Hall tower may have been my last, for the German shells were falling about incessantly.

7 May
The Gas Atrocity in Flanders

The following extracts from a letter written by a British officer at the front speak of the terrible suffering of soldiers who were 'gassed' during the Germans assaults on Hill 60: 'Yesterday and the day before I went with *** to see some of the men in hospital at *** who were "gassed" yesterday and the day before on Hill 60. The whole of England and the civilised world ought to have the truth fully brought before them in vivid detail, and not wrapped up, as at present. When we got to the hospital we had no difficulty finding out in which ward the men were, as the noise of the poor devils trying to get breath was sufficient to direct us. We were met by a doctor belonging to our division who took us into the ward. There were about twenty of the worst cases in the ward on mattresses, all more or less in a sitting position, propped up against the walls. Their faces, arms, and hands were of a shiny grey-black colour, mouth open and lead-glazed eyes; all swaying slightly backwards and forwards trying to get breath. It was the most appalling sight, all those poor black faces struggling for life. What with the groaning and the noise of the efforts for breath, Colonel ***, who as everybody knows, has had as wide an experience as anyone all over the savage parts of Africa, told me to-day that he never felt so sick as he did after the scene.

'In these cases, there is practically nothing to be done for them, except to give them salt and water to try and make them sick. The effect the gas has is to fill the lungs with a watery, frothy matter, which gradually increases till it fills up the whole lungs and clogs up the mouth; then they die. It is suffocation – slow drowning – taking, in some cases, one or two days. Eight died last night of the twenty I saw, and most of the others I saw will die, while those who get over the gas invariably develop acute pneumonia.

'It is without a doubt, the most awful form of scientific torture. Not one of the men I saw in hospital had a scratch or a wound. The nurses and doctors were all working their utmost against this terror, but one could see from the tension of their nerves that it was like fighting a hidden danger which was overtaking everyone.

'A German prisoner was caught with a respirator in his pocket. The pad was analysed, and found to contain hypo-sulphite of soda with one per cent of some other substance. The gas is in a cylinder, from which, when they send it out, it is propelled a distance of 100 yards. It then spreads. English people, men and women, ought to know exactly what it going on.'

The Preparation for its Manufacture

It is now, of course, perfectly clear that the Germans have been preparing for some time to use asphyxiating gases in the present campaign ... according to the latest reports, the Badische Anilin und Soda Fabrik Company was displaying great activity, the number of its workpeople having been increased from 10,000 to over 20,000, and that the nature of the work in hand was being kept as secret as possible. The reason for this secrecy is now obvious, for the Badische Company is one of the largest German makers of liquid chlorine – which is what the troops are using to produce poisonous fumes – the other large concern similarly engaged being the Chemische Fabrik Griesheim Electron, at Frankfort-on-Main. It is significant, too, in this connection that it is the share of these companies which have attracted most speculative interest in Germany during the last few weeks and have risen most in price.

Gas increased the horror of the war, and imposed fresh restraints on the combatants. In May the Manchester Guardian *editorialised about a vain hope.*

10 May
Poison as a Weapon

From the accounts of medical men and others which are now reaching us it appears that the effects of the poison-gas which is Germany's latest weapon of war are beyond description painful ... It is, in fact, by far the most cruel instrument of war yet invented ... And yet we are told, and told in quite reputable quarters, that there is nothing for it but that we ourselves should do likewise – in other words, that we should emulate the crimes which we condemn. If that indeed were so, then it would be idle to pretend that we can henceforth place any limit to the atrocities of war. War, it is true, must always be atrocious, but there are degrees of atrocity, and it is worth something – it is worth very much – to maintain such poor restrictions as the conscience and pity of mankind have sought to build up ... If we are driven to emulate this latest German atrocity, and thus to give to it the sanction of the fair fame of our country, it will mean that we abandon henceforth – so far at least as this war is concerned, and it may be permanently – every restraint on the conduct of war which the slow progress of mankind has imposed. Is it not worth some effort and even some loss to avoid that?

The allied response came that autumn at the battle of Loos, as Philip Gibbs reported.

18 October
The British Gas and Smoke Attack

France, Saturday 25 September: On Wednesday ... an attack was made after a bombardment and under cover of a cloud of smoke and gas upon the enemy's trenches from a point south-west of Hulluch to the Hohenzollern Redoubt ... Owing to the character of the battleground and the fine, clear day it was possible to obtain a view. Large numbers of villagers living around the slack heaps and pitheads of this mining district did actually watch the terrific bombardment, roused to a new interest in the spectacle of a war which has become a monotonous and familiar thing of their lives. 'The English are attacking again,' was the message brought out to these poor people. They climbed to the black peaks of their slag-hills and stared into the mist, where, beyond the brightness of the autumn sun, men were fighting and dying.

To the left the ruins of Hulluch fretted the low-lying clouds of smoke, and beyond a huddle of broken lines far away was the town of Haisnes ... Pit 8 and the Hohenzollern Redoubt were black hills looming vaguely through drifting clouds of thick and sluggish vapour. On the edge of this great battleground the fields were tawny under the golden light of the autumn sun, and the broken towers of village churches, red roofs shattered by shell-fire and trees stripped bare of all leaves before the wind of autumn touched them, were painted with clear outlines against the grey blue of the sky.

Our guns were invisible. Not one of all those batteries which were massed over a wide stretch of country could be located by a searching glass. But when the bombardment began it seemed as though our shells came from every field and village for miles back behind the lines. The glitter of those bursting shells stabbed through the smoke of their explosion with little twinkling flashes, like the sparkle of innumerable mirrors heliographing messages of death. There was one incessant roar, rising and falling in waves of prodigious sound. The whole line of battle was in a greyish mirk which obscured all landmarks, so that even the 'Tower Bridge' of Loos was but faintly visible.

But presently, when our artillery lifted, there were new clouds arising from the ground and spreading upwards in a great dense curtain of a fleecy texture. They came from our smoke shells, which were to mask out infantry attack. Through them and beyond them rolled another wave of cloud – a thinner, whiter vapour, which clung to the ground and then curled forward to the enemy's lines.

'That's our gas!' said a voice on one of the slag heaps amidst a little group of observers. 'And the wind is dead right for it,' said another voice. 'The Germans will get a taste of it this time.'

Then there was silence, and some of those observers held their breath as though that gas had caught their own throats and choked them a little. They tried to pierce through that great bar of cloud to see the drama behind its curtain – men caught in those fumes, the terror-stricken flight before its trapped in advance, the sudden cry of the enemy trapped in their dug-outs.

Later from our place of observation there was one brief glimpse of the human element in this scene of impersonal powers and secret forces. Across a stretch of flat ground, beyond some of those zigzag lines of trenches, little black things were scurrying forward. They were not bunched together in close groups, but scattered. Some of them seemed to hesitate and then fall, and lie where they fell, others scurrying on until they disappeared in the drifting clouds ...

The enemy were firing tempests of shells. Some of them were curiously coloured, of a pinkish hue or with orange-shaped puffs of vivid green. They were poison shells giving out noxious gases.

All the chemistry of death was poured out on both sides. Below it and in it our men fought with a fierce valour. The enemy were strong as usual in machine-guns, and held on to some of their trenches with a desperate courage, while those which we had captured come under the fire of their batteries.

There were many acts of magnificent courage and a superb endurance by the officers and men in this difficult position. Only by the most resolute valour have they held to the ground which was gained at the cost of many lives.

The initial British gas attacks had, disastrously, blown back on to British lines. The battle of Loos dragged on into early November. It was a learning process for the allies, bought at a catastrophically high cost. Part of that process was the deployment of air power. By November, Philip Gibbs was examining the Royal Flying Corps.

15 November
The Warfare above the Flanders Lines

British General Headquarters, 11 November: Of the courage of these men of the Royal Flying Corps it is impossible to write too much praise ... A typical episode happened on 4 November. A flight captain and a second lieutenant were engaged in artillery observation when they were attacked by a large hostile 'pusher' machine – that is a machine with its engine and propeller behind the wings – closely followed by three tractors – or machines with forward engines and propellers. Our officers immediately opened fire upon them, using one drum containing the cartridges of the Lewis gun.

The 'pusher' was hit and flew off at once followed by two others. The remaining one engaged our aeroplane, chased it in full flight, and then, while it was manoeuvring for position, dived underneath its wings and fired as it passed. The flight captain was wounded in the right arm and the petrol tank was pierced. Two other flight officers of ours on patrol duty saw the machine mentioned above closely pursued by a German monoplane, and they made a steep dive towards it, like a swooping hawk. The Germans saw their danger, and making a swift turn flew straight beneath the wings of the British aeroplane, passing at about thirty yards below.

Half a drum was fired at them, but they turned again and spiralled three times round our men, while both machines were dropping rapidly. Suddenly the Germans decided to make off and flew away at a great pace, but they were followed at about eighty yards distance by our machine, which fired the remaining rounds in the drum … The German monoplane turned right-handed and banked steeply, then toppled upside down and plunged to earth just inside our lines. The pilot and observer were both killed.

'FROM THE POLE TO THE TROPICS'

When war broke out in 1914, Italy was part of the 'triple alliance' with Austria-Hungary and Germany but, having declared its neutrality, its government attempted to wring out the best deal for its support from the rival belligerents. On 26 April 1915 Italy signed the secret Treaty of London. Britain and France agreed territorial concessions to Italy, following an allied victory, in return for Rome's declaration of war on

Austria-Hungary. Among those clamouring for war were the Futurist Marinetti, lately of London artistic salons, and former revolutionary socialist Benito Mussolini.

13 April
The Moment of Decision Drawing Near

Dr. EJ Dillon, Rome: The Government is resolved to put down all attempts on the part of demagogues and agitators …to excite the masses for or against war … To-day, meetings of partisans of war and neutrality having been convoked in Rome, elaborate measures were adopted to prevent their taking place … Several orators attempted to harangue the populace from chairs outside the cafés, but were arrested on the spot …Signor Mussolini, and the leader of the Futurists, Signor Marinetti, were arrested by the police.

3 May
War and Soho

Our London Correspondence: It would be untrue to say that the war excitement in the papers has communicated itself to the Soho Italians. They showed, indeed, all the characteristic phlegm which they are popularly known to possess … In the afternoon, when there is not much doing anyway in the hotels, the waiters in their best clothes – the poorest Italian youth would not feel himself respectable without a fancy vest and a silver topped stick – formed groups in the foreign-smelling streets, and talked stolidly about the war. The Italian green, white and red showed a little more thickly than usual over the cosy eating-houses and those dark and humming social clubs round about Greek Street, where you never hear a word of English. They were quite fatalistic about the prospect of having to go home, but still quite unconvinced that they will have to go … If one looked into the clubroom of the Saffron Hill Italians, one found there the normal atmosphere of friendly conspiracy round the draughts tables in the gloomy corners and over the well-worn billiard table. [...]

Young Italians have not waited for war to join the army. I hear that they have been going home in little parties of a dozen or so ever since the Italian crisis became acute, and of course hundreds of them answered the appeal of the great name Garibaldi and went over to fight in his legion in France. There has never been the least doubt of the passionate desire for intervention on our side since the patriotic meeting in the Queen's Hall, with its pathetic row of old red shirts [veterans of Garibaldi's 1860 campaign for the liberation of Italy] ... Very many of the young waiters would be called upon. It is a flourishing time with them just now, for the departure of the Germans and the French has caused them to be much sought after. It will be an affliction in the back streets of London if the ice-cream vendors are called away just when we are getting hot enough to enjoy a penny cooling. Among all the London Italians, as much among the newcomers as the thoroughly Anglicised, the old Garibaldian spirit has a hold far more real and potent than that of rhetoric.

On 23 May Italy declared war on Austria-Hungary, and the hopelessly ill-equipped, badly led Italian army went into battle amidst the mountains. Stelvio mountain is 2,757 metres high – more than 9,000 feet. In the autumn, WGR Benedictus reported from the Alpine peaks.

2 September
The Top of the Ladder

Stelvio Mountain: The wide Italian front has been compared to many things. The aptest comparison is that to a ladder or flight of steps. It gradually descends from the Swiss frontier to the Adriatic Sea. The highest of these steps is the Stelvio; and it is this point which the General commanding, who only lately has allowed journalists on the front, has decided to show us first. From the Stelvio mountain (High Valtelina) to the now famed Isonzo, the intensity of the battle could be indicated by a stroke of the pen – small and pale at first, widening and darkening gradually to a good-sized black ribbon. The same line would indicate the variation of temperature. From the Stelvio to the Isonzo is a jump from the Pole to the Tropics. Here the soldiers have not known summer. One told me that on the 15th of July the thermometer descended to 14 degrees Centigrade under zero. The soldiers of both sides have to fight against the country and the cold more than each other. Nature keeps the strictest neutrality, and here the fight seems singularly futile. It is waged for the possession of a peak which no human being will ever climb or of a valley whose only inhabitants are pines or a chance chamois.

The scenery is more suggestive of sport than of war. The men whose ant-like forms, bound by ropes, crawl painfully up the white hill seem bent on some excursion. One can realise that anything like a real battle is impossible here – only skirmishes, involving at the most a few hundred men. From a point where I stood yesterday, an officer showed me a small Alpine valley which the other day passed four times in the space of six hours from Austrian to Italian dominion.

From the same spot I looked down upon the territory of three nations. Here Swiss land wedges itself between the contending Italy and Austria. The Swiss mountains seem to my fancy quite different from the others; theirs is not the infinite whiteness broken by jagged, black peaks, but a respectable, monotonous, neutral greyish tint, seeming to say, 'Do not forget I am not of you nor of your kind.' Italy and Austria do not forget it, and neutrality exacts its rights. In fact, the immediate neighbourhood is privileged, and rifles and guns are mute there. The Italian and Austrian patrols pass near without attack. On each side there is an advanced post, which the enemy could easily destroy by artillery but leaves untouched.

In the Stelvio mountains and valleys Italy and Austria are tightly locked in each other's embrace. An Italian peak looms over an Austrian valley. Before the war one of two oxen drawing the plough might tread Italian soil while his fellow trod Austrian. This morning as we motored, 'Here stood the old frontier,' said our driver, pointing to a heap of stones by the way. We traversed a queer country hewn as by a giant's axe and fit for witches' revels – boulders piled upon boulders and a wilderness of snowy crags.

Soon we were chattering and shivering sociably in an officer's little hut. It is the simplest of buildings; its walls of wooden planks are outwardly coated with stones and inwardly patched with newspapers to keep the cold and snow out. 'The press is a fine thing,' says the officer. In spite of it the cold is biting. He tells us, 'The cold is our first enemy, the Austrian second. Snow poisons our lives, eats our flesh to the bone and our bone to the marrow. It gets under the thickest clothes and between the sheets. It needs an effort of memory to think we are in Italy and in August. What will it be in winter? Of course some kind of war can be kept up even then, and patrols of skaters may fight at 3,500 yards' height. But any bigger action must stop.'

The same officer explained the scenery to me. It needs explaining. You can see nothing but white valleys and steep, darker rocks, but the whole country is like a Swiss cheese burrowed with man-holes – innumerable little holes where five to twenty men squat peering, waiting, sometimes with snow up to the belt. Each hole is a little fortress. 'Look at this peak half a mile off,' says the officer. 'Five men are there hidden in a crevice. We cannot see them, but they can talk to us.' At this moment a brilliant spark leaps suddenly from the spot, like the ray of a lost sun sunk deep in the snow. 'It is a piece of mirror with which they signal to us. Those signals and the telephone keep all our little posts together. The whole frozen mountain is alive with them.' Now I began to understand why no real battles can be fought here. Only attacks by surprise – mostly at night – are possible. Nobody could dream of bringing a gun to one of these posts, which can only be reached by hard climbing, often on all-fours. But later in the day I visited a battery situated in the Valfurba, and saw its activity. For months the cannon has not stopped there.

'ZEPPELIN!'

January 1915 saw the first attacks on England by airships, named after their principle creator Ferdinand von Zeppelin. Zeppelin operations continued into 1918, but by 1917 Gotha biplanes were supplanting them. Casualty figures from the air raids were low, compared with the carnage of the second world war, but Zeppelins killed 557 people in England, and the raids had considerable social and political impact. The pilots who shot them down became national heroes.

1 June
The Raid on London

Our London Correspondence: German airships have at last reached the outer districts of London without doing any damage worth mentioning ... what is the meaning of these utterly cruel and utterly futile raids, and why do the Germans risk these extremely expensive and rare engines of war which were understood to be for use along with the fleet, when experience has taught them that all they effect is to alarm a few boarding house localities, and now and then kill a woman or a child? Even as a piece of 'frightfulness' it can hardly pay. But even the most horrible deeds done by the Germans usually have purpose behind them ... military men believe that the chief one is to alarm public opinion so that more and more airmen will be kept in England to fight the Zeppelins, and fewer airmen sent to the front ... After each air raid there is always some sort of outcry about our aeroplane service not doing more. It would be well for those who complain to remember that nothing of the slightest importance has yet been done by these raiders, and that the first importance of our air service is military.

2 June
The Zeppelin Raid on London, Four Persons Killed

Tuesday, 5pm: Late last night about 90 bombs, mostly of an incendiary character, were dropped from hostile aircraft in various localities not far distant from each other. A number of fires, of which only three were large enough to require the services of fire engines, broke out. All fires were promptly and effectively dealt with. Only one of these fires necessitated a district call ... The number of casualties is small. So far as at present ascertained, one infant, one boy, one man and one woman were killed, and another woman is so seriously injured that life is despaired of.

Anti-German Scenes in Shoreditch, Shops Attacked

Probably as a consequence of the air raid, acute anti-German feeling broke out again yesterday in London. Angry mobs surrounded the premises of people suspected of being of German nationality in Shoreditch and attacked shops which suffered in the previous rioting and had been barricaded. In one case the occupants fled when the premises were entered, and were pursued by an infuriated crowd.

3 June
A Little Girl's Death

An inquest was held touching the death of a three-year-old child, Elsie Lilian Leggett, another victim of the Zeppelin raid on Monday night. The jury returned a verdict that the child died from suffocation and burns as the result of an incendiary bomb being dropped from a hostile airship. Mrs. Elizabeth Louisa Leggett said a bomb fell through the roof into the bedroom where five children were sleeping. Her husband got four of them out, and in the excitement he was under the impression that all five had been saved. Her husband and the other four children were all suffering from burns. Lieutenant Evelyn Talbot Cobbett said a label had been found showing that the bomb had been made at Krupps, Essen.

The first airman to destroy a Zeppelin in single combat was Flight Sub-lieutenant RAJ Warneford.

8 June
A Zeppelin Bombed in the Air – British Flier's Daring Exploit

At three o'clock this morning Flight Sub-lieutenant RAJ Warneford attacked a Zeppelin in the air between Ghent and Brussels at 6,000ft. He dropped six bombs and the airship exploded, fell to the ground, and burnt for a considerable time. The force of the explosion caused the Morane monoplane to turn upside down. The pilot succeeded in righting the machine, but had to make a forced landing in the enemy's country. However, he was able to restart his engine, and returned safely to the aerodrome.

The Combat Described by Spectators
Burning Wreck's Fall on a Nunnery

Rotterdam, Monday: In the early hours of this morning there took place over Ghent the most thrilling and important aerial contest in the war – a conflict between a Zeppelin and aeroplanes, which resulted in the total destruction of the former with its whole crew of twenty-eight officers … an opportunity for the aeroplanes to assail the enemy with bombs did not come until the Zeppelin was passing over the Ghent itself and was dropping lower and lower so as to make for the shed outside. As the airship was gradually descending both aeroplanes swooped upwards.

With wonderful skill they got directly above the Zeppelin and began dropping bombs. One or more of these immediately found the mark. There were some small explosions and then a burst of fire. This spread until the whole airship was enveloped in flame and smoke … Then it suddenly fell in a tremendous smother of fire and smoke.

Unhappily it crashed down on to the Grand Béguinage de Ste. Elisabeth, a nunnery, one of the best known in Belgium … The burning mass set fire to the buildings on which it dropped, inhabited just now only by nuns but also by a large number of Belgian women and children refugees.

Terrible scenes followed. Many of the crew were already dead, and their bodies were flung about in all directions. Not one survived. In the Béguinage fire two nuns perished. A brave man lost his life in attempting rescues. With a child in his arms he leaped from the burning room and both were killed. Another man, also in an effort to save a child, jumped from the second floor window and broke both legs.

The Feat and the Men

Our London Correspondence: It is said by airmen here to-night that Flight Lieutenant Warneford's Morane machine turned over more than twenty times before reaching the ground … He only learnt to fly in February at Hendon. I asked an airman who knew Lieutenant Warneford at Upavon what was thought of the hero when he was there. He said: 'Oh, we thought him quite mad then.'

Ten days later Warneford was awarded the Légion d'Honneur *by the allied commander, General Joffre. A Victoria Cross would later follow. But immediately after he received his award, he was detailed to ferry an aircraft to a Royal Naval Air Service base. The plane suffered catastrophic failure and he was thrown out of the aircraft; his injuries proved fatal. Thousands attended Warneford's funeral in London.*

'ALL OUR MONEY ON THE BIG GUN'

When war first broke out, the Manchester Guardian *had editorialised that it would 'be a war at sea'. What had been anticipated was a definitive engagement between the Royal Navy's Grand Fleet and the German High Seas Fleet. Yet both navies found that the threat posed by submarines and mines largely confined the two great fleets to harbour. On 24 January 1915 a German raiding squadron off Dogger Bank was engaged by the British. The armoured cruiser* Blücher *was sunk, while Admiral Sir David Beatty's flagship – the battlecruiser* Lion *– was heavily damaged. The German squadron escaped. On 26 January, Archibald Hurd (great-uncle of the future Conservative minister Douglas) made his assessment in the pages of the* Manchester Guardian.

26 January
The Achievements of the Battlecruisers

The Germans admit that an engagement was fought in the North Sea on Sunday and that the *Blücher* has been sunk ... The engagement is of historical interest, apart from the advantage we gained, by reason of the fact that for the first time Dreadnoughts met in action. They were Dreadnoughts representing somewhat different naval ideas. The *Blücher* was a kind of intermediate type – better than most armoured cruisers, but less powerful than battle cruisers. All the other ships engaged of the British force were either of the *Invincible* class or improvements upon it ... Instead of interning the battlecruiser class 'decently away from the public gaze' the naval authorities, when war came, used them. They were employed with splendid results in the Bight of Heligoland in August, in the action off the Falkland Islands in December, and in Sunday's engagement in the North Sea ... It was a peculiarly happy coincidence that ships of Lord Fisher's design should have brought him such good news to mark the celebration of his birthday yesterday ... so far the naval actions have confirmed in a remarkable degree the wisdom of the constructive policy of the Admiralty, which was inspired by the present First Sea Lord [Admiral Lord Fisher] ...

A few days earlier, Hurd had examined the question of the Navy's diet.

14 January
Are Our Seamen Suitably Fed?

I have by me a naval time-table as described by a writer promoted from the lower desk to warrant rank in the journal of the latter class. He is an impartial witness and he prepared the appended summary of the routine of a seaman. [...]

He starts at 5am with a pint of cocoa. That is meal number one. Number two is at 8am, three hours after the so-called meal, during which time he will have been continuously on the job, often in cold, bitter weather, with beautiful salt water splashing up to his knees and perhaps a pull in a duty-boat for four or five miles. At any rate, we believe the first meal will have been pretty well digested by the time his duties allow him again to refresh himself. The second meal will provide him with a pint of tea or coffee, bread and butter, with perhaps a bloater, kipper or portion of corned beef according to fancy.

Then follows four hours of various work and the meal of the day, consisting of joint, vegetables and perhaps a sweet of some sort to follow. Another four hours and tea is served, which is just a light meal of a basin of tea and bread and butter, sometimes jam. At 7.30pm he has a supper, if so disposed, purchased entirely out of his own pocket – at all events, it is so in 90 per cent of cases. This is followed by any exercise the individual cares for, and he usually retires to his hammock at 10pm.

'THE SCENT OF A CATASTROPHE'

On Friday 7 May 1915, just after 2pm, the U-boat U20 *torpedoed the 31,000-ton British liner* Lusitania. *Of the 1,959 passengers and crew on board, some 1,198 died. Controversy had preceded the ship's departure from New York.*

3 May
Americans Warned by Advertisement
New York, Saturday: The German Embassy has inserted an advertisement in all the principal newspapers to the effect that all British and Allied ships are liable to be destroyed if they enter Germany's 'war zone,' and that passengers sailing by such vessels consequently do so at their own risk.

Lusitania's 1,258 Passengers – The Warning Derided
New York, Sunday: The warning by the German Embassy ... did not have any perceptible effect on passengers sailing on the *Lusitania* yesterday. On the contrary there were 1,258 passengers, a record number for the time of year, and the vast majority joked about the warning, which they treated derisively on the ground that the Cunarder's speed reduced the danger from submarines to

vanishing point. In Washington the action of Germany in trying to injure the Cunard line's trade is harshly criticised on the ground of its extremely bad taste. [...]

It was said yesterday that threatening letters had been received by Mr. Alfred Vanderbilt, Mr. Charles Frohman, Sir Hugh Lane and others amongst the *Lusitania*'s passengers, but I find in inquiry that this statement is incorrect. In view of the persistence of the story and the circulation by German agents here of stories prejudicial to the vessel, a wireless message was sent to Captain Turner yesterday, asking him to question his passengers, and he sent the following reply: 'No passenger received telegrams of the nature mentioned.'

8 May

The *Lusitania* Torpedoed, Submarine Gives No Warning

The *Lusitania*, one of the world's most famous passenger liners, was sunk by a German submarine off the Irish coast yesterday afternoon. The disaster occurred a few miles south by west from the Old Head of Kinsale, in county Cork, and within sight of signal stations on shore. There were on board the liner at the time nearly 1,200 passengers and a crew numbering over 700, making a total of 1,918 persons.

What has happened to the passengers and crew is uncertain; some certainly escaped, but whether all were so fortunate no one can say yet. The attack was made, apparently without warning, soon after two o'clock. At the time the sea was calm and water clear, and although the ship sank very rapidly it was possible to launch the boats. Wireless calls for help were responded to with the utmost speed by navy patrol vessels, tugs, and other steamers.

Late telegrams say between 500 and 600 survivors were landed at Queenstown last night others at Kinsale. There were many hospital cases amongst those rescued. Some have died. A message from the chief officer to the Cunard Company suggests a very heavy loss of life.

Before the *Lusitania* sailed from New York last Saturday the German Embassy issued a warning to all persons who might intend to travel by British or Allied ships that they must do so at their own risk. When questioned about their meaning the German officials said: 'We did it to ease our conscience – lest harm should come to persons misinformed.' The warning took no effect as far as the *Lusitania* was concerned. All her intending passengers persisted in their plans, and she carried to sea a large company, among whom were many distinguished persons. [...]

On the best authority it may be asserted that the *Lusitania* was not armed. An agreement under which the Cunard Company received an annual subvention from the State bound the owners to hold the ship at the disposal of the Admiralty. The naval authorities, however, never sought to employ her, and in recent Navy Lists she did not appear as a fleet auxiliary, as a commissioned merchant vessel or even with the Royal Naval Reserve. The *Lusitania* had a gross tonnage of 31,000, was 785 feet in length, and on occasion had attained a speed of 25½ knots.

Among the passengers on the liner when she left New York were ... Mr. Charles Frohman, the theatrical manager, and Mr. AG Vanderbilt, who is as well known as an exhibitor at international horse shows as for his great wealth.

The name of Charles Frohman lives on in theatrical history. He was the man who first put JM Barrie's Peter Pan, *the story of the boy who would not grow up, on stage – in London in 1904 and New York in 1905. His last words were, apparently, 'Why fear death? It is the most beautiful thing in life.'*

The truth was that Lusitania *had been registered as an auxiliary cruiser, and her cargo – still the subject of controversy – included armaments.*

8 May

Our London Correspondence, Friday Night: It was not until after six, when the streets were full of people pouring homewards, that the calamity bit into London's consciousness. It was a long time before there was anything like a crowd outside the new offices of the Cunard Company in Cockspur Street ... The evening papers' stories sent inquirers there in the hope of finding an announcement in the window, but there was nothing to see except a pathetic notice that the *Lusitania* will sail for New York on 15 May. Inside, the officials were meeting the appeals of the relatives of passengers with: 'We have no definite information – only rumours that the ship has been sunk.' One recalled the afternoon – also in May – when London heard of the *Titanic* disaster, and the far bigger and more excited crowd that besieged the White Star offices across the street. [...]

There were many grimly silent Americans in the crowd that soon filled the [Cunard] office to suffocation ... The Americans came in greater numbers as the evening wore on, and most of them remained in the overcrowded office to wait. They were mostly well-to-do people; many were women dressed in black. They were camping out on chairs and tables, and seemed prepared to wait for hours. The office was to be open all night. The women talked hardly at all; the men talked a great deal. They were asking how it was that the *Lusitania* was allowed to come in unescorted after the warning given a week ago, and one man startled the assembly by saying in a loud voice, 'How much longer is Great Britain going to fight the war with kid gloves?' The conversation circled round the possibility of America joining in the war – 'if Vanderbilt has wet his socks' was one fragment overheard. One man was telling his neighbours that he had advised his wife to travel on the *Lusitania* as she was the only ship fast enough to race the new submarines. A few English officers were waiting with moody expressions.

The scanty bulletins received from Liverpool during the evening were pinned upon the board. They told us that boats were coming into the Queenstown with survivors, but nothing about the racking anxiety, which cannot be allayed until the detailed lists are published. The office windows, almost the only point of light in the gloom of the square, shone on a restlessly shifting crowd on the pavement – the kind of rather vacant London crowd that always gathers to the scent of a catastrophe.

'GALLIPOLI'

On 4 November 1914 the allies declared war on the Ottoman empire (Turkey). With stalemate on the western front, the British attempted to deploy their sea power to control the Dardanelles. Anglo-French forces began landing in March. The ill-managed campaign was a disaster, and in January 1916 the last remnants of the expedition were withdrawn. One political casualty was the first lord of the Admiralty, Winston Churchill, a prime mover in the plan. Yet Gallipoli became a foundation myth both for modern Turkey and for Australia, whose soldiers – alongside New Zealanders, British, Indian, French, Canadians and others – died in their thousands, creating the Anzac legend. Charles (CEW) Bean, official press representative with the Australian forces, was one of several war correspondents whose reportage helped shape Australian perceptions of the campaign.

7 December
War Reports and How to Read Them – 'Success' that Means Nothing, 12 October: First a distant purr, which you in Australia would at once diagnose as a motor car: here in Gallipoli it always means an aeroplane. You look up and see blue sky, and nothing else. Presently there is a very distant report, and you notice one, two,

three, four woolly cloudlets unfolding themselves very high above, and somewhere within half a mile of them will probably be the aeroplane they are shooting at. You watch her carefully circle over the enemy's lines and someone remarks, 'She has laid an egg – there it goes.' You can see the bomb fall, an infinitesimal yellow object.

You must not imagine that life in one of these year-long modern battles consists of continuous bombing, fighting, bayoneting, bombarding all the time. These 'progresses,' 'consolidatings,' 'bomb-droppings' and 'artillery activity' of the war reports are the incidents in long weary months whose chief occupation is the digging of mile upon mile of endless sap or sunken road through which troops and mules can move safely behind the firing line: the driving of whole rabbit warren of tunnels by sweating, half-naked miners, working by the light of candles far into the hearts of hills, as you might see them in any metal mines in Broken Hill or Gobar – indeed the miners are probably most of them from those very same mines. [...]

Every photograph of trenches in France shows us the counter-part of some trench in Gallipoli. Every description of trench-fighting there might have been written in the Dardanelles. And when you find that a vast proportion of the stories of events said to have happened in the Dardanelles are pure fiction, you cannot help the impression that a great part of the stories of other parts of the war is almost certainly fiction too. Indeed, probably this campaign is only different from the rest in that, owing to the authorities allowing war correspondents on the actual battlefield, the proportion of true news is probably higher than in the case of any other theatre of the war ... There is so much real heroism and outstanding self-sacrifice in the history of Anzac, and so much true drama, that it goes against everyone's grain to see so much that is purely imaginary pass, as I suppose it has a good chance of doing, into the nation's history.

13 November

Our London Correspondence, Friday Night: Mr. Churchill has explained his resignation so fully in his letter to the Prime Minister that there is no place for speculation. If he cannot be in the War Council of the Cabinet he declines to be in the Cabinet at all. Looking back over the past year, one sees that his resignation is really the repercussion of the resignation of Lord Fisher over the Dardanelles business. That happened a day or two before the dissolution of the late Liberal Government and the formation of the Coalition. It was believed by Liberals at the time that the resignation of Lord Fisher went a long way towards making the Coalition Ministry necessary. Mr. Churchill was then very much blamed. Indeed, a considerable group of Liberal members gave it to be understood that they thought he ought not to be included in the reconstructed Ministry. This hostility to Mr. Churchill has not diminished since. Rightly or wrongly, the responsibility for the Dardanelles operations has been fixed upon him, and he has never been forgiven.

Once out of the Cabinet, Lieutenant-Colonel Winston Churchill became commander of the 6th battalion of the Royal Scots Fusiliers on the western front.

'THE ANNIHILATION OF OUR PEOPLE'

'Who, after all,' Hitler is alleged to have asked in 1939, 'speaks today of the annihilation of the Armenians?' To this day Turkey denies that the massacres, and deportations from their homeland, that were inflicted on the Armenians from 1915 comprises genocide. In August 1915 the Manchester Guardian *reported on the catastrophe.*

16 August
Armenia without the Armenians, Inhabitants Banished to the Desert

We print below a translation of a letter which gives a terrible account of the treatment now being inflicted on the Armenian population by the Turks. This letter was originally addressed from Constantinople to an Armenian bishop in a neutral country, and a copy had just reached this country.

Constantinople, 13 July: From 25 May events followed hard upon each other, and the misery of our people is now at its height. Apart from some rumours about the situation of the Armenians in Erzerum, we only knew till then of the deportation of the inhabitants of some of the villages in Cilicia, but now we know from trustworthy sources that the Armenians in all the towns and villages in Cilicia have been deported to the desert regions south of Aleppo.

From 1 May the population of Erzerum, and a little later of the province of the same name, began to be taken to Samsoun, where they were put on board ships. The populations of Kaisarieh, Diarbeker, Ourfa, Trebizond, Sivas, Kharpour and the region of Van were deported to the deserts of Mesopotamia, south of Aleppo, down to Mosul and Bagdad.

'Armenia without Armenians' – that is the programme of the Ottoman Government. Already Mussulmans are being installed in the property and homes of the Armenians.

The deported are not allowed to take any of their property with them … The deported are compelled to cover on foot distances of one to two months' travelling, often more, till they reach the corner of the desert which is assigned to them as a home and is destined to be their sepulchre. We hear, moreover, that the roads and the Euphrates are strewn with the corpses of the expelled – and those who survive are doomed to certain death, having neither work nor food nor habitation in the desert.

It is a plan to exterminate the Armenian people without fuss. It is another kind of massacre, a more terrible kind.

Do not forget that the males between 20 and 45 years of age are at the front. Those between 45 and 60 are working on the lines of communication. As for those who paid the regulation tax for exemption from military service, they have been exiled or imprisoned … So that there only remain old men, women and children to deport. These unhappy creatures have to cross regions which in times of peace were considered dangerous. Now that the Turkish brigands, as well as the police and the Government officials, enjoy absolute immunity, the deported are certain to be robbed on the road, the women and girls outraged and carried off. From different quarters we hear of conversions to Islam, the populations evidently having no other alternative if they wish to save their lives. The military courts are busy everywhere.

You must have heard through the papers of the hanging of 20 Hentchakists at Constantinople. The sentence passed on them is not based on any of the laws of the Empire. The same day 12 Armenians were hung at Kaisarieh … Besides the hangings, 32 persons were condemned at Kaisarieh to penalties varying from 15 to 20 years' hard labour. These persons were for the most part respectable merchants who had no connection whatever with the political parties. Further, 12 Armenians were hung in Cilicia. Sentences of imprisonment are everyday affairs. The discovery of arms, books, and pictures furnishes a reason for condemning some unfortunate person to several years of imprisonment.

Many, on the other hand, have been beaten to death. At Diarbekir 13 Armenians have been killed in this way, six at Kaisarieh; 13 others have been killed on their way from Shabin-Karahissar to Savis. The priests of the village of Kurk, with five fellow-travellers, suffered the same fate on the way to Sousherk-Sivas. [...]

I do not speak of the other outrages committed on different occasions almost everywhere on the pretext of looking for arms and revolutionaries.

No house has escaped search; not even the religious institutions and the schools. Hundreds of women, girls, children await their fate in trembling in the prisons. Churches and monasteries have been looted, desecrated and destroyed.

Even the clergy has not been spared ... Father Meguerditch, the locum tenens of the Bishop of Diarbekire, has succumbed to the beating he received in prison. No news has been received of the other bishops, but I presume that far the greater part of them have been imprisoned.

We are now living isolated as if in a fortress; no means of corresponding either by post or telegram. The villages round Van and Bitlis have been plundered and their inhabitants put to the sword. At the beginning of this month the inhabitants of Karahissar were pitilessly massacred with the exception of a few children, who, it is said, escaped by a miracle. Unfortunately the details of all this news came in to us too late or with difficulty. But you see that the days of the Armenians in Turkey are numbered.

If the Armenians abroad do not succeed in interesting the neutral States in our plight there will only be a few Armenians in Turkey left out of a total of a million and a half. The annihilation of our people will be complete.

'MR CHAPLIN'S ART'

Despite – or perhaps because of – the horrific news filtering in from abroad, the British public continued to seek distraction through entertainment. In 1912 a London music-hall artist, Charlie Chaplin, began his second American stage tour. While in Kansas City, an offer came through to Chaplin from the Keystone Film Company in Los Angeles. By 1915 the 'little tramp' had become the world's first global star.

31 July

Miscellany: A young soldier, home on leave, went to make an unexpected call on his sweetheart. When her young brother said she had gone 'to see Charlie' the warrior's expression became troubled, and more so when the youth ingenuously added, 'She goes every week – twice sometimes.'

'Where?' demanded the distracted soldier.

'Oh, at the Grand or the Magnet or the Arcadia. They're sure to have a Charlie Chaplin film somewhere!' […]

Almost any lad in almost any school, if asked to mention the funniest thing he had seen, would promptly answer, 'Charlie Chaplin.'

August 12
Chaplin in the Street

Our London Correspondence: Last Sunday in Euston Road a youth, out of sheer love of art (for he did not ask or receive a penny), acted a Charlie Chaplin turn on the broad pavement before a large and critical audience, each of whom seemed by the remarks a Chaplin expert. He had the ineffectual Chaplin cane – never raised save by the way of kindness or balance – little false moustache, 'practicable' hat and a not bad imitation of the boots. He performed that great passage when Charlie Chaplin has been pushed by a heavy man and stutters back on his heels, evading disaster and plaintively enduring. He did other turns, and generally gave a not bad impression of that brilliant and forgiving worm. It was a striking public tribute to genius.

Later that year, the Manchester Guardian *devoted an editorial to the subject.*

7 December
An Important Problem

What is the correct interpretation of the popular interest in Mr. Charles Chaplin at this time? Apparently so many people nowadays see so much of the contributions which he has made to the art of the kinematograph theatre – and even those to whom, like ourselves, Mr. Chaplin's art is, unfortunately, completely unknown, inevitably hear so much of that artist – that there is a real tendency abroad to make a devotion to him and his art a symptom of one of the war phases of our national character. Unfortunately, it is a little difficult to ascertain precisely what the symptom indicates. In a contemporary yesterday, for instance, a letter from an anonymous officer at the front is given great prominence. In that letter, among many other complaints against the people at home which are given as the universal feeling of the men who are fighting for them, occurs a reference to the resentment felt 'at the general rottenness of taste and feeling in a country which can amuse itself with "Charlie Chaplin" in days like these.' From this reading it would appear that the practice is equivalent to fiddling in the face of a burning Rome. On the other hand, in the admirable instalment which appears in the November number of *Blackwood*'s of the experiences at the war of 'The Junior Sub,' the present public devotion to Mr. Chaplin is noted at some length and with exactly the opposite moral. The major at the front, who has had this new devotion described to him by a colleague returning from leave, 'put down his glass with a gentle sigh and rose to go. "We are a great nation," he remarked contentedly. "I was a bit anxious about things at home, but I see now there was nothing to worry about. We shall win all right."' Is Mr. Chaplin, then, a national menace or benefactor; a symptom of frivolity and decadence or of the undaunted spirit which, jesting in the proper time and place, keeps the native hue of resolution uncontaminated by the pale cast of thought? Of the two expressions of opinion quoted we are personally more impressed by the manner of the second than of the first. But in the interests both the nation and its historians this matter should be settled one way or the other without delay.

'THE SMALLEST SOLDIER WHO EVER WALKED INTO SUSSEX'

Britain was a shelter for (not always popular) Belgian refugees – and for convalescents, as Helen Roberts explained.

25 August
Sussex in War-Time

We have taken the same house as usual. It faces the English Channel, and behind it there is a garden full of hollyhocks whose rosy tints are sometimes pleasant to the eye after all the blueness and whiteness of the sea and shore. Owing to the absence, 'somewhere in France,' of one member of the family, we have this year a spare room. Somebody has suggested an invitation – either to a great aunt or a convalescent officer. It seems a pity to waste a spare bedroom in Sussex just now. For Sussex is very old, and very steady, and very restful. 'It hasn't changed a bit,' we said cheerfully on the first day.

We got into the car and went to see. At Storrington, where Francis Thompson's hills look over to the south, the heather is twice as good as usual, because of the great fire that burnt it up a year or two ago. In the big hollow just below the vanished white mill it lies like a great lake of wine. At Pulborough the anglers sit along the river in attitudes expressive of perfect peace. I suppose that in the act of catching a fish an angler may cease to express repose. Yet in the search for satisfaction on this point I have before now walked in vain behind the rounded backs of fishermen from Pulborough to Arundel. Just half an hour before sunset, when the town on the hill is a grey, turreted outline against the yellow, and the woods behind it very soft and black, I have certainly seen (or felt) a sort of tremor – a tenseness – a whisper … 'Hush, hush, my soul, the secret draweth near!' Yet, apparently, the mystic moments slips and is gone, and the angler remains passive. And perhaps this August the fishes have all gone down to Littlehampton, or perhaps they have been attracted by the great doings at Amberley.

For at Amberley, where we stop to buy postcards at the grocer's, we are told that never before has the place been so thronged with August visitors. There is literally not a place to be had: the place overflows! Thrilled, we go out into the main street; half-way up an old sheepdog snores and dreams. We see no other living thing. We know that a Royal Academician lives at Amberley, and decided that this or that is his house because of the window-curtains. We go on to Chichester, where there are many convalescent soldiers. In the porches of Norman churches are lists of names – the fighters and the fallen; one or perhaps two cottages out of every three show a blue painted Maltese cross in the window; some show a row of blue crosses. You may add another cross if you have another son.

Sussex, with its round-headed down and chalk-pits and marshes and red villages, is unchanged. In the Weald the orchard and the harvest fields are full of richness. The dear, unfruitful Downs are full of silence and sweet peace. And we are having just the same holiday as we had last August – and the August before. And even the spare room has filled of its own accord. There was no trouble about an invitation. He merely walked in by the open window on Monday while we were at dinner. He wore a bottle-green coat, khaki breeches, black puttees, and a green cap with a shiny peak; and he must be quite the smallest soldier who ever walked into Sussex. He has a strong, grave, fair-complexioned little face, unspoilt by the scar of a healed bayonet wound below the chin. He has strong, sturdy, capable legs. Minute but inflexible, he might have come to us merely as a symbol of his country. But he is not merely a symbol. He has come to stay with us for six days – for his first leave since the beginning of the war and a year's fighting, including the affair of Liège. He could not go, he explains in careful French, to his own home, since this was, or had been, at Louvain. For a year he has received no news of his parents. So he has decided, even as we have done, to come to Sussex. And he is glad that he has come. 'It is as I expected,' he says. 'Here it is *chic!*'

We request him to dine. His appetite is abnormally small. He is now accustomed, he says, to only a little food. He refuses wine. 'It is not permitted,' he remarks simply. He puts the gifts he has brought for us on the dinner table – three *bagues broches* made from the aluminium of German shrapnel, and a dented German cartridge belt. He apologises politely for the absence of a pickelhaube. It is pleasant, but curious, that out of all the houses in England Joseph should have selected ours. Later he explains that among certain British gifts of tobacco forwarded to his regiment he had picked up a piece of brown paper which happened to bear the name of this house and this town. It was necessary that the paper signed by his commanding officer should announce his destination. Joseph had supplied the single destination that was within his knowledge. These are the things that happen in wartime, even in Sussex. Joseph's age was recorded as twenty-two; his eyes as *bleu-vert*. We verified these particulars.

After the Yser, Sussex is certainly a good place. Joseph walks on the sands or he sits very stiffly in a striped hammock chair. He is very quiet during the day, but in the evenings he talks much and picturesquely. He tells us about strange and terrible things that happened a year ago; of an action that lasted three days; of the time when there was great shelling during a great storm. '*C'était chic!*' he says, and he illustrates the noises and flames of war. And we listen to the tiny man in his shabby green uniform and reply, 'Yes, Joseph, indeed it must have been very *chic*.'

He will return to his duties on Saturday, and I don't know whether he will come to Sussex again. Having now become used to the idea, he is not afraid of being killed – his exceptional smallness should also add to his chances of being missed by German bullets. Meanwhile, in Sussex, he cultivates the arts of peace. Walking between the hollyhocks, he composes a poem upon the Kaiser. When in 'the next world' Joseph and William II stand face to face (the precise locality is not specified) the German Emperor will receive no salute from Joseph. That will be a bitter day for William II. On the beach Joseph makes a picture of Sussex with coloured chalks. Here is the smooth, blue sea, with a white undulating line to show the Seven Sisters running out to Beachy Head. Tomorrow he will go motoring, perhaps to Midhurst by the way of Cowdray Park, and when he sees the blue crosses in the cottage windows he will know that Sussex men have gone to fight for a fair country, and a country as yet unscarred.

Unscarred? And yet I suppose even in Sussex things are a little different. Last year in Sussex we were further away from the Yser. Meanwhile it is good to hear that Joseph agrees with us that Sussex in August is *chic*. It is comforting, too, to know that his simple soul believes as plainly and as steadfastly in the ultimate redemption of his own country as in the might and friendliness of ours. And if Joseph has brought, for our profit, a little bit of Yser to Sussex, we are grateful to know that he will take with him next Saturday a little bit of Sussex back to Yser.

'OUR LONDON
CORRESPONDENCE'

1 September

Outside a London Hospital: An eager crowd, chiefly of women and children, was gathered to-night watching the windows of the wards where three hundred British soldiers, wounded or merely worn out, are lying. The women moved along the railings in front of the huge dingy façade searching the half-opened windows for the sight of a familiar face, but as likely as not there was nothing to be seen except a red flannel sleeve of a hospital jacket. One 'Tommy' was code-signalling with his tobacco-box from a top window to a friend on the pavement. 'Not much the matter with him,' said the friend in a grumblingly affectionate voice. The soldiers were completely isolated from the cheerful street, and they looked a little bored in their isolation, but in a side street the people found a half-open window on the ground floor low enough to let them talk with a few of the men, whose honest countenances glowed in the light of admiration. They were chiefly anxious for more cigarettes, and eager youths were running across the road to a tobacconist's to supply them. 'Food and rest is what most of 'em wants, poor lads,' said a woman with a baby, and she said she had had a letter from her man telling how he fought two days on an empty stomach – 'a shell destroyed the food just when they was goin' to 'ave it,' she said. None of the soldiers was allowed out of the hospital to-day, however slightly wounded they might be, and visitors were not allowed inside, so that this silent street gathering was all that was possible in the way of communication. The wounded are men of all regiments, and the women outside had no reason to suppose that their particular men-folk were among them. 'He might be, for all I know,' one said as she slowly searched the windows. The onlookers were a little reassured by the sight of a dray loaded with beer going towards the hospital gate. A thin woman in black by the main entrance refused to be reassured or to go away. She has sons among the fighting men, and she though it safer to wait. 'Maybe they'll let us in to see.'

22 September
'Busmen with Wounds

The other day a spruce young man out for the day with his sweetheart was annoyed because the 'bus gave a violent jolt. 'What's the matter with your driver,' he asked, 'and why isn't he doing his duty at the front?' The conductor was tremendously pleased with his own retort: 'He has been at the front, where you ought to be, and he's got a hole right through his leg same as you ought to have.'

1915 was the year that the controversy about quantity and quality of British munitions was at its fiercest, and debate became part of the moral panic around the 'liquor problem'. In February 1915, the then chancellor of the exchequer, David Lloyd George, told an audience in Bangor that 'a small minority of workmen' refused to work full-time because of 'the lure of drink'. They were doing the country more harm than 'all the German submarines put together'. Restrictions on the sale of alcohol had been part of the original DORA in 1914, and a control board was soon imposing more restrictions, including a ban on buying rounds of drinks without food. The hangover effect on opening hours persisted into the 21st century.

12 October
Effect of No Treating

London has begun life under the no-treating order to-day with characteristic resignation. All the same, the order is highly unpopular, especially with the large floating population of 'minesers' – the 'whatlers' are probably less disturbed. The immediate effect has been a big drop in the takings at every public house … An incident described by a publican to-day was probably repeated in most London bars many times. The publican said: 'There are three customers, who always come in about luncheon-time, and each of them stands a drink, making nine drinks in all. To-day they came in as usual. They each ordered one drink. Then one of them, still feeling dry, ordered another, but the others did not think it was up to them to do the same. The result was – four drinks instead of nine.' […]

On the great question as to what is a meal, the general view with publicans is that nothing short of a plate of meat and vegetables is a legal meal. They say that bread and cheese might well be a meal, but that brings in the plate of sandwiches question, so it is much simpler to make it something that is beyond a quibble. A few of them, however, allow treating with bread and cheese. Ingenious persons were going about to-day citing all sorts of conundrums to the worried licensees, such as the man who brought his dinner with him and asked whether he could not treat his friends while he ate it at the bar.

'GOD DAMN THE ARMY'

Britain's war was being fought by volunteers, but during 1915 the press clamour for conscription was moving towards a crescendo. Unionist (Conservative) ministers threatened to resign from Herbert Asquith's coalition government if it was not introduced, and they were backed by David Lloyd George. When conscription was established, it provided an impetus for the anti-war movement – whether liberal, pacifist or, as in the case of John Maclean (as his name is usually spelled), revolutionary socialist.

11 November
Socialist Speaker Fined £5

From Our Correspondent in Glasgow: John McClean, a prominent member of the British Socialist party in Glasgow, was to-day fined £5 or five days' imprisonment for having, in speaking at an open-air meeting, uttered words likely to be prejudicial to recruiting. McClean, who is a school teacher, has addressed a meeting in Bath Street, the thoroughfare in which the Glasgow recruiting headquarters are situated. Someone in the crowd shouted to him, 'Go and enlist.' He retorted, 'I have been enlisted in the Socialist army for fifteen years. God damn the army, and God damn all other armies.'

The trial ... was marked by strange scenes. At the close a large crowd of McLean's supporters who were present in the court joined in cheering, sang 'The Red Flag,' and departed amid much commotion.

James McDougall, secretary of the British Socialist party, in giving evidence for the defence, was closely questioned by Sherriff Lee on the attitude of the society towards recruiting ... The Socialist party (the witness added) believed in international action, and consequently were entirely opposed to singling out of any country for attack because of the fundamental principles of Socialism.

The Sheriff: 'Joining the army is contrary to your principles?' 'It is.'

'And the view you take is expressed in the words of the accused as "God damn all armies"?' 'Yes.'

Despite his imprisonment, the 'Scottish Lenin' (who is one of the most famous revolutionary socialists in British history) never relented in his battle against capitalism. Appointed Bolshevik consul in Scotland in 1918, he died five years later, but not before becoming a key figure on 'Red Clydeside'.

'BEFORE ANOTHER COMES'

Back on the western front, as the year drew to a close, the troops faced a second Christmas on foreign soil. But, as Philip Gibbs reported, optimism persisted.

27 December
Christmas Feasts in Billet

Here where I am tonight, near our General Headquarters, it is very quiet. But in some of the farmhouses round about where some troops are billeted after a long spell in the lines there are Christmas feasts in progress, and out into the wild, wet night comes the sound of laughter and song. The officers are visiting the men's messes.

'Well, my lads,' says the colonel of the battalion (they had a bad time in the Ypres salient), 'a happy Christmas to you and good luck in the coming year.' His eyes rove down the table as though searching for faces that are not there, and for a moment there is just a little sadness in his smile, remembering all those who have gone. Then he raises a glass and says heartily and cheerily: 'A happy Christmas, and may we beat the Boche before another comes.'

All the men are standing. It is the sergeant major who answers the colonel's speech. 'A happy Christmas to you, sir, and all the officers. As for the Boche, we've got him beat. It'll be a poor Christmas for Germany, in my humble opinion, sir ... and we'll follow you to the big victory, sir, and the other officer here present, and I'm sure the men and myself included will give the enemy what for, whenever the next chance comes.' ('Hear, hear. Three cheers for the colonel.')

And now as I write, the sing-song has begun with the aid of mouth organs and concertinas, and the funny men (there are two or three in each platoon) have cheered up the boys who went a little sad when it was the tune of 'The Old Folks at Home' and 'Auld Lang Syne.'

CHAPTER 4

1916

Conscription was introduced in January, and Herbert Asquith departed as prime minister in December, to be replaced by David Lloyd George. At Easter, Great Britain, whose self-proclaimed reasons for going to war included defending the rights of small nations, set about suppressing a revolt in a small nation that it ruled: Ireland. This was also the year the British empire deployed a huge and undertrained citizen army to the western front, and incurred huge losses accordingly. The German assault on Verdun ended in failure, at great cost to both the Germans and the French. The long-predicted clash between the British and German fleets finally took place – and left both sides dissatisfied, yet both claiming victory. Conscription spelled increasing dissent at home, while labour shortages drew more women into the workplace. In Vienna, Franz Joseph I, who had ruled as the emperor of Austria and king of Hungary since 1848, died. The nonagenarian was succeeded, briefly, by Karl I, but the new emperor's domain was collapsing. And while the armies of his fellow ruler, Nicholas of Russia, did achieve a few notable victories, the criminally incompetent and defeatist tsarist bureaucracy was buckling under the pressure of war.

'THAT PUSHING EX-AIRMAN'

The war plunged British citizens into a world where the coalition government sought to control the news, and personal accounts from *the front – and the occasional Zeppelin – provided glimpses of reality. The no man's land in between was a breeding ground for fantasy and rabble-rousing. The most famous demagogue was Horatio Bottomley, but his sometime ally Noel Pemberton Billing, initially utilising the wonders of flight and the terror of the Zeppelin, prospered. This was a time when by-elections were accompanied by electoral truces between the main parties.*

21 January
Lively By-Election in Mile End

The election which has been forced on Mile End by that pushing ex-airman Mr. Pemberton Billing has no reality as a contest, but it has some value as an entertainment. Mr. Pemberton Billing is one of the liveliest candidates we have had for some time. The big white aeroplane which he trundles about with him serves as a platform and draws big crowds at his open-air meetings, and he brightens the walls with huge red placards showing the bombing of a Zeppelin. He is the anti-Zeppelin candidate, of course, and he has broken the truce at elections for the purpose of advertising his views on the need for more efficient air defences. He bases his right to do this on the fact that he was until recently an officer in the Naval Air Service ... many electors agree with Mr. Bertram Straus, the Liberal candidate at the last election, that 'Mr. Billing would be more useful, if he wants to prevent air attacks, if he remained in the Air Service.' [...]

He is setting himself up against the somewhat more important experts who are advising the Government. The demand that the lights of London should go up is naturally popular with the shopkeepers of Mile End, but as to the rest of his programme – the creation of strong aeroplane force to attack the Zeppelins in the air, and so on – its importance is such as to justify his label as the 'hot air candidate.'

In this matter of air defence Mr. Pemberton Billing has no advantages over Mr. Warwick Brookes, the Coalition candidate. Mr. Brookes, while refusing to concentrate on one subsidiary issue, is just as anxious as his opponent to protect London from Zeppelins. 'I would stop at no expense,' he says, 'to get the best inventions, the most expert administrators, the strongest air commander-in-chief … ' It is interesting to note that Mr. Horatio Bottomley has claimed for Mr. Billing that he has invented an aeroplane, 'which carries an armament before which a Zeppelin would turn back and never come here again.' One hopes that the Government will have the benefit of this wonderful invention.

Mr. Brookes … [is] fighting the election on what may be called the general patriotic programme … Mr. Brookes will be returned, of course. He will be supported by the mass of electors on both sides. There are about 2,000 Jews in Mile End, and Mr. Leopold Rothschild [a banker and leader of the British Jewish community] has issued a letter calling for support to Mr. Brookes.

In fact, Pemberton Billing won more than 44 per cent of the vote, and was just 376 votes behind the winner.

The vote in Mile End was followed by the East Herts by-election. The 'Raemaker Cartoon' that featured on the election posters depicted a broken father and daughter by the deathbed of the mother, who has been killed in a Zeppelin raid.

4 March
The Air Candidate and His Policy

Mr. Pemberton Billing now says he is 'not going to be so foolish' as to guarantee that in the event of his being returned for East Herts there will be no more air raids. It is difficult to reconcile this prudent disclaimer with the vehement posters placarded over the 240 square miles of the constituency bidding electors. 'Vote for

Pemberton Billing and no more Zeppelin raids,' reinforced as this exhortation is by pictures of wrecked homes and a reproduction of Raemaker's drawing. 'But Mother had done nothing wrong, had she Daddy?' The latter is surely a heartless appropriation of that poignant cartoon. There is no occasion to bring home to people in this part of the country the ravages of the Zeppelins.

In place of 'a strong air policy' Mr. Pemberton Billing now advocates 'a great' air policy, whatever the difference may signify, but at present he refuses to produce his plan – not, at any rate, till he gets into the House of Commons. To do him justice, he has confided to an audience in this remote town – remote, though only twenty-five miles from London – that he has designed a machine for fighting Zeppelins in the air. 'The Germans have no machine like it.' […]

But Mr. Pemberton Billing is not to be taken alone in this fight … he has the powerful backing of three or four London journals of the widest circulation. 'The wonderful one-man fight against a powerful caucus he is waging in East Herts is astonishing the electors,' says one of these organs. Another speaks of his great fight 'against the Coalition machine,' and a third of the way in which he is 'rousing' the whole constituency, the interference from which would seem to be that the real desire is to deal a blow to our Coalition Government.

Pemberton Billing won the contest. In parliament he expounded conspiracy theories – the 'Unseen Hand' was thwarting allied war aims, training homosexuals to bring down the nation, etc – and in 1918 won a sensational libel case and was re-elected, before resigning in 1921. By contrast, his by-election campaigns during the second world war flopped.

'OUR LONDON CORRESPONDENCE'

Allowing for the vagaries of propaganda, this comparison between living conditions in England and Germany has the ring of accuracy. German living conditions were worsening under the pressure of the Royal Navy's blockade.

17 March
London after Berlin

The first few days spent in England by the Englishwomen who have been living in Germany during the war months, and absorbing German views of England's position, are days of astonishing enlightenment. One woman, who was prepared to find London sunk in gloom, tells me that her first few hours in London were among the happiest she has lived. The people looked so happy and walked so confidently, instead of looking, as the German soldier now does, desperately conscious that he is up against a very big thing.

It delighted her to walk past the butchers' shops, looking at such meat as she had not seen for nearly two years. It was a year, she said, since she had seen any fat, and if she asked her Berlin butcher to supply just a little fat with her mutton chops, she used to be told that, 'the animals hadn't got any.' It shocked her to see that in her Bloomsbury hotel, more bread was cut than the visitors were likely to require. She preferred the rigid care exercised in Berlin about every crumb, though it was very awkward sometimes, as when, for instance, a lady wishing to have a few friends to tea could only get a supply of bread and butter by ringing up her convenient friends and begging for any bread they could spare from their individual bread tickets. The number of taxi-cabs and motor-cars was another surprise, since Berlin, with its rubber famine, is now very short of cars. The overwhelming question was whether a people so serene could understand the magnitude of the war. Berlin has light and music and entertainments, but her people walk very gravely.

Kinema in Drury Lane

Tonight it is announced that next Wednesday Drury Lane will be handed over to the kinematograph ... The film to be produced at Drury Lane Theatre is *The Birth of a Nation*, an overpowering American representation of the brighter features of its own developments. This is the production which raised so much controversy because of its handling of the black-and-white problem when it was first screened in America.

DW Griffiths' The Birth of a Nation *(1915) remains one of the most controversial films of all time. A racist portrayal of the US civil war period, it inspired the revived Ku Klux Klan. It was the first film to be shown at the White House, where it was viewed by the Virginia-born President Woodrow Wilson.*

20 May
Economy v. Fashion

There is an outbreak of small dances in the West, invitations for which are issued on the telephone after this fashion: 'Is that you, dear? We are dancing to-morrow night. If you can bring a man be sure and come.' The principle is that if each girl provides one dancing man, then there will be enough to go round and no one sitting out. Usually the hostess or some friend plays the piano; there is no sit-down supper – only light refreshments. But frocks and more frocks are needed. The opinion in these regions is that no frocks can last more than four evenings under modern dancing conditions.

Another point for expensiveness is the new fashion in day blouses. The opening in the shape of a V is cut lower than would have been thought decorous twenty years ago in an evening frock for a married woman, yet all the 'nicest girls' wear them. These, too, are new, and have suddenly appeared with the sunshine. Fashionable men, like other men, are nearly all in khaki, which they manage to make somehow very smart, while the elderly men are properly dingy. The Duke of Norfolk goes about Pall Mall in a frock coat that symbolises the antiquity of the Howards. Lord Curzon thinks nothing of appearing in a Homburg in Piccadilly.

'NOXIOUS COWARDS'

With sections of Fleet Street targeting 'slackers', pressure for compulsory military service intensified in autumn 1915. The Liberal and Labour parties were hostile towards conscription, while the secretary for war, David Lloyd George, and the Conservatives were in favour. There was only one certainty, a Manchester Guardian *editorial argued on 8 September 1915: conscription would divide the nation.*

The paper's editor, CP Scott, was one of the opponents of the Military Service Act, which became law in January 1916. In the first six months after the law was passed, voluntary enlistment fell by more than 50 per cent. The law stipulated that conscientious objectors could make their case before a local tribunal. They did so, and the court confrontations led to more controversy.

Founded in 1914 by the pacifists Fenner Brockway and Clifford Allen, the No-Conscription Fellowship became a key organisation in the opposition to conscription – and to the war.

6 March
Conscientious Socialists

At the Huddersfield Tribunal on Saturday a weaver and twister-in, aged 22, said he belonged to an organisation which in all times was opposed to military warfare. This was the British Socialist Party.

Captain Bradbury: They are different from German Socialists, aren't they? – Yes, they are supposed to be.

The applicant stated that he had held his conscientious views four or five years. The Clerk to the Tribunal (Mr. T Smailes) had been his Sunday school teacher, and had heard him argue as he was arguing now. (Laughter.)

Mr. Smailes: I disclaim all responsibility for his personal views. It is true he was in my class for seven years, but he has not imbibed my doctrine. That is his own particular doctrine. (Laughter.)

Answering Captain Bradbury, the applicant admitted having had to handle khaki materials. 'I have been forced,' he said, 'to do so, or walk the streets. I had notice given me for not joining the army, and I should have been walking the street but for the trade unions standing by us.'

The Tribunal granted exemption from combatant service only.

Captain Bradbury: These men are a great evil, and will hinder recruiting if they are left.

The Case of a Lion-Tamer

A lion-tamer applied for exemption at the Stockton Tribunal on Saturday. He was a coloured man, a British subject born in the West Indies. He stated that there being no demand for menageries at present, the one he was engaged with was not travelling, and his duties consisted in attending to the wants of five lions and two wolves. No one else could attend to them, and this was the reason for his application, as he otherwise was quite willing to fight for his country.

The military representative remarked that the difficulty might be got over by a member of the Tribunal adopting the animals as pets.

Three months' postponement was given, and the applicant was told that at the end of that time he could apply again if necessary.

20 March
Appeal to Join No-Conscription Fellowship

Yesterday afternoon a meeting of unattested men was held on the Burnley market ground. Mr. JT Beilby put in a plea for those who objected to military service on moral, ethical and religious grounds, and said that conscientious objectors were being most unfairly treated at the local tribunals. (A Voice: They deserve it.) He had seen nothing like the bullying, cajoling, and tricking of these men and the tribunals, which were constituted to give them a judicial hearing. The tribunals were a perfect farce.

Mr. F Robinson said he was the only young man in his Sunday school who was not in the army to-day. (A Voice: Are you not ashamed of it?) If married men had been bluffed, that was no reason why they should try and force on this country the atrocious system of general conscription. Mr. Pilkington appealed to the audience to join the No-Conscription Fellowship and thereby do their utmost to prevent the enlargement of the conscription machine in this country. A man in the audience: If you are opposed to fighting, what is your remedy in face of Germany's action against us? Mr. Beilby: We are not here to answer that question.

30 March
Catechisms at the Town Hall

Conscientious objectors were before the Manchester Tribunal yesterday. All the cases were taken in the court over which Mr. Edgar Brierley presided. [...]

A bank clerk gave as his reason that victory by force produced no peace. He was, he said, a member of the Church of England, and he was following the doctrines that he had been taught all his life.

Mr. Brierley: What doctrines? Are you not prepared to defend your Church, your life or your country, whatever the authority may be? I presume your parents are educated people. Would you say that at no time in the world's history has it been lawful to take up arms under any circumstances whatever? Supposing the Mahometans commenced a crusade against Europe. In former times Christian countries were overrun by barbarism owing to non-resistance.

The Applicant: You are asking me to take up arms and murder people in cold blood.

The Military Representative: If the Germans came into this country that is exactly what they would do.

'I believe all disputes are capable of being settled by arbitration,' said another applicant.

Mr. Brierley: But what is the good of talking about arbitration when a country declines to observe its treaties?

The Applicant: I object to taking up arms, and I do not believe that any civilised country would invade an unarmed country.

Mr. Brierley: Do you seriously think if Belgium had been unarmed that the German soldiers would not have walked through it?

The Applicant: If I had been a Belgian I would not have resisted.

Mr. Watkin: Would you allow the Germans to invade this country and murder your father, your mother or sister? Many competent authorities are still of the opinion that the enemy will land here.

The Applicant: That has nothing to do with it.

Exempted from combatant service.

In June, a group – including Philip Snowden, the future Labour chancellor of the exchequer (and future defector to the 1931 National government), Liberal MP for York Arnold Rowntree and the suffragist and Manchester councillor Margaret Ashton – wrote to the Manchester Guardian.

22 June
The No-Conscription Fellowship

The authorities have apparently decided to embark upon a campaign of suppression against the No-Conscription Fellowship by prosecuting its national committee, raiding its head offices and fining or imprisoning many of its branch officials. [...]

The No-Conscription Fellowship is acting to-day according to the same policy which has established for the Quakers a security that would prevent the Government even contemplating the suppression of their society. Genuine conscientious objectors ... are not confined to the Society of Friends. We are personally acquainted with many of the fellowship leaders of the No-Conscription Fellowship, and can vouch for their high characters. [...]

We cannot believe it was the intention of the authorities to add to the uneasiness created by the persecution of conscientious objectors the further mistake of attempting to suppress an organisation which is claiming for it[s] members and other genuine objectors the relief intended by the Military Service Act. Its object should surely command the support of all those who desire the retention on our national life of that principle of toleration and that respect for liberty which has been threatened by militarism in other continental countries.

'I WILL GIVE YOU THE BEST THRASHING YOU EVER HAD'

Some 1,500 'absolutist' conscientious objectors were drafted into the army during the war.

14 October
Conscientious Objectors Court-Martialled,
More Allegations of Torture

The court-martial appointed to try seven conscientious objectors of the Cheshire Regiment who had refused to obey orders resumed its sitting at Birkenhead yesterday. Major WB Beamish, of the Royal Welsh Fusiliers, again presided. The cases left over for hearing were those of Privates Charles Dukes, of Warrington, and George Benson, of Disley. Dukes is an organiser of the Gasworkers' and General Labourers' Union, the secretary of the Warrington Trades Councils, and also a member of the Executive of the British Socialist party. Benson has associations with the Independent Labour party ... Mr. SR Dodds, a Liverpool solicitor, appeared for the accused.

Dukes was charged with failing to appear at the place of parade appointed by his commanding officer on 19 September, and in view of the ruling of the Court on the day before, as to the admissibility of certain evidence, he pleaded guilty.

The accused ... said that he was ordered to report at Chester Castle on 18 August. He was arrested on that day, fined £2 by a civil court, and taken by an escort to Chester, where he refused to sign attestation papers. Next day he again refused to sign, but submitted to a medical examination, and was placed in Class A. He refused to take any part or to arrange for allotment. In the afternoon he refused to sign for his kit or to carry it, and a sergeant swore at him. He refused to put on military clothes, and was forced into them. On the following day a commissioned officer tried for a long time to persuade him to give in, but he refused, and said that he did not intend to soldier. The officer replied, 'You will obey orders as long as you are here.'

He was taken to the Birkenhead camp next day, and on arrival a sergeant major asked him if he was Dukes, the conscientious objector, and on what ground his objection was based. A crowd of soldiers gathered, and an orderly corporal said, 'You must have your hair cut.' He was placed astride a form, and clippers were used. His hair was torn so violently that the clippers were put out of gear. Several non-commissioned officers abused him and said, 'We can tame ******* lions here. We have already broken others in.' Next morning he arose with the other men at six o'clock, but declined to go on parade. He was forced out by a corporal, and when he refused to obey orders an officer said, 'Well, you continue to refuse. I do not care a continental so long as you know what you are doing.' The accused asked if he was not entitled to a court-martial, and the officer replied, 'You have no right at all under military law.' Later he was marched to the park with his arms held behind, and he resisted as hard as he could.

He was forced into line and handed over to a gymnasium instructor, whose orders he refused to obey. The instructor said to two men, 'If he doesn't move, kick his feet.' They did this, and he was chiefly kicked on the heels. He continued to resist, and three men then held him. He was ordered to double, and was run about the park. As one set of men grew tired another took hold of him, and at the end of each five minutes they were ordered to throw him on the ground. One man sat on his legs while another raised his body and bent it forward. After several repetitions of this his head was held down and his legs were doubled from the hips several times. The whole process was repeated several times.

He was set on his feet, and a fresh set of men continued the doubling. He was then taken to a horizontal scaffold pole about 3ft. high and when he refused to jump it he was thrown over. He was pushed about the park to the water jump, and as he was pushed from behind he was compelled to jump to avoid falling into the water. Each time someone tried to kick his feet from under him as he jumped. The third time this succeeded and he fell in. The doubling began again, and while he was on the ground the colonel went up to him on horseback and asked him why [he] refused to drill. He replied that he was a conscientious objector and demanded a court-martial. The colonel said they could not give one, but would break his resistance down. At the end he said, 'Take this man away,' and the doubling was resumed. When he was thrown on the ground two or three officers were gathered round. He asked for a drink, and one of them said, 'He is only shamming; give him some more.' The treatment was continued for some time until he was semi-conscious, and he was then given ten minutes in which to consider his position.

He still refused to drill, and the treatment was continued until they returned for dinner. In the afternoon he was taken to the park again, and handed to the gymnastic instructor. He was treated as before until they got to the water jump, when he agreed to go through the rest himself. On 22 August he drilled under threat of personal violence, and he did that because he was warned that the abuse would be continued, and would be more severe.

Benson's Story of Torture

The charge against Benson was that he refused to obey an order to fall in at Bidston Camp on 22 September. He pleaded guilty.

The accused read a statement in which he said that after several appeals the Stockport Tribunal took away a non-combatant certificate granted by the Disley Tribunal, and gave no reason for so doing. He was arrested and handed to the military authorities on 14 September. He was first put into the Lancashire Fusiliers, but when an officer of the regiment heard that he was a conscientious objector his transfer to the Cheshire Regiment was arranged. He heard the officer say: 'They will put him through more quickly there.'

He was removed on the same day to Birkenhead, where a number of sergeants told him they would 'break him, tame him,' etc. Later he was told that other 'COs' had given in, and that he would; also that if he refused to drill he would be taken into a hut alone and drilled by two special instructors, by force if necessary. 'You were sent to us to be drilled,' he was told, 'and we shall drill you. We shall not court-martial you.' Later on the same day he was removed to Bidston, and there taken before a sergeant major, who said, 'We will soon tame you.'

Next morning he refused to fall in or stand to attention. He was knocked into position and his ankles were kicked. They were kicked again when he refused to stand at ease, and he suffered great pain. Later he was taken to a hut, where he was pushed along at the double and punched repeatedly in the small of the back. His heels were kicked, and he was tripped up and pulled up by the scruff of the neck. This continued until he was in a state of great exhaustion, especially from the blows in the back. In the afternoon his ankles were kicked again, and when he refused to shoulder a rifle it was hung round his neck by a piece of thin string so that the whole weight fell on his throat and caused great pain.

A Sergeant's Threats

[Benson] was told continually that what he was undergoing was only a foretaste of the treatment that would be, and that they would break his heart. Seeing no alternative to further physical torture, he decided for the time being to drill under strong protest. On 19 September, feeling fit for another lot of ill-treatment, he did not appear on parade after breakfast. As a result he was 'crimed' and put into the cells. 'That afternoon,' Benson continued, 'a sergeant of police came in and told me that he would see I did not get a court-martial, but 21 days under him. He would break my heart or kill me in the attempt. He said, "I will get the three men to strap you to a plank. I will give you the best thrashing you ever had in your life. I will make your ribs sore, and there will be no witnesses present." Next morning when I refused to clean out my cell he took me by the throat, thrust his knuckles into my throat, and shook me. He did it again when I refused to clean my boots.'

Dukes and Benson were sentenced to two years' penal servitude. Four of their assailants were court-martialled but acquitted, Dukes and Benson having refused to testify.

'THE DOMAIN OF DREAMS'

After catastrophic defeats at the hands of the Germans, the Russians were more successful on the Galician front against Austria-Hungary in June 1916, taking 500,000 prisoners. It was one of the last successes of the tsar's armies. Another had been at the expense of the Ottoman empire, with the capture, in February 1916, of Erzerum in eastern Anatolia.

17 February
How the Russians Took Erzerum

Petrograd: Russia has accomplished one of the most dramatic and momentous feats of the war. Less than a month ago her advance guards, chasing the Turks from Hassankala to the shelter of the guns of Erzerum, fired the first shot at the outer defences of that fortress. Foreign estimates put the garrison of Erzerum at 80,000. [...]

Decisive fighting for the precipitous gorges and rugged steps which form the eastern breastwork of the fortress seems to have begun on 25 January. On that day, the Turks, having hurried together all their available forces, made a desperate attempt to stem the Russian advance by an attack directed from villages which are situated to the north-east of Erzerum, a mile or two beyond the outer forts. This move was covered by a hurricane of fire from the fortress artillery, but was checked by the Russian advance guard. When the Russian main force came up the enemy was not only rolled back, but was pursued into the hills, where a strongly entrenched village which formed part of the scheme of fortifications was captured.

With untiring energy the Russians followed up their advantage by a sudden night attack. Further villages were taken by storm, and by dawn the Turks found their assailants firmly entrenched close to the fortified line. These operations probably decided the fate of the fortress. So far General Yudenitch's Caucasian campaign has certainly been a model, both in conception and execution … It has been put into execution with iron energy and lightning speed, and has thus effected a transformation which can hardly be without a very weighty influence on the further course of the whole war.

It was not to be so. Two months later the Russians had arrived in Trabzon, on the Black Sea coast. But a year later the tsar's empire collapsed, and in March 1918 the Turks were back in Erzerum.

A fantasia on the battle came later that year with the publication of the classic war thriller Greenmantle *– a book that, capturing something of Anglo-German rivalries in the near east, climaxed at Erzerum.*

18 November
Mr. Buchan's War Romance: *Greenmantle* by John Buchan

In a dedication prefixed to his thrilling romance Mr. Buchan warns us, 'Let no man or woman call its events improbable. The war has driven that word from our vocabulary, and melodrama has become the prosiest realism.' Whether when he has turned the last page of *Greenmantle* the reader should be inclined or no to acquiesce in such a view, two things at least we believe he will admit – that Mr. Buchan is a born story-teller, and that the improbabilities of this his latest tale come with such a rush and whirl of excitement, such a stirring up of the flaming dust of adventure, that we are, if not temporarily blinded to them, at any rate perfectly willing to forgive and forget. *Greenmantle* is certainly the most exciting story we have read for a long time. It belongs quite frankly to the class of sensational fiction, but in that class we must rank it very high. For its heroes are more than mere puppets, and if they are endowed with a remarkable share of luck, such as the average mortal cannot hope for, they are at the same time men of flesh and blood and intellect, very much alive, and quite distinct from the heroes of the ordinary 'shocker,' while their bold adventure is admirably planned and told in 'honest, plain words.'

That adventure is the discovery and frustration of a mysterious prophet who has arisen in the East and is being secretly exploited by the Germans, and in particular by the terrible Hilda con Einem, with the aim of gathering the entire force of Islam into one huge, irresistible wave which shall sweep over the Allies and destroy them. The movement is already in progress when Richard Hannay, the hero of *The Thirty-nine Steps*, is sent on his perilous mission; and how, with the help of three gallant friends, he discovers the secret of its power and stamps it out, thus bringing an almost impossible task to a triumphant conclusion, is the subject of the book. *Greenmantle* is the sort of book to keep the most stolid reader from his bed to a quite unconscionable hour, the sort of book to hold him breathless and spell-bound till the last chase is ended, the last plot baffles, and the long deferred victory won.

'ALL MILITARY HONOURS'

In November 1915 in what is now Iraq, a largely Indian force, commanded by General Sir Charles Townshend, was falling back to

Kut-al-Amara, pursued by the Turkish army. The siege of Kut began on 7 December and a succession of British attempts to break the siege led to 23,000 casualties. On 29 April 1916 Townshend capitulated.

4 May
As the Germans See It; The Fall of Kut

The fall of Kut has naturally aroused great jubilation in the German press. The *Frankfurter Zeitung* speaks of 'an irreparable blow to British prestige in the East and especially in India,' and the *Könische Zeitung* breaks out into the following tirade:

'Kut has fallen. Turkey has once more given proof of her vitality. The conquest of Mesopotamia by England has certainly receded once for all into the domain of dreams, and the political success which London expected from the capture of Bagdad is on the side of the Turks.'

The defeat at Kut, one of the most shameful in British military history, ended with 13,000 Indian and British troops marched into captivity. Few would survive. One who did was General Townshend.

12 June
General Townshend Well Treated

Amsterdam, Saturday: The Constantinople correspondent of the *Tageblatt* learns that General Townshend was delighted with his reception by Turks when he arrived at Constantinople, where he was received with all military honours. At one of the finest spots in Constantinople the Turks had prepared a house for him and his two aides-de-camp ... Shortly after his arrival General Townshend was allowed to visit the American Ambassador.

After the war, Townshend wrote a whitewashed memoir, My Campaign in Mesopotamia, *and was an independent Conservative*

MP from 1920 until 1922, by which time his war record had been exposed. His reputation destroyed, he died in 1924.

'ONE OF THE MOST FANTASTIC AND HOPELESS REVOLTS'

On Easter Monday, 24 April 1916, the British government paid a price for its pre-war vacillations around the Home Rule Bill of 1914. In Dublin, a handful of nationalists seized the General Post Office and proclaimed the Irish Republic. The Easter Rising had begun. Five days of fighting ensued – and cast James Connolly into the limelight. Liverpool-born, County Down-raised Connolly had worked alongside James Larkin at the time of the bitter battle for union rights in the 1913 Dublin Lockout.

29 April
The Larkinites' Leader

Our London Correspondence: James Connolly, who is said to be the leader of the rioters in Dublin, has so far figured in that city as 'Larkin's lieutenant'... Larkin himself is of the fire-brained type, ignorant, bustling and voluble. Connolly is quieter, better educated, far more intelligent and consequently far more dangerous ... His self-imposed mission in the Irish capital was to bring socialism ... He was always as extreme and uncompromising as his singular leader. Substituting 'strike' for 'war,' both would have accepted their ally Nietzsche's saying: 'You say that a good cause sanctifies even war; I say that a good war sanctifies any cause.'

On Saturday 29 April, the first provisional government of the Irish Republic, represented by Patrick Pearse, surrendered to the British authorities.

2 May
The End of a Hopeless Struggle

Dublin, Sunday Night: I was permitted to leave the Gresham Hotel in Sackville Street under a military order for half an hour last night, after three days' close confinement, and this morning there is a general, but still limited, permission to see the sunlight. There is no official authority so far, but we have hopes that communication with the rest of the country will be restored to-night, and it is clear now from the state of the streets, where people are hunting for pieces of shell and other remnants of the reign of terror, that the army have at last established full control.

Since last Wednesday night no non-combatant has been seen in the central part of Dublin. Crossing to Greenore on Wednesday morning, after a day's delay at Holyhead, I got to Drogheda by train without much difficulty and without any signs of the trouble which has strewn the streets of Dublin with dead. [...]

At Drogheda I managed to get a motor-car to Drumcondra, a suburb of Dublin, but the driver, who had heard of the wholesale confiscation of cars by the rebels of Monday, prudently refused to go further. We passed several barricades with the soldiers in possession on the way.

Walking into Dublin from Drumcondra I found the central part of the city in possession of the rebels. At the Parnell monument at the end of Sackville Street bullets were whistling down from the Post Office, the principal but not the only seat of the insurrection, and a Sinn Fein sentry ordered me to put up hands. On submission he was obliging enough, after borrowing a cigarette, to conduct me to the back door of the Gresham Hotel, where after a long parley behind barricaded doors they gave one shelter. Since then until this morning the guns have never been silent, and though the military have no complete possession of the city one still hears of desultory sniping.

Liberty Hall, the headquarters of Mr. Larkin's Citizen Army, who make the great bulk of the insurrectionists, was shelled by a gunboat from the river on Tuesday, and several other snipers' nests, including the YMCA buildings, just opposite the Gresham have been partially destroyed by light field artillery. The rebels, who felt the increasing pressure of the military cordon drawing in from the outskirts, set fire to the Post Office on Friday, and the place and several hotels and shops near by are gutted.

The troops, strongly reinforced from England and acting on a careful plan of convergement, have established full control to-day, and Mr. Pearce, who has described himself as the Commandant General of the Republican Army, and Mr. James Connolly ... have formally surrendered with 700 or 800 followers. Mr. Connolly is badly wounded. These people, who were quartered in Sackville Street and the Four Courts, laid down their arms last night in front of the Parnell monument, and to-day the rebel garrison in St. Stephen's Green, where they had entrenched themselves, and Jacob's biscuit factory have also surrendered. Terms were asked for, but unconditional surrender was insisted on. The Countess Markievicz, formerly Miss Gore-Booth, a well-known leader of the Irish extremists, surrendered with the St. Stephen's contingent. [...]

The authorities are satisfied that the trouble is now almost over ... There are still a few homicidal maniacs on the roofs who fire indiscriminately on soldier and civilian alike, but these are being gradually rooted out, and organised resistance is clearly at an end.

Initial reactions to the rising among the general population of Ireland were largely hostile. And there was a substantial southern Irish contingent in the British army.

1 May
Loyal Irish in Battle

France, Sunday: Whatever comfort the Germans may get out of their plot to stir up trouble in Ireland they found only cold steel and machine gun-fire when they came up against the Irish race in the field of battle. It was a splendid coincidence that on the very night when the Sinn Fein was trying to besmirch the honour of Ireland in the streets of Dublin some of the Irish battalions here should have been in the fighting line at one of the points of the German attack, and should have given by great gallantry a proof to the world that the heart of Ireland is true and loyal.

The Irish gentlemen in the trenches and billets belong to the old families whose names are heroic in Irish history. The soldiers in the Irish division are boys from Leinster and Munster, from Connaught and Ulster – from Dublin or Cork, Galway or Donegal, Catholics and Protestants stand shoulder to shoulder forgetting old feuds. There are no politics in the trenches, but the old fighting qualities of the Irish race and the fine spiritual fire in the Irish heart have been revealed on many days of great ordeal, so that the folly of a rebellious rabble is made ridiculous and hateful to the men out here. [...]

These Irishmen kept cool. I have seen them in the trenches, and they are as stolid as their English comrades, with a grim joke on two when the shells come crying overhead ... Slowly on a light north easterly wind there came from the German trenches a thick, sluggish volume of smoke 'Poison gas! ... Put on your helmets!' 'And I wish Sir Roger Casement could get a taste of it down his throat,' said an Irish soldier.

Roger Casement, the Irish-born British diplomat, exposed Belgian atrocities in the Congo and the slavery of Putumayo Indians in Peru. Knighted in 1911, he had by then embraced Irish nationalism. Having failed to enlist German support for an uprising, he reached Ireland by a German U-boat in 1916, aiming to put off the insurrection. He was quickly arrested, and his case became enmeshed in the controversy surrounding the executions of the leaders of the rising, which had boosted Irish and international support for the rebels.

Following court martial, some 15 people were shot between 3 and 12 May. These were the signatories to the proclamation of independence and all but one of the volunteer commandants – the stateless Eamonn de Valera. On the last day of the executions, the Manchester Guardian *made an editorial comment.*

12 May
The Danger for Ireland

Mr. Asquith yesterday made the welcome announcement that the executions are now to cease, except in the case of two out of the seven signatories of the manifesto of rebellion, against whom alone the death sentence has not yet been carried out. These two are James Connolly, commonly regarded as the real leader of the whole movement, and one other not specified but presumably 'Sean MacDiarmida,' of the manifesto. Connolly was severely wounded in the street fighting, and presumably MacDiarmida, or MacDermott, is also incapacitated. Both are under sentence of death ... Presumably it will be some weeks at least before Connolly is strong enough to stand up to be shot. What conceivable gain will there be in shooting him?

13 May
Connolly Shot Yesterday

An official report issued at the military headquarters in Dublin yesterday afternoon states that the trial of two prominent leaders in the rebellion whose names appeared in the proclamation issues by the so-called 'Provisional Government' – namely, James Connolly and John MacDermott – took place on 9 May, and sentence of death was awarded in each case.

The Manchester Guardian *commented editorially again that day.*

The Outlook in Ireland

The execution of Mr. Connolly and Mr. MacDermott has been carried out as a tribute to that sense of symmetry which stands in the place of justice in times of rebellion and repression ... We can only trust that these will be the last, that if there are common murderers to be tried they will be brought before a civil court, and that a definite end will now be put to the disposal of men's lives by military courts. That end once reached it is possible for both British and Irish to look the future – a future which not only affects our fortunes in the present war, but still more vitally enters into the whole of our prospective development ... Ireland in the main has been won from her attitude of distrust and hostility to a peaceful and to the verge of a cordial and sympathetic relationship with England. The outbreak of the war, though it dashed Ireland's hopes, was nevertheless used by the imagination of the Irish leaders to foster the new spirit. Ireland forgave the delay of Home Rule, though it was a dashing of the cup from her very lips, and for the first time in a great European crisis associated herself heartily with Great Britain. Then came a number of untoward events working on the feelings of the little group of ill-balanced enthusiasts, men and women, who date from those days before the war which we can still with an effort remember, days when in all countries there was a sudden shoot of disbelief in government and a gospel of doing things for ourselves – 'ourselves alone,' or in Irish 'Sinn Fein.' Some of this group were poets, literary men, idealists, dreamers, even pacifists like Mr. Sheehey Skeffington, but there were others of that 'robuster' type which everywhere exists and which believes in shooting without much caring why you shoot or what you expect to come of it. These men carried arms in imitations of the other bands of organised volunteers and finally a few of them organised one of the most fantastic and hopeless revolts known to history. This revolt found the two great parties that divide Ireland united in the determination that it should be repressed, and that law and order should reign. [...]

Thus it came about that the revolt, which seemed for an hour to threaten the whole fabric of good feeling which statesmen have been patiently building up, in reality revealed the solidity of the new structure. But good-will was to be subject to a more dangerous assault. There are few loyalties that can stand the rule of martial law for any length of time. What effect the executions have actually had, how much is now irretrievable, how much may still be saved, we cannot tell.

On 5 July CP Scott wrote to Lloyd George, asking for Sir Roger Casement's life to be spared. Nonetheless, Casement was hanged at Pentonville Prison in London on 3 August 1916. The Irish war of independence began on 21 January 1919. The Irish Free State was created – without the six counties of northern Ireland – on 6 December 1922.

'A FRIGHTFUL MELODRAMA OF BLOOD AND DEATH'

In 1915 Londoner Philip Gibbs had become one of five correspondents officially assigned to the British Expeditionary Force (BEF). In 1920 he was knighted for his coverage of a war he said had 'changed him utterly'. The following reports reveal his optimism as the army expanded.

1 January
Army's Confidence and Hope

British Headquarters: 'Will 1916 drag poor human nature through new agonies and leave us still bleeding and fighting?' There is not a man here who thinks that possible. There is an absolute faith along our whole line of trenches and in the French lines ... that those who live will see both victory and peace.

As far as some of the officers and men are concerned that faith is founded upon small details which lead to optimism in sections of the line ... But generals who have wider sources of knowledge hold the same view, and they have told me with a grave sincerity, weighing but significant – of deterioration in the enemy's man power. His reserves of strength are not so great and not so good. The *moral* of the men is weakening. [...]

But these generals of ours see also something of greater hope for us – our steady increase of strength in men and in guns, and in the food of guns. They feel behind them a growing power, making defence more certain, so that there is no longer that growing anxiety which bit into their souls last year, because at any moment the thin crust of our security might be broken through and let in an overwhelming tide. That can never happen now unless the gods are against us. It is the sense of relief and of increasing might of the machine behind them which gives our officers a steady hopefulness, not only in the strength of their defensive, but also in their power to strike. [...]

'Next time!' they say, and those words hold a promise. The armies which will fight for victory and peace after the New Year will not be the same as those who fought mainly for defence a year ago and in the months that followed. There are new men, and the machinery of our war has changed as well as grown.

12 February
How the Clerks Are Sticking It Out

I had not seen much of the London men since Loos until yesterday, when I went to see how they had been getting on ... Eighteen months ago these young men wore black coats and white collars, and travelled from Streatham Hill or Lewisham or other quiet suburbs by morning trains without guessing for a moment that this little life of theirs was but the prelude to a frightful melodrama of blood and death. They pushed through the swing-doors into Government offices and did a few hours of leisurely futile work about elementary school and Board of Trade returns and had games of dominoes on tea-shop tables and discussed books and plays and the ideals of human progress and the suffragette problem and the Territorial system, till suddenly everything broke and England called upon her men of fighting age, and there happened – this!

'Do you think fellows of your kind – men who have done clerical work – can stick it out as well as mechanics and agricultural labourers and men of outdoor life not requiring much head work?'

'It looks like it,' said one of them simply. 'The Londoners did all right at Loos. On the whole our nerves are steady enough under bombardment, though we don't like it any better than other people. Pride helps – London pride.'

There are many well-to-do men in the ranks ... In some of the battalions university men march shoulder to shoulder with actors, music-hall singers, commercial travellers, and shop assistants. All the types of London life are here in the ranks, and it is 'London pride' that makes them good fighting men.

In 1916 Erich von Falkenhayn, the then German commander on the western front, aimed to inflict such a blow on the French as to drive Paris to seek terms. An onslaught on the fortress at Verdun followed, with the intention of bleeding the French army to death. The barrage began on 21 February. By December, when the battle concluded, 162,440 French and 143,000 Germans were dead. The two sides had incurred more than 400,000 other casualties. French losses were slightly higher, but the Germans had not made a breakthrough. Philip Gibbs's report appeared in March.

4 March
Desperate German Assaults near Verdun

The renewed German attack north of Verdun was another furious effort to capture the commanding Douaumont ridge, made, as had been expected, by simultaneous assaults on the north-western and eastern sides. The latter, directed against the village of Vaux, broke down, with the Germans, it is stated, 'leaving heaps of dead in the barbed wire.' The former had, by the official reports of yesterday afternoon, carried the Germans, in spite of frightful losses, in to the village of Douaumont. According to the French report, the struggle was continuing desperately in the village – across its single street, said a semi-official account. The German Headquarters claimed to have cleared the village and pushed the line west and south, thereby reducing the 'encirclement' of the fort on the plateau above, and to have taken over 1,000 prisoners and six guns … Berlin is far from elated over the Verdun battle, and the depression has been heightened by a remarkable article by the most respected of the German military critics, Major Moraht, who laments that 'a generation of warriors,' French and German, should be going to their graves under the shadow of Verdun.

'COLONEL CHURCHILL'S HELMET'

John Brodie patented his steel helmet in 1915 and by 1916, after protests from officers, the British army was taking delivery of them – before then,

'A huge inspector plucked Mrs Pankhurst out of the struggling group and ran away with her in his arms.' Suffragette Emmeline Pankhurst arrested at Buckingham Palace, 21 May 1914.

'A Serb student fired a revolver at the car' – and set fire to the world. The Archduke Franz Ferdinand, heir to the throne of Austria, and his wife, just before their assassination, 28 June 1914.

'It was just like ten thousand thunderstorms all coming at once.'
The German navy shells Scarborough, 16 December 1914.

The ultimate deterrent, that wasn't: the British Grand Fleet, 1914.

On their way. By the end of August 1914, the British Expeditionary Force had arrived in France.

'Those Indians looked all like kings.' By November 1914, Indian Army units had joined them.

The White War: 'The men whose ant-like forms … crawl painfully up the white hill seem bent on some excursion.' Italian soldiers in the Alps, 1915.

'Italy and Austria are tightly locked in each other's embrace.'
Austrian soldiers during an early battle of the Isonzo, 1915.

A new world of women: shell-making in Sheffield, May 1916.

'If the War Office could appoint her colonel, one could
imagine her recruiting a battalion in record time.'
Vesta Tilley as the Tommy in 1916.

'The most cruel instrument of war yet invented.' Repairing telephone lines during a gas attack.

'If you know a better 'ole ...' A Tommy at supper, 1917.

'The awkward efficiency of the tank.' The arrival of the 'monstrous insects' in 1916 would transform warfare.

'A long tide of life, streaming forward for an affair of death.'
Scottish troops advance at Arras, April 1917.

'Weary and soaked and partly numbed, covered with slime.' Passchendaele, August 1917.

'American troops seem to have distinguished themselves finely' – but at a cost.
An American Red Cross nurse at work in France, October 1918.

An irresistible force: Charlie Chaplin atop Douglas Fairbanks,
promoting Liberty Bonds in Manhattan, 1918.

'It was as though people had heard the news and wanted to breathe it.'
Londoners, 11 November 1918.

the troops wore cloth caps that provided no protection from bullets or shrapnel. Churchill was at the front – in a French helmet.

31 March
The Steel Helmet

Our London Correspondence: The steel headpieces for protection against shrapnel, which were demanded so dramatically by the officer who reached the floor of the House of Commons yesterday, have been very slow in coming to our troops, although the French reported, as the result of their experience in the Champagne battles, that they have made a reduction in the casualties of almost 10 per cent … In the Verdun fighting General Pétain is never seen without his helmet. Colonel Churchill has his own helmet, and has been seen wearing it out of as well as in the trenches … The French helmet is not only serviceable but is also very handsome. Many of the young men at the French front look like statues of Mercury.

'THERE CAN BE NO DOUBT UPON THE MATTER'

On Wednesday 31 May 1916, off the coasts of Norway and Denmark, the long-awaited 'decisive battle' was fought between the German High Seas Fleet and the Royal Navy's Grand Fleet. The majority of the almost 250 ships involved were British. Communications were chaotic. The reality of the battle of Jutland – Skaggerak, to the Germans – was that the British sustained substantially higher losses, in ships and men. However, the High Seas Fleet would not challenge the British again, and the naval blockade on Germany was sustained. For the British the appearance of victory was reassuring.

6 June
The Navy Certain of Victory

A Port of the North-East Coast: I am writing by the shores of a channel which leads to a most important naval base. During the last two days there have passed many of the ships that fought in the great fight, proudly bearing their scars, and men from those ships have come ashore almost as proudly and silently and have gone about their business and their pleasure. They have said little, but a great joy fills this town and an exultations of feeling caught from the men returning from battle with high spirits and victorious mien. It is a joy that rises superior to many fine ships and such glorious lives. It is not modified though a little chastened by the cautious, unboastful statement issued by the Admiralty. It turns to contempt the jubilation in Berlin …

It must be admitted that this deep and confident joy is not wholly to be accounted for. Its springs are mostly out of sight, but it is highly infectious and persistent. It is an emotion without a reaction. Had it been a thing of one day and gone the next it would have been negligible, but its force has been constant, ever increasingly, as ship after ship has come in bringing its report to confirm others. […]

Some of our smaller ships show signs of damage, but there is no cause for alarm in the wreckage, for example, of the bridge of a destroyer that arrived here yesterday. That destroyer was in the act of launching a torpedo at a German cruiser when a shell carried the bridge away bodily. But the boat was not vitally hurt, and the remainder of the crew brought her safely back to port.

'WELL WITHIN THE WAR ZONE'

By 1916 the British naval blockade was wreaking havoc on Germany's home front. The British had declared the North Sea a 'war zone' in

November 1914; in February 1915 the Germans declared all approaches to Britain a war zone. Over the course of 1915, U-boats accounted for the loss of nearly a million tons of allied shipping. The total loss the following year was over a million.

On 18 September 1916, Blake Barton provided an account of a fraught transatlantic crossing at a time when cavalry and horse-drawn transport were at the heart of the global war machine.

18 September
Getting Through

The nervous stamping of fourteen hundred tired and hungry horses came to me in my storeroom at the bottom of No. 3 hatchway. I was squatting on a pile of empty sacks, working by the swaying light of a villainous ship's lantern at my inventory of salt, meal, halters, shovels, forks, blankets, and the innumerable other accessories of a horse transport in his Majesty's service. The air was vile and choking.

'Hey, below there! A pail of linseed, three hay-nets and a sling. Get a move on!' And Red Nickerson received the stores and my rejoinder with his customary grin. 'Red' had played cowboy parts in a Los Angeles kinema company, and had met Grace [*sic*] Pickford and Charlie Chaplin (so he said). At any rate, he and I were friends because we had both learned to love the cattle country. We had spent many an off-duty hour smoking together and telling tales of the old days of the range and of famous cattle thieves. That morning at seven bells we had been assigned to the same cutter at boat-muster, and had been exchanging submarine jokes ever since.

'Sorry to hurry yer, mate; I'd forgot you was tryin' on yer life-belt,' and he dodged a handful of rock-salt and was off forward.

We were well within the war zone, doing more than fifteen knots, east-bound, Boston to Liverpool. One of the line's biggest boats had been torpedoed just before we sailed and Captain B was determined that they should not get his ship. It was in the summer of 1915, before the Big Sayville wireless station had been closed, and when ostensibly innocent news items could carry information of the most valuable kind to the enemy. Only two piers away from us as we loaded in Boston the *Kronprinzessin Cecilie* had been docked, and was marking well every dray-load of shrapnel and every remount that passed. We carried a hundred-thousand worth of war material. Captain B would never heave to if a shot came across his bows, and we all knew it.

I had finished my inventory before the horsemen were through feeding in our hatch-way. The wind, which had been south-west and astern, changed to easterly. The big ship began to roll so heavily that at each swing five thousand hoofs would rattle as the horses braced to meet it. Turning out my pitching lantern light, I stepped into the open hatchway before closing my storeroom to see whether there were any more orders. A beam wave slapped against the starboard side just then, and came rushing down the hatch. I jumped in time to avoid broken bones and a ducking. The horses were thoroughly wet and frightened. One big grey, an especial friend of mine, for whom I used to steal sugar, slipped and got badly cast.

'I say, feller, some spray! What?' said the gang boss of No. 3, as he staggered by to attend to the grey. The horses were knee-deep in the wash, being below the lowest scuppers; and No. 3 gang spent a profane hour bailing out between decks.

Meanwhile I made my way aft to the galley cautiously, for we were rolling badly now. As I passed the pantry I stepped in to say good-evening to Jack, and to take a look at the weather out of one of the port-holes. The light was still good, but the weather thickening.

'The thicker the better,' said Jack. 'The — shar-r-ks can't see us then.'

'The Old Man'll have coffee and toast on the bridge,' said Victor, the Captain's 'tiger,' swaying in. 'What do you blighters know about real work? I've been up and down the — bridge till I'm done out. I say, the wireless chaps have been running up every other minute with code for the Old Man. Something doing. They say there's two U-Boats waiting for us this side of Tusker. But there'll be no need of lifeboats mate. The Boss'll run for it or ram hell out of them.' And Victor was off with his pot of coffee, proud to be so necessary to the one upon whom every life on board depended.

That night 'Red' and I went up on deck at six bells for a pipe and a look at the weather. A blanket of fog lay over us, and settled down even among the horse-stalls. It was dark on deck. Every porthole and doorway was muffled. The ship was pounding along at top speed. There was a moon somewhere for now and then the fog shimmered. We stood forward on the starboard side looking into it. Unexpectedly it began to lift a bit, and the two look-outs at the bow raised their night-glasses. We could see several hundred feet ahead and as far aft.

The wireless operator scurried forward along the hurricane deck with a code message for the Old Man, who stopped to read it and then went to the starboard side. He levelled his glasses right abeam, and then ahead. It was lifting all about us now. A faraway fog-whistle sounded, whence we could not tell. A bell rang sharply down in the engine room, and we slowed to half speed – too late if the stranger had been dead-on. Again the toot came, this time clearly from the starboard. Another bell-handle snapped from the bridge, and we resumed speed, the old ship trembling with the full-engine drive, and sending a phosphorescent wake far behind. A dozen cattlemen and stewards came on deck, sensitive to the change in speed. A subtle excitement was in the air.

As we looked back and abeam, straining our eyes to make out the passing ship, we changed our course abruptly to port, and left a well-defined, glittering white right angle of wake to starboard. We were zigzagging!

There was no panic, only intense interest and suppressed excitement. Again the distant toot, this time clearly to starboard and receding. The fog was lifting fast now, uncovering the moon, which was right above, with a brown ring of mist. Now we were clear of the fog, driving ahead at full speed. Again we swerved, this time to starboard.

'Two trawlers, sire, a point off the starboard bow,' the look-out called with the regulation monotonous drawl. Had he said, 'The British Fleet,' the words could not have been sweeter to us. The tense silence was broken by a murmur of relief. The Old Man had 'got by' again.

We went below and slept till morning, life-belt regulations and submarines forgotten. As we steamed up to the bar of Liverpool the pilot brought news that they were towing a captured U boat into Queenstown. We had been followed by three. Slowly we made our way up the Mersey, the Captain still on his bridge, hollow-eyed from his vigil but happy. I looked back toward the Irish coast. A score of hulls were veering and manoeuvring there – his Majesty's trawlers, the very picture of a peaceful fishing fleet.

'THE ADVANTAGES WE HAD GAINED'

On 14 February 1916, the British Commander General Douglas Haig and Joseph Joffre, the French commander-in-chief, agreed on an offensive to be launched in Picardy at the meeting point of the French and British lines, although Haig's preference had been for Flanders. The larger plan was that Britain, France, Russia and Italy would simultaneously attack the central powers in the summer. But on 21 February the German attack at Verdun threw the French army on to the defensive.

And while on the eastern front a Russian offensive towards Vilna failed, from 4 June the onslaught of General Alexei Brusilov's forces, in what is now the Ukraine, shook the fighting spirit of the Austro-Hungarian army and led to the taking of 200,000 prisoners, which helped to ease the pressure on Verdun. Friends and foes learned from the tactics used in Brusilov's initially successful operation.

12 June
Battles Raging on the River Styr

With the capture of a general and 35,509 officers and men on Saturday, the Russian total of prisoners for the first seven days of the attack on the Austrian front reaches just under 108,000 together with 124 guns and immense quantities of war material.

After 'smashing in' the Austrian northern wing as far as Lutak and crossing the Styr at several points, the Russians are now engaged in furious battles on that river. In Galicia they have carried the Strypa line from Butchatch to the Dniester and have driven the point of their wedge here to a village seven miles west of the Strypa. It was announced from Petrograd last night that in Bukovina the Russians on Saturday captured 18,000 men and put the Austrians to rout. As the main fighting line here was only about a dozen miles north of Tchernovitz, news of the re-entry of the Russians into that city may not be long delayed.

Then came the Somme offensive. It was the vastly enlarged BEF, and its Commonwealth troops, which provided the bulk of the manpower. The allied artillery bombardment began on 24 June. On Saturday 1 July, amidst much hope, battle commenced. On Monday 3 July, this Press Association report was filed, and published in the Manchester Guardian *the following Wednesday.*

5 July
On the Battle's Fringe

Today I had a chat with an officer who had been 'having a look round' in Fricourt and spent an hour in the old German strong point of Danzig Alley. He related his impressions as coolly as if he were describing a visit to the Probate Court. True, he admitted, the place was 'a bit unhealthy' at times, which was the equivalent to saying that there would be twenty flashes of flame a minute within a radius of 200 yards, shedding bullets, steel splinters, and a blinding, suffocating smother of fumes. Another officer told me that he had just returned from Montauban, where 'the strafing was certainly a bit thick'. In as much as it had taken him an hour and a half to get away from the *rafales* of fire ... These adventures into the battlefield are accompanied by some grim and tragic discoveries, more particularly in the tracts where the grass is tall and thick. One of these will form a haunting memory. It was the sight of several men, almost in a row, leaning forward in various motionless postures upon their rifles, the bayonet points of which were buried in the ground, and between two of them a seated terrier with its drooping head, faithful unto death in its devotion to its soldier master. One need not be told that it was the work of a slowly swinging machine gun which had wrought this dreadful tableau. [...]

Few things have impressed me more than the deep enthusiasm which the British offensive has kindled amongst the French ... One is unmistakably conscious of the fact that it is good to be an Englishman in France just now. In a great historic town not 20 kilometres from the front I have been watching the endless ambulance trains bearing our wounded back from the battleground. The wide central boulevard is lined the day long with spectators – most of them, alas! women in mourning – and you instinctively feel the depth of their sympathy with the men who have suffered in the cause which has welded the two races into an indissoluble kinsmanship. [...]

Let it not be supposed at home that only 20 miles of the British army is now fighting. The whole 90 miles of the khaki line is bearing its full share in the terrific brunt ...

I am told that an astonishing proportion of the 5,000 odd prisoners thus far accounted for have plaintively asked ... what they are fighting each other for; and Tommy, who is not easily posed, cannot get behind the explanation that it is because the Kaiser wants to boss the earth. [...]

The first assault on the Gommécourt salient, although not succeeding in its purpose, is described as one of the most gallant feats of the entire war. The enemy on the opening of our bombardment put down a terrific barrage both in front of his own trenches and in front of our own, as well as behind the latter, to prevent the bringing up of reserves. No-Man's Land at this spot is about 200 yards wide – an exceptional depth across which to deliver an assault. On the word to charge being given, the infantry left their cover and advanced through the infernal fire as coolly as though on manoeuvres. Then the German did a very gallant thing, getting out into the shrapnel-swept zone of our own artillery and bringing machine-guns with them, which they played with deadly effect even as they themselves were being mown down.

4 July
Signs of the Offensive

Our London Correspondence: One sign of how Londoners have reacted to the great weekend news is the new feeling in the little crowds that gather at the stations to see the Red Cross trains arrive. Very few of the wounded from the great battle have reached London yet, although it is difficult to learn always from what battlefield come the men swathed in blankets who lie in the smooth-going ambulances. Nevertheless the people who watch the deft unloading of the trains at Charing Cross and Waterloo do so less than ever, one is sure, from mere curiosity, but as a way of showing a glad sympathy for the men who have done all they knew for England.

This afternoon at Waterloo there were women in black who have already given someone to the war – there on the off chance of getting news of some other man of theirs ... From the people less intimately concerned one noted a disposition, absent during the everyday processions of wounded, to cheer and wave handkerchiefs as the ambulances went by. We hear from the front of the cheerfulness of the wounded after a victory, and even here, at the end of a long and trying journey, there was the same gay spirit, for often a man lying prone on his narrow berth would respond to the cheers by waving his hand from among the blankets.

At Charing Cross, where there is always an amazingly mixed and vital crowd, the London greeting was especially cordial to-night, and you saw women buying up the street sellers' roses and tossing them into the taxis that brought the slightly wounded away. Those few who had a chance of a chat with one of the Somme fighters learned how the spirit of man – wounded man – can survive a hell of artillery and shell-hole fighting such as makes the battle of Loos a mild anecdote by comparison.

Everywhere to-day one finds that Londoners, refusing to be foolishly elated by 'big-push' headlines and the rest, are taking the news coolly, even critically, saving up the big enthusiasm for the big result. A sign on the quickened interest is the crowds round the map shops, where the battle front is marked across Europe by a procession of Allied flags. Those flags have been in the old positions so many weary months the pavement-goers had ceased to glance at them, but now people gather and stare at the line with the hope, deep in all hearts, that the little flags will march on before long.

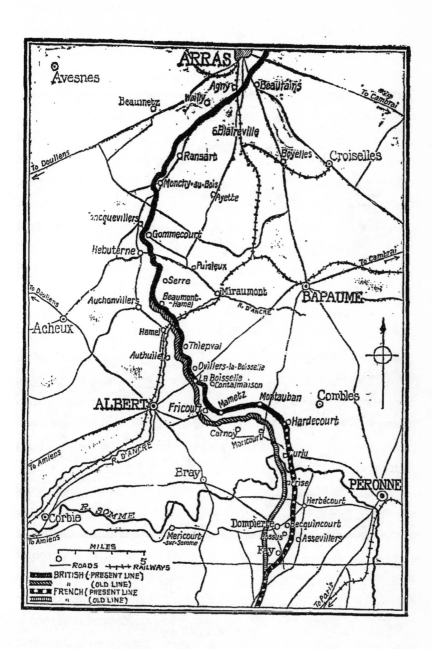

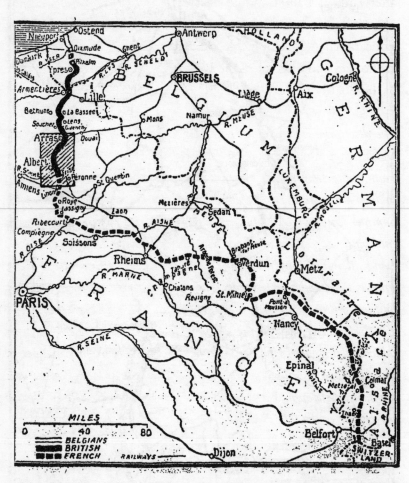

The map illustrates the relation of the present British-French
attack to the whole western front. The small shaded oblong
is the area of the large-scale map [*on the previous page*].
Appeared 3 July 1916

14 July
Sgt. RH Tawney (wounded)

Sergeant RH Tawney is in hospital at Tréport with machine-gun wounds in chest and abdomen. He was a scholar at Rugby and afterwards at Balliol. While Lecturer on Economics at Glasgow University he started the tutorial evening classes for the Worker's Educational Association. He was the author of several books of economics and director of the Ratantata Consultative Committee of the Board of Education.

The description of Richard Henry 'RH' Tawney's fate appeared in the Manchester Guardian *under the headline 'Heavy Casualties, Over Four Hundred Officers, Lancashire Losses'. More than 19,000 British soldiers are estimated to have died on the first day of the Battle of the Somme. Tawney had led his troops from the 22nd Manchester regiment into battle at 7.30am and was rescued, in acute pain, from No Man's Land after spending more than a day there. The armies of Germany, France, Austria-Hungary and the Russian empire had been incurring vast losses from the early days of the war, but the first day on the Somme effectively marked the arrival of the mass British Empire citizen army which set the pattern for the rest of the campaign. Tawney was one of almost 40,000 casualties on the bloodiest day in the history of the nation's arms, a catastrophic event which has, for good or ill, defined British perceptions of the war ever since.*

Tawney, a Christian socialist, had enlisted in 1914 – and declined a commission. The year before he had become head of the Ratan Tata Foundation at the London School of Economics – funded by a member of the Indian industrial family – which conducted research into the relief and eradication of poverty. His army experience confirmed his worst suspicions about the class system.

A great educationalist and economic historian, he was a key intellectual inspiration to the Labour party – and a regular Manchester

Guardian *contributor. Pain from the wounds he suffered that first morning on the Somme persisted until his death in 1962.*

The battle itself raged on into the autumn. At Flers, on 15 September, a new weapon appeared. The first tanks were extremely unreliable – but offered the prospect of a weapon that would, eventually, end the stalemate of trench warfare.

21 September
Voyages Made by the Tanks beyond the German Front
From a Correspondent with the British Army in the Field: The more I hear about armoured cars – the 'tanks' – and their amazing adventures in battle, the more I am convinced that the entire Empire will consider their crews worthy of very special praise ... Like the submarine voyagers, they are locked in a vessel, which is exposed to a variety of lurid dangers. They control great forces, but by the very reason of their power are subject to perils which do not beset the ordinary soldier. Yet single-handed one of these strange craft is prepared to engaged an entire battalion, an entire battery, a trench crammed with machine-guns, and come out of the fray victorious. All these exploits have been performed. [...]

Let me begin haphazard with the story of an 'emergency' tank, thrust into the order of battle at the last minute, with a 'scratch' crew, and with instructions to fight on our extreme right above Combles. Through no effort of the frightened Boches, the steering-gear went wrong and the pilot could only travel straight ahead. This he did. He eventually found himself astride a German trench on the outskirts of Combles, a little out of his reckoning. Here he halted, enfilading the trench repeatedly until a chance shell of large dimensions hit the car, making it impossible to move forward or back. For five hours the crew of the 'tank' worked their guns while parties of German and British bombers lobbed their missiles across from opposite sides. Eventually the Germans were killed or driven off, and the crew of the 'tank' returned safely through a deadly enemy barrage.

A second 'tank' had a wonderful experience in Bouleaux Wood. It travelled about halfway up the wood to a position from which it could enfilade the enemy's trenches. Then the commander discovered that the infantry were not coming up behind him, so he went back for them. Again he went forward with the infantry following, and passing over the enemy trenches continued his journey to the outskirts of Morval. Later the commander found that he was again alone. Not wishing to keep all the fruits of victory for himself, he again turned and went back to find the infantry for whom he was acting as a kind of chaperon. He made a return journey of more than 1,300 yards in their direction, and then discovered that the infantry had been held up by a group of machine-guns which had been turned on them from a trench previously reported as unoccupied.

Calmly hoisting itself astride the trench, the 'tank' took a hand in the firing, knocking out one machine-gun after the other until the trench was cleared. Unfortunately the 'tank' became wedged in an unusually deep crater, and the crew could not extricate it, even though they emerged and tried to dig it out, while the enemy were firing at them from another trench seventy yards away. Then the fun really started. Parties of German bombers worked around to one side of the car while British bombers from the infantry took cover on the opposite side. The ensuing duel lasted an hour and a half. The Germans tried to drop their bombs on the roof of the 'tank' without success. A corporal of the 'tank's' crew seized a German bomb which fell among his companions and tried to fling it back, but it exploded, blowing him to pieces. Eventually the German bombers were driven off and the crew returned to the British lines. [...]

There is a nautical atmosphere about the 'tanks.' Their officers salute navy fashion. As one of them said to me, 'You have to be everything from a mechanic to a sailor,' and I am inclined to think they are as handy men as ever sailed the sea. Their land craft – some of them christened with strange names – are surely breeding a new type of soldier which will become as distinct as the sailors of the air.

29 September
Great Deeds by the Tanks

The greatest tank story of the day: ... It ambled on its lonely advance towards a deep, broad fissure in the tumbled earth, which was the obvious lodging-place of many armed men. The 'tank's' intention was to sit astride this trench and play its machine-guns freely. But suddenly it halted, the engine stopped. Instantly the Germans swarmed out of the earth. They buzzed around the 'tank' like bees. One must give them credit for unusual courage. Although the hidden batteries rained like bullets at them they made a desperate attempt to storm the travelling fort, to pierce its hide with rifle-fire, and to kill the crew within.

They might as well have attacked a battleship with spades. The machine-guns whirred incessantly, and the pile of dead Germans grew steadily around the 'tank,' but still there were rushes by these foolish men. They clambered on the steel roof, they hoisted each other up in the hope of finding loopholes or joints in the armour of the beast, some of them carried dead men on their shoulders before them themselves were killed by the hidden gunners. It was a fearful and indescribable sight, this futile combat of men with machinery. The 'tank' fought stolidly. Inside, the crew were filled with astonishment. Never in their wildest dreams had they conceived the possibility of Germans crowding forward to be killed. Never did gunners work their pieces more franticly. All they asked for was more Germans.

The strange tumult drew the attention of infantry engaged in 'cleaning up' odd corners in Gueudecourt. They ran to the rescue. Now the tank will tell you that it did not need rescuing. It was quite happy. But the infantry took a hand and beat the Germans off – or rather what was left of them – and seized a few discouraged prisoners. The field of battle was thick with corpses. At least 300 Germans lay dead around the 'tank.' And the 'tank' itself? The passing indisposition of the monster was attended to, and it went its way. The crew came back to marvel at this inexplicable occurrence. We shall never know what sudden blind enthusiasm sent these Prussians mad, and caused them to fling away their lives as recklessly as any fanatics that ever lay down before the Juggernaut.

At the beginning of October the rains came down on the Somme, and the miserable weather persisted for over a month.

9 November
How the Advance Has Been Held Up

For a whole month now rain and the condition of the ground have prohibited operations of any magnitude. Records of the last 100 years are said to show that in the Somme valley October is the wettest month of the year, and one can believe it, for in the whole month there have been only 11 days on which some rain did not fall. Unfortunately the October weather has now continued over the first week of November, and the outlook to-day is even less promising than it has been at any time since the wet weather began. [...]

The amazing spirits of our men, the splendid work of our artillery, the superb audacity of our aviators – these things may be robbed of their fruits by natural conditions which no one can control, but they are as wonderful as ever. It is not surprising that we cannot get on faster. What might be surprising is that during these last thirty days we have got on at all, that we have continued to make ground as we have made it.

The second phase of the battle of the Ancre, between 13 and 18 November, marked the end of the battle of the Somme. On Monday 13 November, the village of Beaumont Hamel was finally taken by the 51st Highland division. It had been a target on the first day of the battle, back in July. Though they were defeated, the sophistication of Germany's underground workings during the Somme were revelatory.

16 November
Uncounted Booty

From a Correspondent with the British Army in the Field: Monday's victory – already the most complete and least costly that we have won since the Battle of the Somme began – is hourly enhanced ... We have stormed three villages, captured and held the commanding double-ridge north of the Ancre, and overlook the German positions at Grandcourt and Miraumont. [...]

I must say something of the battlefield – one of the strangest and thorniest and most novel in history. Fiction is quite baffled by fact at every turn. The men who stormed the positions north of the river and along it might have been advancing over roofs in a street fight. Underneath them were rooms upon rooms containing hidden and unsuspected groups, and down in the street-trenches below – some nearly empty, some crowded – the enemy lifted their hands and shouted for mercy, or occasionally fired into the air.

The battlefield is still unsearched or unplumbed. Pickets of men, dumps of stores, reserves of weapons lie hidden here, there, and everywhere. It is not improbable that even cannon, and certainly mortars, will be among the treasure trove. The scale of these hiding-places is on the scale of a town of many streets and well-cellared houses. Seven hundred prisoners all together in one row were clean passed by in our first advance. The trenches themselves are as tangled as the pattern of a quick-set hedge in winter, and the maze of crooked lines interspersed with dug-out holes extends to a breadth of over a mile. A section of ground cut through Oxford Street would hardly be more intricate.

I have been writing of the country north of the River Ancre, but the crowning marvel of the German defence lies just across the river on the south side. If you slip along the river road you come to an opening about seven feet high in the cliff, and when you have penetrated into the secret place you find a new world – a Monte Christo world. Even the guns which thunder to madness outside are blurred to a murmur – indeed are often wholly inaudible. A sickly reek pervades the place – though not the reek of dead bodies, though a few wounded men from the battle, vainly seeking shelter, here lie where they have fallen in the passages. Meat and bread, perhaps, have mouldered in the stores, and the volatile dust of the fungus blends with the pungent dampness of the clay.

On 15 November the Manchester Guardian *published an optimistic editorial on the concluding stage of the battle.*

15 November
The British Victory

The news from the west front has several folds of goodness. It is good because important ground was won and more prisoners captured than the British have yet captured in any single-handed engagement. It is better because the ground has been won north of the Ancre, which has hitherto defied our efforts. It is best because it shows that our offensive in the west need not be stopped by the winter. To take this last and best point first, it needs no elaboration that a victory won now is worth much more than the same victory won six months hence. The central military and political idea of the Germans now is to transfer the war to the eastern front in the hope of achieving peace by decisive victories over Russia. For good or evil – more for evil than for good so far – we have determined to make our main effort in the west, and the German plan of transferring the war to the east rests on the assumption that, even if we gain ground in the west, we cannot gain enough or gain it soon enough to embarrass their eastern schemes. Hence the intrinsic importance of the victory that we have won is vastly enhanced by its being won now … We shall embarrass their preparations for the east in the winter, and they will be in two minds about their offensive against Russia in the spring. Not only so, but if they do advance east in the spring they will constantly have to be looking round over their shoulder to see what progress we are making in France. This is clear gain – strategical and not merely tactical. Multiply it by the number of weeks or even months in the winter, and we shall soon have grounds for confidence of being able to strike at a vital spot next year … . How thin the German lines have been worn at some points was shown by the French successes at Verdun … Our infantry is superb, but while we use [it] let us beware of abusing and overworking its splendid valour. Forethought and fore action can save thousands of lives.

The staged documentary The Battle of the Somme *was a huge success in the summer of 1916.* The Battle of the Ancre and Advance of the Tanks *would be released the following year.*

23 December
Film Records from the Ancre

Our London Correspondence: The War Office films of the Battle of Ancre and the tanks in action, shown for the first time at the Scala Theatre to-day, are an improvement even on the famous Somme pictures. The climax – the advance of the Scottish regiments on Martinpuich – comes out far more sharply than anything of the kind seen before. We get at last a true impression of the great masses of men used in the seizure of a village … There are none of the horrors of the Somme record. The operator, Mr. GH Malins, took them faithfully, but the Censor has taken them out. The omission of the more terrible things results in an amazingly sustained cheerfulness throughout the three acts of the drama – the massing and preparations, the assault, and the clearing up the debris, human and other. The packed soldiers in the advance trench, many of whom must die in a few minutes, have the heart to enjoy the joke of being photographed as they clamber up the mud wall over the top into the rain of bullets.

The attack is revealed as groups of soldiers trudging slowly through mud, like ploughmen going to work, nearer and nearer to the line of white puffs that marks our barrage. One grasps the neatness of the artillery work as the men methodically creep close to the barrage, then pause before the final tramp into the ruined German trenches. This attack of the Scots, photographed at the greatest risk – a shell bursts twenty feet or so from the camera – is the best war picture one remembers in its combination of close detail and panoramic effect.

The series include[s] the first films of tanks on the move. The photographer speaks of seeing our men recklessly exposing themselves over the parapet and laughing hysterically as they watched the creatures crawling on. You see a tank thoughtfully flattening barbed wire and shoving itself astride a trench, moving its guns like the eyes on stalks of some monstrous insect. There are always round the tank a following of soldiers, grinning at the wildest joke of the war.

This film throws a better light than the most imaginative correspondence on the awkward efficiency of the tank. There is a glimpse of domestic tank life – the small-sized crew, who wear a special brimless helmet, squirming in at the back door, followed by the officer with his mascot, a frightened black kitten. A tank comes strolling back, its work finished, with sulky pride written all over it.

Repairing Broken Soldiers

Our London Correspondence: An important movement for training partially disabled soldiers is on foot in Wales. The Lord Mayor of Cardiff, who is very active in this matter, has called a conference of the Education Committee there and representatives of the South Wales technical institutes, to devise a scheme, with the co-operation of the War Office, for taking these soldiers from the hospitals and training them in the use of their limbs in institutes while still convalescent, and so avoiding the present waste of time between the hospital and the return to civil life.

30 December
Sir Douglas Haig's Account of the Great Campaign

Sir Douglas Haig's despatch describing the part played by the British armies in the Somme campaign from the preparatory bombardment, which began on 24 June, to the capture of Beaucourt and Beaumont-Hamel in the middle of November was issued last night.

Sir Douglas Haig admits that the extremely bad weather of October and the early part of November disappointed his hopes of securing much greater results than were actually obtained … incessant rain came to the enemy's aid, and it became impossible 'to exploit the situation with the rapidity necessary to enable us to reap the full benefits of the advantages we had gained.'

None the less, the British commander holds that the three main objects of the offensive were achieved – 'Verdun had been relieved; the main German forces had been held on the western front; and the enemy's strength had been very considerably worn down.'

In February the intention had been for the French to play the leading role in the offensive. Verdun put paid to that idea. As for relieving pressure on the French, Brusilov's armies did that. The German commander General Ludendorff observed that the offensive had left his army 'absolutely exhausted'. The British army had learned some lessons during the battle, at great cost. These lessons would be applied in the summer of 1918.

'THE COMMON GERMANIC HORROR'

Partly emboldened by the success of the Brusilov offensive in June, Romania declared war on the central powers on 27 August. This was a catastrophe for the kingdom, which, after initial success, was beaten out of the war by the end of 1917 – at a cost of 220,000 fatalities. It

re-entered the conflict again on 10 November 1918, just one day before
the end of the fighting in western Europe.

29 August
The Tenth Flag

Our London Correspondence, Monday Night: One after another, the Powers of Europe have been compelled to unite against the common Germanic horror which threatens civilisation ... Roumania, who at the beginning seemed for historic and economic reason much more likely to join with the Austrians than the Russians, has added her flag to the march of the Allies. These events must be as disheartening to the Germans as they are inspiring to the Allies. The end of the second rubber is approaching, and the tricks are all falling to the Entente – even though the King in this deal is a Hohenzollern.

The East End Roumanians

Our London Correspondence: There was rejoicing to-day in that little East End Roumanian restaurant whose customers have clung for many months to the belief that Roumania would, in her own good time, join the Allies. The centre for London's 600 Roumanians is a homely little place in Whitechapel, the one window distinguished by its strange fruits, huge chilis and deeply-coloured cheeses. You step from the street into the small front room, where artisans are dining on preserved fish, and pass through the doorway under the tiny flag, like Belgium's, but with dark blue instead of black into a smaller room still, where you may talk with the people in the cottage kitchen as you wait. The proprietor told me this evening that there are 20,000 of his countrymen in England to-day – not nearly as many as there were before the war drew them home. They are nearly all Jews, and one of the chief centres is in Manchester, where they have entered into all branches of the industry. Those in London are mostly tailors, cabinet-makers, bakers or bootmakers, and among them he did not think there were more than twenty or thirty pure Roumanians. He said they had all been hoping that Roumania would come in, and a great many, unwilling to wait for her decision, had enlisted in the English army.

'OUR LONDON CORRESPONDENCE'

29 August
Experiences of the Girl Conductors

The girl conductors on the London 'buses have now nearly completed six months' service. They are looking even jollier than they did the day they started, and they have certainly become very popular with their public, for they are polite, considerate, and without favour or fear. They talk very happily about their work, and say that people as a rule are very nice to them – especially the soldiers – but they all draw a distinction between the ordinary passengers and those they meet 'east of Mansion House,' for in those greyer districts, they say, the passengers sometimes talk to them very roughly. In other districts they have a good time, and while there does not seem yet to have been any really romantic story of their adventures – nor do they look out for persistent admirers to join the 'bus at stated hours, as they say happens on the Manchester trams – they get many little gifts of flowers and confectionary from appreciative friends … One girl from a little country town who had been too timid to ride on top of a 'bus when she first came to London, expecting it to run into everything it met, spoke delightedly of her work, especially when she was on routes that took her from the City far into the country.

In 1916, 46-year-old Marie Lloyd, queen of the music hall, suffered a nervous breakdown. Her great rival, Vesta Tilley, ended her days as Lady De Frece and married to a sometime Tory MP, but Lloyd's fate was rather different. She collapsed on stage at the Edmonton Empire in 1923 and died four days later, aged just 53. Her death was a 'significant moment in English history' wrote TS Eliot.

11 September

Miss Marie Lloyd: Whatever her shortcomings, she was known to be off the stage the ultimate expression of vitality, generosity and good-fellowship, the qualities of which naturally appeal most to the hearts of the struggling, hard-working and moneyless multitude that comprise the main part of our population. 'She has a kind heart and makes three hundred pounds a week,' is the common East End eulogium of this lady – an unconscious criticism implying the rarity of the combination of riches and kind hearts.

When fastidious people began, some ten years ago, to take the music-hall seriously she was discovered to be a great artist … Marie Lloyd can make the meanest London street a ballroom, and the hot-chestnut sellers, the costers, the charwomen and the pub-loafers gay and entertaining partners and sitters-out. She brought the East End streets into carnival – no more innocent than any other carnival. But Jan Steen and Van Ostado have their place in art as well as Watteau and Fragonnard … No one else can be mentioned in the same breath with Marie Lloyd for the spontaneity, raciness, and real inventiveness of her best work … To the older music-hall public she still is the essential genius of the music-hall.

CRW Nevinson, a pre-war Futurist, briefly served as a volunteer ambulance driver (1914–15) and later became an official war artist. His painting La Mitrailleuse *is a renowned depiction of the first world war, and was much praised by critics at the time.*

27 September
Art and the Soldier

Mr. Nevinson gives you the black gloom, the horror, the feeling of despair that make even death and mutilation seem trivial incidents in an epoch of horror ... There is only one really cheerful picture in the exhibition. That is a characteristic 'Camden Town school' version of a factory at night, painted in the pointillist style of Pissaro. The firework diagrams of bursting shells, which echo a futurist formula that has done duty for various emotions in the past, are the least happy of Mr. Nevinson's various styles ... But it is the pictures of the trenches, of wounded lying in rows in patient agony, or exhausted troops lying tired-out, devoid of all life and expression, which are the most characteristic and the most genuine things in the exhibition.

13 November
Evening Dress at the Theatre

In the first year of the war evening dresses became scarce even in the stalls, but recently there have been signs of the partial reassertion of an old habit. No other manager has followed Mr. Gerald Du Maurier's lead at Wyndham's in printing on the programmes, 'Evening dress is optional, but not fashionable.' Custom varies greatly according to the theatre; in one or two theatres few people have even been so bold as to sit in the stalls in ordinary clothes.

Still, it is now fairly well established that you need not dress for the theatre, and tweeds have been seen without a sensation in the stalls of some extremely well-attired theatres. The breakdown of the convention has been generally welcomed. Most people work longer at their offices in wartime, and have less time to go home to dress, and nowadays by no means all buyers of expensive seats dress for dinner at home and go straight to the theatre – the custom, supposed or real, on which the dress convention was based ... It cannot be said that women dress more plainly for theatre-going than before the war. Of course most of the men who would be in evening dress in normal times now wear khaki, which is full dress anywhere.

14 November
The Lady Chauffeur

The arrival of the private lady chauffeur is creating domestic problems that will not be easily solved, for her position is even more undefined that that of a governess, and it is prejudiced by the fact that the man who preceded her was always treated as one of the servants. He might take rank even above the butler, he probably had his own rooms, but there was no difficulty about arranging where he should have his meals. He was not infrequently handy man, and ladies applying for his vacant post have been startled by being asked whether they were willing to clean the boots. The servants in certain households, rendered more exacting than ever, have refused to wait on the chauffeur if she were to have her own room, and for various reasons employers prefer to have a woman chauffeur acting as chauffeur-companion, chauffeur-secretary, or else to employ one of the still newer class, the superior servant who has taken her certificate. The girls themselves prefer to live out. Many London girls continue to live at home. Others have rooms assigned to them near the car. There are instances where several bachelor girls engaged in similar work have clubbed together and established themselves very comfortable in a mews or garage in the rooms above the car.

'A GOVERNMENT OF
NATIONAL DEFENCE'

By November 1916 there was major disaffection towards the coalition among Conservative backbench MPs. The collapse of Romania and the uncertain results of the battle of the Somme further depressed morale. 'The crass stupidity of the military chiefs', wrote CP Scott to a fellow Manchester Guardian *journalist on 25 November, 'and the incompetence of the Government are enough to make one despair.' The Liberal secretary of state for war, David Lloyd George, precipitated a challenge to Herbert Asquith's conduct of the conflict and in early December, Asquith, having lost the support of Lloyd George and the Conservative leader Bonar Law, stepped down as prime minister.*

7 December
Paris and the Crisis

Our London Correspondence, Wednesday Night: The crisis in Downing Street is being anxiously watched by Frenchmen. The general French opinion is on the side of Mr. Lloyd George ... His visit to Verdun produced many stories that were relished by the French, and his eloquent speeches made a great impression, more particularly as English generals had created a belief that Englishmen have no words to spare for the dramatic appreciation of military events and great moments ... His forceful personality has become more and more appreciated as one of the great assets of the Entente ... It must also be said that there is a very large section, especially among officials, which sees Mr. Asquith as the typical Englishman, with all the traditional qualities of steadiness, four-squareness and tenacity that they associated with all England's victories in the past.

Outside the Palace

The passer-by this afternoon could not realise anything of the importance of the conference which was taking place at Buckingham Palace at the King's invitation ... The Ministers who attended ... passed into the courtyard of the Palace almost unnoticed, and remained for about an hour and a half ... a little group of pressmen kept the company of the sentries outside the Palace, and competed with them in marching up and down to keep warm. ... A grey mist hung around the Palace as the afternoon wore on, and it was hardly possible to see anything of the Ministers ... The Queen, accompanied by several ladies, drove into the courtyard of the Palace in a motor-car at a quarter past four, and was not even noticed by all of the waiting scribes.

On 7 December, the day David Lloyd George became prime minister, the Manchester Guardian *published an editorial on the political crisis.*

7 December
A New Ministry

As we write, the arrangements are going forward for the formation of a new Ministry. It will be a Lloyd George Ministry, of which Mr. Bonar Law will be a leading member and in which Mr. Asquith will not take a place ... Whether any other of the Liberal members of the late Cabinet will be included in it is as yet undetermined. Unquestionably they will be asked, but it is not known what will be their decision, though the expectation is that they, like their chief, will decline ... The Labour party adjourned its meeting yesterday and has not yet decided what position it will, as a body, take up, and whether it will permit or will not permit any of its members to take office in the new Government. It is impossible at present to say how much support Mr. George may be able to obtain for his Ministry from either of these sources, but whether it be much or little there can be no doubt that he will persevere with his task, and we see no reason to suppose he will fail … It will be a Government of National Defence, eschewing, like its predecessor, all merely party issues and claiming the support of all patriotic men in carrying on its supreme task of efficiently prosecuting the war. By the test of its success in that vital undertaking also, like its predecessor, it must stand or fall.

It is impossible to watch the formation of a new Ministry from which nearly all its Liberal members will have been eliminated without a heartfelt acknowledgment of the devoted service which each and all of them have rendered, and, above all, an expression of deep respect and esteem – there are many who will add the word affection – for the brilliant chief who for so many years has piloted the fortunes of the Liberal party, and for more than two years has led the nation in the greatest of its wars. We have often dissented from the political action or inaction of Mr. Asquith as Prime Minister, but no one could have obtained the extraordinary hold which he possesses on the House of Commons, or could have won the personal allegiance not only of his political friends but in almost if not quite an equal degree that of his political opponents in the composite Government which has now come to an end, without very remarkable qualities not only of intellect but also of temper and of character which have endeared him to his associates. It is something of a tragedy that so great a career should have met with so sudden a check, and that qualities in many ways so remarkable should have failed to enable him to rise to the special and supremely taxing demands of the conduct of war. It is this relative failure, and this only, which has led to the fall of his Government. For the war is to us at present everything, and by its side neither persons nor parties count. For this reason we are convinced that should Mr. Lloyd George form an Administration, as there is no reason to doubt that he will, it will receive a fair trial at the hands alike of the House of Commons and of the nation ... The desire of the House, as of the people, will be not to embarrass but in every way to assist the new Government to perform its task efficiently and to redeem the fortunes of the war. [...]

Of course the change of persons, even though it be not accompanied by a change in party colour, cannot be made without exciting much feeling and even hostility. It has not been due to any initiative in the House of Commons itself, but to divisions within the Government. For his share in these and for the change of Ministry which they have brought about, Mr. George will have to bear the blame of many of his old friends and colleagues, and if, as seems almost inevitable, he should appear to profit by the crisis which he chiefly has provoked, there will be found plenty of people to allege that a desire for this result and not any more disinterested and patriotic motive has guided his action. Such imputations are, we believe, as unfounded as they are uncharitable. Yet none the less it is not without a certain emotion that we shall see Mr. George become the head of a predominantly Unionist Administration, and we shall join all who wish him well in the hope and the exhortation to him to walk warily and to permit no sort of provocation, should provocation come, to goad him into antagonism to the party to which he still owes allegiance, and to preserve for the future of Liberalism all the treasure of his soul.

CHAPTER 5

1917

The year 1917 was the pivot on which the 20th century turned. The United States declared war, and began its progress to global pre-eminence. Halfway across the world the Russian empire imploded, underwent two upheavals and attempted to declare peace. As the exhausted French army recuperated from a wave of mutinies, the responsibilities of the armies of the British empire expanded, and at Passchendaele that autumn and winter endured a hell of mud. In the Middle East the British conquered more and more of the Ottoman empire's Arab territories – and in London, Foreign Secretary Arthur Balfour backed a 'national home for the Jewish people' in Palestine.

'THE BANQUET GIVEN TO RASPUTIN'

In Russia, the 'monk' Grigori Rasputin symbolised the medievalism at the core of the tsar's rule. Rasputin's murder on the night of 29 December 1916 anticipated the collapse, for a time, of tsarist despotism.

25 January
Rasputin's Death: Last Dinner Described by an Eyewitness

Apparently the Petrograd newspapers are now permitted to talk about Rasputin, and to give fairly freely some details of his death, without even concealing the quality of the people chiefly concerned in the affair. One of these stories appears in the *Outro Rossii* ... and it is written by one of the guests at the banquet given to Rasputin just before he was murdered.

Rasputin had been invited to meet Purishkievitch, the deputy of the Right, who hoped to convince him that his political influence was a danger to Russia, and to persuade him to turn his energies to producing better results. To this end, then, this dinner was arranged. From the beginning, however, several members of the nobility, including Purishkievitch, had resolved to put Rasputin out of harm's way more effectually than that. Then Prince Yussupoff went to fetch Rasputin. In the meantime M. Balk, the chief of police in Petrograd, received a telephone message from M. Protopopoff ordering him to go immediately to Prince Yussupoff's house, to ensure Rasputin's safety. He told the Prince of his mission, but he was assured that Rasputin need have no qualms at all, and asked to leave the house, which he did. The dinner was in full swing when a violent dispute arose. Prince Yussupoff declared that his rights as host had been wounded by certain remarks made by Rasputin, and demanded explanations. Rasputin refused. The quarrel became extreme, and one of the guests held out a pistol to Rasputin, telling him to shoot himself. Others, threatening him with death, ordered him to swear on the spot that he would henceforth renounce all political action, and would leave Petrograd without delay.

At this juncture Rasputin, who had taken the pistol, suddenly pointed it at one of the guests. Yussupoff and – it is claimed – Purishkievitch, considering that they were legitimately defending themselves, fired at Rasputin, wounding him mortally.

Accounts of the murder differ. Repeated attempts were made both to shoot and to club Rasputin to death. That night his body was dumped in the Neva. Yusopov died, in Paris, half a century later.

'ENGLAND HAILS THE NEW RUSSIA'

In the winter of 1916–17 food shortages in the cities of Russia grew worse. In March troops refused to suppress disturbances – instigated by women in bread queues – in Petrograd (St Petersburg). The tsar was prevented from returning to the capital.

16 March
Tsar Abdicates: Troops Side with People

News comes through Copenhagen that the Duma has placed itself at the head of a revolutionary movement and that, supported by the troops in Petrograd, it has declared a Provisional Government. The Tsar has abdicated, and his brother, the Grand Duke Michael Alexandrovitch, has been appointed Regent ... Petrograd was yesterday stated to be calm and orderly. In the early days of the week there had been firing in the streets, but no very serious loss of life. The bloodshed was chiefly caused by the police, not the soldiers, and the soldiers and the people have freed political prisoners and burned police stations and police papers. Reactionary leaders, including members of the Cabinet, have been arrested.

The Revolution in Russia

The sympathy of every man in this country will go out to the Russian people in this supreme hour. If they win and establish their liberty upon an impregnable basis, then they will have given a new aspect to civilisation. Already the first workings are visible in the speech of the German Chancellor to the Reichstag, in which he promises internal political reorganisation to Germany and a less illiberal franchise to Prussia. The revolution in Russia promises to isolate Germany, bureaucratic, despotic and militarist, in the European world, not only during the war but after it, unless Germany follows a similar course. Already the anxious question faces Germany, the Germany of the Junkers, how they can hope to stand, and faces the German people, why they should be shedding their blood and their treasure for reaction against liberty. The revolution in Russia is the deadliest blow to the war *moral* of Germany that has been struck. That it will strengthen Russia in the further conduct of the war as well as liberalise the spirit and purpose for which she wages war – these are certainties. It is the reactionaries who have now been struck down, who worked for a separate peace and an alliance with Germany. They were kindred souls with the Junkers. They feared liberty in Russia much more than the German enemy, and to stave off free institutions they were prepared to lop off provinces. It is the Liberals of Russia who have resisted these unholy temptations, and now that they have taken over the control we have hope that a new vigour will energise the war, springing from a sincere idealism. Revolution has before now proved a great mother of efficiency, and there is no finer dynamic force than a passion for freedom. England hails the new Russia with a higher hope and a surer confidence in the future not only of this war but of the world.

Our London Correspondence, Thursday Night: The expected news has come, and the world now hears of the Russian revolution, for the whisper of which all ears have been strained for so long. It is not the revolution that so many Russian exiles here have dreamt of, but a revolution from the centre – of all parties from the Grand Duke Cyril and the Octobrist leaders of the Duma, including the aristocratic Colonel Engelhardt, to the revolutionary workers' societies. Russians here who have received the news with great emotion are astonished at the suddenness and scale of the movement, which has surpassed their wildest hopes. They were prepared for something rather different. The social effect of the change cannot be estimated. It may be more and it may be less than what was expected, but one thing, anyway, is certain. It means that Russia now is whole-souled with the Allies in the war.

'Inevitable'

The astounding news from Russia was known to a limited number of persons early this afternoon, and rumours began to percolate in Fleet Street towards evening. Though startling, it was not unexpected by the student of Russian affairs ... it was well-nigh the conviction of everyone who knew anything about Russia for months and months past that a revolution was inevitable if Russia was not to perish ignominiously from internal chaos and external misfortunes.

The view was taken at the same time that to be entirely successful – 'national' in the true sense of the word, and free as much as possible from bloodshed and internal friction – the revolution must be led by the Duma itself, which had the sympathies of all the sections of the population as well as of the majority of the army leaders. This, it seems, has been the case and in this, one may safely say, lies the pledge of the final and complete success of the colossal transformation which has now taken place.

In Petrograd, alongside a national provisional government made up of liberal politicians, a council of workers and soldiers was set up called the Petrograd Soviet. The war against Germany continued, albeit with dissension. Following the agreement of General Ludendorff and the German general staff, the Russian communist revolutionary Vladimir Lenin was transported to Petrograd from Zürich, where he had been living in exile. He arrived on 16 April 1917.

30 April
South Russian Armies for Victory: German Agents in the Capital

Petrograd, Saturday: I have just returned from the south, where I obtained the impression that conditions there are different from

Petrograd. I talked to numerous soldiers from the Roumanian and south-western fronts. All underline that the revolution was made by the army. Most desire complete victory ... The soldiers in the south are evidently unaware of the tendencies of the Petrograd Social Democrats; but in Petrograd the soldiers are growling against Lenin, the refugee whose return was facilitated by the German Government. A disciple of his, while attempting to dissuade the Lynsky Reserve Battalion yesterday from going to the front, was arrested.

Michael Farbman was one of several distinguished journalists who reported on revolutionary Russia for the Manchester Guardian. *Yet, as the following extract indicates, his assessment of Lenin's role would not be borne out by events.*

1 May

Revolutionary Russia: The Truth about Some Illusory Dangers
Petrograd, Saturday: My first impressions of the new Russia surpass my most sanguine expectations. The revolution has by no means reached its end, but its victory is accepted on all hands, and the new regime must be regarded as definitely established. Russia's public life still contains many potential disturbing elements. There are demagogues on both the Right and the Left who try to stir up panic by suggesting that the danger still looms of a counter-revolution. But the whole life of Russia is pervaded by an enthusiasm for the revolution which is almost religious. Russia's public life is full of exaltations, and there is the greatest confidence that the victory which has been won has been won forever.

The political maturity and soundness of judgment which are being displayed exceed what was anticipated even by those who know the Russian masses well. It gives the assurance that the nation is organising on the solidest basis the freedom it has conquered, and it justifies the widest hopes for the future. In the revolution of 1905 the leaders of the various parties were for the most part demagogues and their following among the masses equally irresponsible. To-day the power of the demagogues is largely held in check by the sound judgment and the ripe political sense of the masses.

Liberal newspapers and the survivors of the reactionary press, as well as the correspondents of some foreign papers, attribute more significance and importance to the agitation of the demagogues than to the whole weight of the revolutionary democracy. The truth is, however, that the revolutionary extremists are controlled by the astonishing critical capacity of the great democratic masses.

My arrival coincided with the sensational reappearance in Petrograd of Lenin, the famous Socialist leader, who has been in exile for many years. Lenin's return was looked for with interest by all parties and with anxiety by not a few. He is not only the most eminent among the revolutionary philosophers and agitators but is the greatest of all Russian demagogues. People had not forgotten his activities during the revolution of 1905, and these afforded good reasons for expecting and for fearing what they might be now. His programme, as he has now announced it, is to overthrow the Provisional Government, to proclaim the dictatorship of the proletariat, to establish it by force if necessary, and to continue the present war with the purpose of extending the social revolution throughout the whole of Europe. Such a programme constitutes the greatest possible danger in the revolutionary days.

As a matter of fact, Lenin lost ground the moment he arrived. The twelve years since 1905 have left Lenin entirely unchanged, but Russia had changed immensely. I cannot say that all danger from Lenin's anarchic propaganda has disappeared, but it has lessened considerably. In the disturbances at Cronstadt some regiments were guilty of excesses, and there have been isolated cases of agrarian troubles. These episodes have been fostered by his party and by his irresponsible and violent organ, the Pravda. Other disturbances of the kind are pretty sure to follow, but they should not be exaggerated. The great driving force of the revolution is beyond the influence of Lenin or any other attempt at a counter-revolution from the Left.

2 May
The Russian Socialists and Their Leaders

The Social Democratic Labour party has for its principal leader M. Lenin, a man of fanatical devotion to his ideals, of considerable talent for organisation and agitation, with an iron and ruthless will ... His knowledge of and influence over the proletarian masses is very great, and just as he agitated before the war in favour of revolutionary political strikes (with considerable success) and preached during the war the gospel of defeat and revolution, so he is now advocating 'dictatorship' of the proletariat, a wholesale expropriation of all lands, and the immediate cessation of the war by means of an international revolution, including fraternisation in the trenches ... M. Lenin and his followers are not be despised, but must be regarded as the Jacobins of the Russian revolution, at present not very numerous, but exceedingly powerful and likely to grow.

2 July
Lenin and Zinovief: The Russian Extremists on the Platform

M. Ludovic Nandeau, the special representative of the Paris *Temps* in Petrograd, sends his paper an interesting and descriptive account of a meeting of Russian extremists, which seems to have caught very clearly the peculiar atmosphere of one side of Russian Socialism. We translate the following from it:

At last the famous Lenin was seen moving towards the dais, and a number of voices called out, 'Lenin! Lenin! Lenin!' He is a little man with a huge skull. He has a striking, clear-cut diction, and one feels that he does not doubt for an instant that he is the advocate of a higher truth, and that he had nothing but disdain for the retarding elements of humanity who are stopping at national conceptions.

He recited us his articles in the *Pravda*, and repeated in a different tone what Zinovief had told us. He quoted Jaurès, Liebknecht, and declared that Tseretelli, Kerensky, Skobelef, though quite good fellows, had committed a fatal error in agreeing to collaborate with the bourgeois in the Coalition Ministry. He wanted to sweep all the bourgeois out of the Ministry. The Workmen's and Soldiers' Council was to have all the power, a council composed of true revolutionaries … Lenin continued his argument. He became animated. Suddenly his eyes blazed, and took on a wild and sinister expression; his mouth contracted and became cruel. Then we had before us the type of monomaniac, the fanatic, the type of visionary, argumentative maniac.

Yet this man, whose words are so useful to the Germans, is not so ingenious as to ignore the tricks of public oratory. When the audience applauded the end of his speech a sailor raised his arm and asked to put a precise question to Tovarish Lenin. The latter frowned. In the same moment one of his acolytes, with a head like a spaniel, rushed on to the stage and barked: 'Tovarishchi, remember that Lenin is tired. He has spoken in three meetings to-day already!' Murmurs of approbation; the sailor is rebuked. But Lenin does not retire. Another acolyte puts little bits of paper into his hand, upon which 'honest citizens' had scrawled some questions. Lenin accepts these. He looks confidently at the scraps of paper, and begins again his insinuations against the Allies and his poisonous phrases. He ends by passing a unanimous vote by lifted hands declaring that: 'All the German workmen are brothers, and all the English and French *bourjouis* are enemies.' Then this enemy of the *bourjouis* departed with his satellites in a superb motor car. [...]

Can one deny the influence of Lenin, Zinovief, and Kamenef? Within a few weeks they obtained by subscription from their readers 250,000 roubles, with which to buy a printing press for Finland. Crews of cruisers, regiments, and thousands of factories sent along their obol. The garrison of Kronstadt, capital of the 'independent' island of Kotlin, recognises Lenin only as its prophet.

By summer 1917, Alexander Kerensky had emerged as leader of the provisional government and the Kornilov right-wing coup was thwarted, but swathes of the Russian army were deserting.

'TOWARDS ULTIMATE HARMONY'

Back in Britain, opposition to the war invited local hostility and national surveillance. Peace campaigners were denied permission to travel abroad, while conscientious objectors died in prison. Among the most notorious of wartime prosecutions were those brought against the Derbyshire socialist suffragette Alice Wheeldon, her daughters Hettie and Winnie, and Winnie's husband Alfred Mason, who were accused of attempting to poison Lloyd George. In 1916 the Wheeldons had been visited by one 'Alex Gordon', a supposed conscientious objector, who embroiled the family in a plot to liberate a Home Office work camp and planted evidence on them. It was finally confirmed 80 years later that the man was an MI5 agent named William Rickard. Hettie was acquitted; Alice, sentenced to 10 years' penal servitude and amnestied 18 months later, died in the 1919 flu epidemic.

12 March
The Wheeldon Poison Trial

Our London Correspondence: A friend who attended the poison plot trial at the Old Bailey writes: ... Politically its chief interest was that it has exposed and broken up a daring underground intrigue for helping fugitives from the army to evade the law. Apart from any question of a plot to poison the Ministers, what was discovered would have certainly landed the Wheeldon family in prison if the Crown had chosen to prosecute them on this charge. On the human side we had the experience of hearing able and well-educated women calmly expounding to a hostile court an amazing series of revolutionary opinions (in the case of the mother, criminal opinions.) For defiant courage there has been nothing like the evidence of the Wheeldon women since the old militant suffrage days.

Restrictions on peace campaigners extended to the deliberations of the Nobel Committee.

24 April
What the Nobel Committee May Not See

The National Peace Council were asked by the Secretary of the Nobel Committee of the Norwegian Parliament to make for the Committee a general collection of recent publications bearing on peace and representative of all opinion. The collection was made and a permit applied for to send it to Christiania. The Chief Postal Censor at the War Office replied as follows: 'I am directed to inform you that it is considered undesirable, that any of the following should be included in the consignment: (1) Any publications of the National Labour Press. (2) Any publications of the Union of Democratic Control. (3) Any publications containing the writings of any of the following authors: Messrs. Bertrand Russell, Arthur

Ponsonby, ED Morel, GM Trevelyan, Norman Angell, Philip Snowden, CR Buxton, and A Lowes Dickinson. (4) The following publications specified in the list which you have forwarded: *Common Sense, The Herald, The Tribunal, War and Peace, What are we fighting for?, Peace this Winter,* the *Socialist Review, Towards Ultimate Harmony.* I am accordingly to request that you will forward to this department a written guarantee that none of the foregoing will be exported.'

'WOMEN'S COMPETITION'

Meanwhile, women continued to exert a greater influence on British society as the war carried on.

16 March
'Down Cabs' Again

Our London Correspondence, Thursday Night: The London taxi-drivers are again threatening trouble – this time because the Home Office refuses to give way on the question of licensing women drivers. Sir George Cave told a deputation of the Licensed Vehicle Workers the other day that there is no intention at present of licensing women as tram and 'bus drivers, but that competent women will certainly be licensed for taxi-driving. The men are holding indignation meetings on Sunday, and threaten to bring all the cab, 'bus and tram drivers of London out on strike – about 20,000 workers, inclusive of garage men.

In this matter the men appear to have a thoroughly bad case. It is based frankly on the fear of women's competition. They say that the men drivers are not fully employed, and that there is no need to bring in women. They will have no public sympathy. Women drivers have proved themselves thoroughly efficient for army work

BATEMANS' SPECIAL FEBRUARY OFFER

In order to keep our staff fully employed during the quiet season, we are again making our Special February Offer of COSTUMES and GOWNS at REDUCED PRICES. All orders placed during February will be executed at prices as below, which represent a very considerable saving. The styles are of the new spring modes, and the cut and fit of the usual high "Bateman" standard.

You save nearly 20 per cent by placing your orders in February.

Orders received March 1st can only be executed at usual prices.

The MALVERN.—Tailor-made Costume in fine cloth. The skirt is full, and finished with rows of the new pearl stitchings. Effective Coat, with long roll Collar, finished at the waist with gilt clasp. In Navy, Bottle Green, Nigger, &c.
February Price . . 3½ Gns.
Usual Price . . 4 Gns.
The Hat.—Becoming Hat for Young Lady, in Silk and Velvet, trimmed feather mount.
Price 17/9.

The BRISTOL.—Dress in New Spring Materials. Bodice trimmed Silk, Vest of Ninon and Embroidery on Belt. Skirt with pleats sides and back.
February Price £3 19 9
Usual Price . . 4½ Gns.

BATEMANS LTD.
Oldham Street,
MANCHESTER.

The CH STEP.—Tailor-made Costume in fine quality Gab. Cloth, with full skirt. Smart Coat finished with collar to stand up or turn down, hand embroidered. In Navy, Bottle Green, Nigger, &c.
February Price . . 4 Gns.
Usual Price . . £4 19 9.
The Hat.—Smart Hat in Black Panne Velvet with rich embroidered crown. **Price 19/9.**

and in scores of other kinds of motor work, and there is no reason why they should not have their opportunity at taxi-driving. The taxi-drivers have always shown themselves a somewhat aggressive class, and they do not stand much chance of closing another avenue of employment to women at this time of day.

10 April
Variety Theatres

The New Palace: This music-hall makes no demands upon Miss Vesta Tilley for new songs. It never tires of the old ones. But Miss Tilley sings a song this week which is not only new in form but departs a little from the singer's convention. It drops the happy frivolity and the light-headed 'swank' which by a subtle and entirely feminine art have been endowed with charms not always associated with them in real life, and it adopts a humour which is ironical but not heavy. In this song Miss Tilley is a soldier straight from the trenches, equipped with a woolly coat, full kit and rifle, and the inevitable German helmet which dangles inconveniently about his knees. He had discovered that the joyfully anticipated 'six days leave' is a snare and a bitter delusion, and he tells us about his troubles in a song. Most of us have heard soldiers talking like it, and Miss Tilley, who always seems to be guided more by intuition than by observation, has got the manner of the 'grousing' Tommy perfectly and his relish for jokes upon his own misfortunes. And under his cloud of troubles one sees familiar flashes of spirit which will make him strut and tell a bold tale in serener times.

8 May
The Bazaar for the Blinded Soldiers

Our London Correspondence: Queen Alexandra, who opened the Albert Hall bazaar in aid of St. Dunstan's Hostel for blinded soldiers this afternoon, made a young artilleryman who was blinded at Suvla very happy. The ladies at the Duchess of Sutherland's stall learned he was very anxious to present the Queen with a purple bag he had netted especially for her, but could not approach her. They arranged the matter, and when the Queen visited the stall the soldier had his chance. As he stooped to pick up the bag Queen Alexandra patted his shoulder, and assured him earnestly that she would treasure his gift all her life. It was a remarkable bazaar. Royal Princesses, duchesses, and famous beauties, all of whom are taking ten hours of daily duty, presided over stalls loaded with beautiful or very useful gifts. Princess Louise displayed on her stall a miniature *escritoire* she had used when a child. Lady Robertson sold soldiers' comforts. Lady Alexander, wonderfully dressed, made a speciality of flowery hats and smocks for women land-workers. Lady Rothes offered an original copy of the Scottish Covenant of 1620, bearing as first signature that of the Earl of Rothes. The pride of one duchess was a Stradivarius, but it did not compare with the potatoes just arrived from the Transvaal, sold at the Duchess of Somerset's stall for sixpence apiece.

30 May

Deansgate Picture House: To obtain the atmosphere essential to [the French propaganda film] *Mothers of France,* Mme. Sarah Bernhardt 'ventured into the trenches and exposed herself to the perils only hardened soldiers are called upon to face.' The result is certainly as convincing a piece of realism as it is possibly to convey by the means of film. There is much in the play that is familiar now – the village farewells, the glimpses of fighting in the trenches and No Man's Land, the pathos of the hospital, and the work of women in the harvest field; but these are mere incidents in a moving story of self-sacrifice from which not a little of the power of Mme. Bernhardt and of her fellow artists shines out.

'SELFISH AUTOCRATIC POWER'

In early 1917 a political crisis developed with America on one side and Mexico and Germany on the other. The previous year the Mexican revolutionary Francisco 'Pancho' Villa had led a raid on Columbus, New Mexico. The United States responded by sending a force, commanded by General John J Pershing, into Mexico to capture Villa. It failed. The German Foreign Minister Arthur Zimmermann concluded that Mexico might warm to the idea of a German-backed invasion of the US, in the event of US–German hostilities. Telegrams to this effect were sent to the German ambassador in Washington, DC. The British intercepted them, and leaked the contents to the US ambassador to London on 19 February 1917.

2 March
German Government Shown Up – Proposal to Mexico

New York, Thursday: The Washington correspondent of the *Associated Press* is enabled to reveal that Germany, in planning her unrestricted submarine warfare and counting on its consequences, proposed an alliance with Mexico and Japan in order to make war on the United States. If that country had not remained neutral, Japan, through Mexican mediation, was to be urged to abandon her allies and join in an attack on the United States. Mexico for her reward was to reconquer Texas, New Mexico and Arizona, and to share in the victorious peace terms which Germany contemplated … These instructions were as follows:

Berlin, 19 January 1917: On 1 February we intend to begin submarine warfare without restriction. In spite of this it is our intention to endeavour to keep the United States neutral. If this attempt is not successful, we propose an alliance on the following basis with Mexico. That we shall make war together and together make peace. We shall give general financial support and it is understood Mexico is to conquer her lost territory of New Mexico, Texas and Arizona. Details are left to you for settlement. You are instructed to inform the President of Mexico of the above in the greatest confidence as soon as it is certain there will be an outbreak of war with the United States, and suggest that the President of Mexico shall on his own initiative communicate with Japan, suggesting the latter's adherence at once to this plan, and at the same time offer to mediate between Germany and Japan. Please call to the attention of the President of Mexico that the employment of ruthless submarine warfare now promises to compel England to make peace in a few months.

(Signed.) Zimmermann.

The Zimmermann telegram has gone down in history as a significant reason why the United States entered the war on the allied side.

In December 1916, a month after his re-election to the presidency, Woodrow Wilson contacted Germany, Britain, France, Austria-Hungary, Russia and the other belligerents to state their terms for bringing the war to an end. While the allies had offered a relatively liberal settlement deal, Germany's plans involved holding on to much of the territory they had seized since 1914.

On 1 February 1917, Germany gave the US less than 24 hours' notice of its intention to resume unrestricted submarine warfare, meaning German submarines could attack neutral American passenger ships without warning. The German gamble was that, even if the US entered the war, Britain could be brought to its knees before the Americans could play a decisive role. On 3 February the US broke off diplomatic relations with Germany. The leaked Zimmermann telegram – which followed on 19 February, thanks to British intelligence – was the final straw.

On 2 March the tsar abdicated, and in the first Russian revolution in 1917 democracy appeared to be on the march. On 6 April the US declared war on Germany, its decision bolstered by the sinking of the

Lusitania, *the revelations contained in the Zimmermann telegram and Germany's submarine warfare policy. On 4 April the* Manchester Guardian *editorialised on the impending US decision.*

4 April
The Entry of the United States

'Our object,' says President Wilson, 'is to vindicate the principles of peace and justice in the life of the world against selfish autocratic power, and to set up amongst the really free and self-governed peoples of the world such a concert of purpose and action as will henceforth ensure the observance of these principles.' Language could not be clearer. The German people, with whom Mr. Wilson is careful to say America has no other quarrel, are here branded with the stigma of being unfree and politically backward. They think they are fighting for their liberties; they are, in fact, fighting for their chains. And so badly has their Government mismanaged their affairs that it produced a kind of Holy Alliance of free peoples against them. 'A steadfast concert for peace can never be maintained except by the partnership of democratic nations.' Hug your chains, Mr. Wilson says in effect to the German people, and you will always be political outcasts, unfit for the fellowship of free men; break them, and you may have both peace and freedom. What incompetence on the part of their rulers it is that has brought the most conceited people on earth to a pass when even Russia, so long despised by them, can pity them as slaves. It will not be for their moral vices that the future historian will castigate Germany, but for their intellectual forcible-feebleness. Think of it. Here is a nation which wants some sort of an empire in the East, and the way she sets about it is to invade Belgium, to unite Englishmen of all shades of opinion against her, and finally to bring in the United States against her ...

It would be unfair not to acknowledge the great contribution which the Russian revolution has made to the great moral victory for the Allies which Mr. Wilson's speech is. Before the revolution a great part of Mr. Wilson's speech could not have been delivered, or if it had could only have been read as an attack on our eastern ally. It is impossible to exaggerate the difference that has been made by the establishment of a free Russia. It has made this war quite unequivocally one between those who love freedom and those who do not. It has made Germany what Mr. Wilson calls her, 'the natural foe to liberty.' At the same time it has opened up for the German people a war of escape from their present troubles. If they stand by the masters whose gross incompetence is now revealed, they will suffer the penalties of slavery; if they achieve their own freedom, they will also win a place for their country amongst the great nations of the world. The arch-enemies of Germany are not the Allies but her own rulers; it is they, not we, who are dragging her down and ruining her body and soul. Mr. Wilson goes even farther. This war, to his mind, is one for the liberation of all the peoples of the world, including the German people, for the privilege of everyone everywhere to choose their way of life and obedience. 'The world must be safe for democracy,' says Mr. Wilson; 'its peace must be planted upon the trusted foundations of political liberty.' There are thus two ways in which the German people can work for peace. One is by offering themselves up as sacrifices to stupid and incompetent rulers. That way is the peace of bondage, the dull, heavy sleep of slaves. The other way is achieving their own liberty.

'SICK AND HUNTED ANIMALS'

In 1916–17 the 'Siegfriedstellung' (the British called it the Hindenburg Line) was constructed on the western front, shortening the German line by 25 miles and providing more defensible positions for an army devastated by casualties and facing severe manpower problems. Imposing a savage scorched-earth policy, the Germans began a withdrawal to their new fortifications.

On Monday 9 April British Commonwealth troops launched an offensive at Arras, supporting the imminent French attack on the Aisne. While the massive 'Nivelle Offensive' was a disaster – triggering mutinies in the French army – the preceding Canadian triumph at Vimy Ridge became emblematic of the country's nationhood. The initial modest and well-organised attack at Arras anticipated victories in 1918.

13 April
In the Caves of Arras

War Correspondents' Headquarters, Wednesday: 'This is King Street,' said a voice in the darkness to-day, 'the third to the left is India Lane.' A moment later I collided violently with a dark figure, moist with mud, and our steel helmets rang sharply. We were in the caves of Arras, tunnelled out centuries ago, when rich merchants built the houses in the Grande Place and mansions guarded within grand walls, all pierced now or quite destroyed by two years of German shell-fire. But the caves and the tunnels have not been touched by any shell. They are very deep and wander in a maze far below the ruins of the cathedral city and out in the open country.

On Sunday night last, before our advance across the German lines, thousands of our soldiers waited in these caves for dawn, and before the dawn, marched down the tunnels, pressed close in a long tide of life, streaming forward for an affair of death. Hour after hour the supporting troops followed the first waves of assault, and from the world above came down the first of the wounded. They passed their comrades closely, touched them with the blood of their wounds, and steel helmets clanked together. There was not much talking. The men going up asked a question or two. 'How's it going, mate?' 'Fine; we're through the second line.' 'Badly hit?' 'It hurts, but it ain't much, old lad.'

The long tunnel was only dark at its entrance. Further along was the glimmer of electric bulbs, set along the walls at even distances. I passed on a long way and heard a throbbing down in a deep pit and felt a sudden warmth come up to me. Here was the power-house for the electric plant. Further still I looked down other tunnels leading away to unknown places. Men slouched down them and talked in low voices. Cigarette-ends glimmered, a rifle fell with a clatter. I had a sense of bring in a subterranean world inhabited by men doing uncanny work. [...]

I turned down India Lane, climbed a long flight of chalk stairs, felt the wind blow on my face, and heard the infernal clangour of great guns. My steel helmet caught in a strand of barbed wire. Before one stretched the battlefields of Arras. Down across the battlefields came the walking wounded. They were not in a company, which makes suffering more tolerable ... but in single figures, lonely, after being hit by chance shells up by a village where fighting was then in progress.

I hated to pass these men without an offer of help, but I could do nothing for them. They walked very slowly, avoiding the litter of brickwork flung up by shell-fire, drawing breath sharply when their tired feet stumbled against a stone, hesitating with a look of despair when they came to the edge of broken trenches. They were 'light cases' – the lucky ones – but their way was a Via Dolorosa. An officer came along in a private's tunic. He was wounded in the arm and very white and weak looking. 'Feel bad?' I asked. He smiled. 'I'm all right ... but it's slow going.'

A comrade with me pulled out a flask and said, 'This will do you good.' The officer lifted it to his lips, and the colour came back into his face a moment. 'Thanks very much,' he said, '*elixir vitae* at a time like this.' A German crump cracked a score of yards away from us with a howl and a roar. The wounded officer struck half right. 'Not out of it yet,' he said. I watched him stagger a little and then straighten himself and trudge on – a gallant man, needing all his courage for that walk.

The German prisoners huddled together for warmth until they were given shelter. The officers were … grateful for their treatment and were polite to their captors, saluting punctiliously with a click of heels. They were mostly young men and not professional soldiers before the war, and nearly all of them Bavarians and Hamburgers. Some of them excused themselves for being unshaven and dirty. 'We had to keep close to the dug-outs,' they explained. 'Your drum fire was frightful. Up above it was certain death.' 'The waiting was worse than death,' said one young officer whose hand trembles as he lit a cigarette. […]

'We could do nothing. We were trapped,' said the Brigadier, who was taken with his whole staff. The Brigadier wept a little. He confessed to the humiliation of being captured with such little loss among his men. 'We thought the Vimy Ridge impregnable,' he said.

But his greatest grief was not for the defeat or for the capture or sufferings of his men. 'My little dog,' he said again and again. 'Has anyone seen my little dog? It has been with me ever since the beginning of the war.' He had lost his little dog when he had come out of his dug-out and held up his hands and then come down with his mob of men.

'THE BIGGEST THING EVER'

In 1915 British sappers began digging 19 mines under the Messines ridge in Flanders. At 3.10am, on Thursday 7 June 1917, the mines were detonated.

8 June
Million Pounds of High Explosives – The Biggest Mining Feat Ever Attempted

Correspondents' Headquarters, Thursday: At the prearranged moment the biggest thing ever attempted in mining operations rent the sky with a terrible glare and an ear-splitting crash, as a long series of mines, some of which were dug over a year ago, were blown along the enemy positions. The aggregate total of the charges touched off in these earth-shattering eruptions was well over a million pounds of high explosives ... For the past seven days a 'preliminary bombardment' of appalling intensity has been in progress. [...]

The existence of these German soldiers for the past week baffles all efforts of the imagination. Prisoners taken in the wholesale raids we have carried out in this period state that no food worth speaking of has reached their front since the terrific bombardment began. They were reduced by hunger to the lowest ebb of *moral*. For the past two days our destructive shoots have been devoted to counter-battery work, and, thanks to the magnificent co-operation of the airmen, this has largely curtailed the volume of the German artillery fire. [...]

A week ago I telegraphed that our artillery army had the Germans very busy guessing. I could not say more at that time. Well, since dawn this morning the Germans are no longer under any uncertainty. They now know that we are out to drive them off the Messines Ridge, an eminence from which they drove the handful of British cavalry that held it down to 14 October 1914, and from their positions along which they have since dominated the Ypres salient. [...]

People who saw Vimy Ridge after the Canadians had taken it said that the worst of the Somme battlefield could not compare with the much-pocked surface of that famous hump. Those who see the Messines Ridge will draw a similar comparison between it and Vimy. The spectacle this morning is incredible. The whole geography of the district has been churned and blown and furrowed out of recognition, and how many dead Germans lie amid the hecatombs the Recording Angel alone can tell. The enemy has been expecting this attack for days past, and had brought up masses of troops to try to withstand the onslaught.

The attack of this morning was heralded by a night-long rolling of thunder and by every variation in the whole range of lightning effects. It was a most impressive and fitting accompaniment to the perfect tornado of gunfire which swelled up as the appointed hour approached. It was shortly after three o'clock that the infantry went forward to the attack. The moon, peering rayless through a film-like cloud, shed a sort of mystic sheen over the land, which was heightened by the almost concealing flashes of the guns and signal lights and the pale violet glare of the lightning.

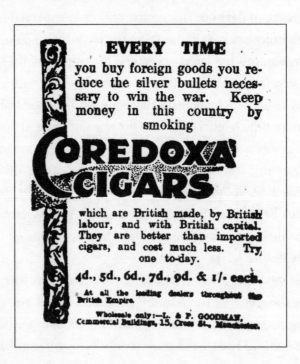

'IT CAN ONLY BE A DRAW'

In 1917 the working class of Germany had just endured a 'turnip winter'
of privation, strikes were commonplace, there was a naval mutiny at
Kiel, and the Russian revolution had transformed perceptions of the war.
The German army was incurring huge casualties. A 'peace resolution'
went through the Reichstag – and was ignored. Having failed to square
the circle, the German Chancellor Bethmann-Hollweg was ousted.

16 July
Bethmann-Hollweg Driven from Office by Militarist Party

Dr. von Bethmann-Hollweg has resigned the office of Imperial
Chancellor ... The German Crown Prince, Field Marshal von
Hindenburg, and General von Ludendorff have been busy seeing
the Reichstag party leaders. The prominent appearance of these in
the affair is generally regarded as of ill omen both for peace and
for German political reform ... Dr. von Bethmann-Hollweg was
unable to stand against the Junkers and other political opponents.

Amsterdam: The greatest danger, according to Herr von
Bethmann-Hollweg, comes from the Germans who still continue
to believe in a German victory. The Chancellor added: 'In the best
case – it can only be a draw.'

'THE AGONY OF MANKIND'

After the success at Messines, German forces were faced with the
renewed offensive in Flanders that began in late July (and concluded
in November) – and the weather. The British fired six times more shells
than the Germans; rain and bombardment turned the landscape into a
quagmire. Mud swallowed humanity, and it became synonymous with
the third battle of Ypres, or as it came to be known, 'Passchendaele'.

2 August
Mile behind Mile of British Guns – Nemesis of Gas

France, Wednesday: A great rainstorm began yesterday afternoon after our advance across the enemy's lines to the Pilkem Ridge and the northern curve of the Ypres salient, and it now veils all the battlefield in a dense mist. It impedes the work of our airmen and makes our artillery co-operation with the infantry more difficult, and adds to the inevitable hardships of our men out there in the new lines, where the ground has been cratered by our shell-fire into one great quagmire of pits.

To the enemy it is not altogether a blessing. His airmen get no observation of our movements, and his gunners do not find their targets, while his poor, wretched infantry, lying out in open ground or in woods where they can get no cover from our fire, must be in a frightful condition, unable to get food because of our barrages behind them and wet to the skin. [...]

The enemy has been rushing up reserves by omnibuses and light railways to the firing line, over tracks which are shelled by us day and night. The suffering of all the German troops, huddled together in exposed places, must be as hideous as anything in the agony of mankind, slashed to bits by storms of shell and urged forward to counter-attacks which they know will be their death.

I saw this morning great numbers of prisoners taken during the past 24 hours and just brought in. They had the look of men who have been through hell. They were drenched with rain, which poured down their big steel helmets. Their top-boots were full of water, which squelched out at every step, and their sunken eyes stared out of ash-grey faces with the look of sick and hunted animals. Many of them had cramp in the stomach through long exposure and hunger before being captured, and they groaned loudly and piteously.

Many of them wept while being interrogated, protesting bitterly that they hated the war and wanted nothing but peace.

They have no hope of victory for their country. An advance into Russia fills them with no new illusions, but seems to them only a lengthening of the general misery. They do not hide the sufferings of their people at home, and say that in the towns there is bitter want and only in the rural districts is there enough to eat. In the field they are filled with gloomy forebodings and live in terror of our tremendous gun-fire. [...]

Among the prisoners I saw to-day I think about a quarter or perhaps a little less were these young boys – anaemic-looking lads with terror in their eyes. The others were more hardy-looking men, though pale and worn. It is certain that they made no great fight yesterday when our men were near them, except when they still had cover in concrete emplacements.

And it is no wonder that all fight had gone out of them. Some even of our own men were startled and stunned by the terrific blast of our own gunfire. Some of them have told me that when they went forward to get into line before the attack they had to pass through mile after mile of our batteries, the heavy guns behind, gradually reaching the lighter batteries until they arrived at field-guns so thickly placed that at some points they were actually wheel to wheel.

The night was dark, but there was no darkness among these batteries. Their flashes lit up their neighbourhood with lurid torches, blinding the eyes of the troops on the march, and all about the air rocked with the blast of their fire, and the noise was so great that men were deafened. As the troops went forward for five or six miles to the assembly lines, flight of shells passed over their heads in a great rush through space, and it was terrifying even to men like one of those I met to-day, who has become familiar with the noise of gunfire since the early day of Ypres and the fury of the Somme. But the worst came when the field guns began their rapid fire of machine guns before yesterday's dawn. It was like the fire of machine guns in its savage sweep, but instead of machine-gun bullets they were 18-pounder shells, and each report from thousands of guns was a sharp ear-splitting crack. [...]

The only men who lived were those who were huddled in sections of trench which were between the barrage lines of our fire. Our men had no fear of what the enemy could do to them. They went forward to find creatures eager to escape from this blazing hell. It was only in redoubts like the Frezenberg Redoubt, which had escaped destruction, that the German machine gunners still fought and gave trouble. Many of the enemy must have been buried alive, with machine-guns and trench mortars and bomb stores.

But there were other dead not touched by shellfire or by any bullet. They had been killed by our gas attack, which had gone before the battle. Rows of them lay clasping their gas masks, and had not been quick enough before the vapour of death reached them. But others with their gas masks on were dead. One of our men tells me that he came across the bodies of a group of German officers – a brigade staff, no doubt – and they were all masked with tin, beast-like nozzles and they were all stone dead.

It is the vengeance of the gods, for that gas, foul and damnable, which they used against us first in the second battle of Ypres and ever since. It is the worst weapon of modern warfare, and has added the blackest terror to all this slaughter of men.

Because there was not great fighting with infantry yesterday it must not be thought that our men had an easy time. The enemy was quick to put down his barrage, and, although it was not anything like our annihilating fire, it was bad enough, as any shell-fire is. [...]

The stretcher-bearers were magnificent, and worked all day and night searching out the wounded and carrying them back under fire. Many of the German prisoners gladly lent a hand in this work on their way back. At the dressing stations to-day I saw them giving pick-a-back to men – ours – who were wounded about the legs and feet.

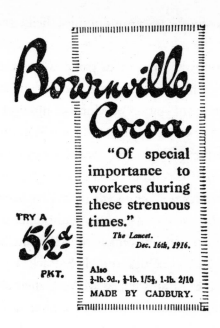

'ARMING THE NATIVES'

Hostilities continued in Africa. Despite the optimism of Jan Smuts, the one-time Boer war general who became a favoured adopted son – and government minister – of Great Britain, the vast numerical superiority of the British empire over Germany in east Africa did not bring speedy victory. The tone of the following report is upbeat, but Major-General Paul von Lettow-Vorbeck's tiny German/African force lived off the land, marched everywhere, struck out of nowhere and continued to outwit its opponents.

12 June 1916
African Invasions Develop

The Secretary to the War Office last night made the following announcement: Telegraphing on 10 June, Lieutenant General Smuts reports that, having bridged the Pangani River at

Mikocheni, the columns operating in the Usambara district have made further progress.

Advancing along the railway, Brigadier General Harrington's column reached Mazinde on 8 June, and on the following day occupied the important station of Mombo, dislodging an enemy force, which retired South.

Having crossed to the right bank of the Pangani at Mikocheni, Major General Hoskin's column advanced on Mkalamo, where the light railway connecting Mombo with Handeni crosses the river, fourteen miles south-west of Mombo. A considerable enemy force was encountered and driven south, and Mkalamo was occupied early on 10 June. Our casualties were slight.

In the direction of Kondis Irangi, Major General Van Deventer was engaged with German forces east of that place. From the Rhodesia Nyassaland border Brigadier General Northey reports that on 6 June one of his columns, under Colonel Rodgers, attacked an enemy party in the Poroto Mountains, capturing a field gun, rifles, ammunition, etc. On 8 June another column under Colonel Murray occupied Bismarckburg.

A key concern of the imperial powers was what would happen when the colonial peoples of Africa embarked on the journey to liberation.

24 May
Gen. Smuts and Native Disarmament
Our London Correspondence: A well-known authority on African affairs draws my attention to some of the difficulties that would be raised by a convention of the European nations prohibiting the training and arming of natives in Central Africa, which General Smuts proposed … yesterday … From the European standpoint it seems doubtful whether France would not hesitate to agree to the reversal of her colonial policy, which has created since 1912 a large

and powerful African army which has been invaluable to her in the war, especially in the defence of Verdun. Opposition to arming the natives has always been a cardinal feature of South African politics, and it is no secret that South Africa imposed a condition on the recruiting of natives for France – that they should not be used in the firing lines. With the exception of the South African Union all the powers in Africa have recruited a native military force as essential to colonisation.

The considerations from the native standpoint are still more serious. If military force is essential to civilised progress – a proposition which the Allies, it is true, could not very well support – the natives would certainly claim that there should be no colour bar to progress in this matter. The natives have been drawn into this war, and have died in their thousands, which ought to entitle them to have their views considered. An even greater difficulty would be the fear of the natives that a complete disarmament would have the ulterior motive of leading up to the exploitation of their countries, particularly in view of proposals that are being put forward by influential people in this country. The natives will not forget that other exploitations by which they have been dispossessed of their land and produce were preceded by humanitarian conventions providing that no arms should be sold to the natives.

30 November
Nearing the End in East Africa

Extraordinary progress has been made towards the close of the East African campaign during the last fortnight … It is unwise to prophesy, but I venture to predict that most members of the South African regiments will eat their Christmas dinners within the bounds of the South African Union; while Colonel von Lettow Vorbeck, the German commander-in-chief will eat his as a prisoner or an exile ... The jungle instinct of the King's African Rifles and Nigerians has been invaluable. They would follow anywhere their white leaders, the mortality among whom has necessarily been heavy.

It was, indeed, unwise of the correspondent to prophesise. Von Lettow-Vorbeck remained at liberty that Christmas. As for the mortality rate, the official death toll (quoted after the war) among British military in east Africa was 11,189; while 95,000 carriers had, officially, died. The historian Edward Paice, however, estimated that at least 650,000 carriers and civilians died in German Ruanda, Urundi and east Africa. By 1917–18, with manpower drained from east Africa and no rain, famine ensued.

'WARDENS OF THE HOLY CITY'

There was a lingering suspicion among the French that while the western front might be the core battlefield, the British were still focusing elsewhere. Following the 1915 Gallipoli disaster and the fall of Kut-al-Amara in 1916 – it was recaptured at the end of the year – the British, combining mobility and efficient planning, made spectacular gains in the Middle East.

12 March
The Fall of Bagdad

Our London Correspondence: At last we can say again: 'the blessed word Mesopotamia.' No great city that has fallen in the war makes such a resounding echo in the world as Bagdad. As the goal of all the German ambitions that beat about the railway to Bagdad the news must be particularly acid to the mouth of the Germans ... It will echo strongly in India, whose brave soldiers have assisted in the capture … this capture is different from all others, for it is like the capture of a place that existed only in a story-book. […]

At a distance, and even when close at hand, the appearance of Bagdad is not unworthy of its ancient fame. Crenelated walls, bastioned gates, numerous towers, a wide ditch, a lofty citadel and a noble river flowing between opposing ramparts give it an aspect rare among the habitations of men. Above the walls appear the gilded domes of mosques and royal tombs alternating with dainty minarets and cupolas.

The interior of Bagdad does not correspond with its outside show. There is no sewerage; water, the unfiltered water of the Tigris, is conveyed from house to house in skins which are the nurseries of continuous generations of microbes. It is not surprising that cholera is endemic, and that there is a special local disease known as 'the Bagdad date mark.' The reforming governor Midhat Pasha wished to grapple with this problem when he was here from 1868 to 1872, but either time was too short or the work too great. Things went on as before … Bagdad has many local industries, but they appertain to luxuries. Choice leathers, silk plush, carpets and curtains figure most prominently in its list of exports, and of natural products dates are the most abundant; but progress and reform may have reached Bagdad for good with the advent of the railway on one side and of steamers on the other. The water storage, which will in time restore its lost prosperity to Mesopotamia, must also revive the opportunities of Bagdad as its most convenient distributing centre, and the time may be coming when it will be no longer true to say that: 'The glory of the City of the Caliphs has departed.'

Early in the war Britain faced a munitions manufacturing crisis. The Manchester Guardian's *editor, CP Scott, was in contact with Chaim Weizmann, the brilliant lecturer in chemistry at Manchester University, and in December 1915 Scott took Weizmann to breakfast with Lloyd*

George. Weizmann's work was of 'vital importance,' said Lloyd George subsequently, and the crisis in cordite production was resolved.

Weizmann, a dedicated Zionist and future first president of the state of Israel, was also introduced to the Foreign Secretary Arthur Balfour, who – like Scott – was passionate about the Zionist cause. In November 1917 came a fateful declaration.

9 November
Jewish Zionists
British Government Support

On behalf of the Government, the Foreign Secretary has sent the following letter to Lord Rothschild [Baron Lionel Rothschild]:

Foreign Office, 2 November 1917. Dear Lord Rothschild, I have much pleasure in conveying to you on behalf of his Majesty's Government the following declaration of sympathy with Jewish Zionist aspirations which has been submitted to and approved by the Cabinet: 'His Majesty's Government views with favour the establishment in Palestine of a national home for the Jewish people, and will use its best endeavours to facilitate the achievement of this object, it being clearly understood that nothing shall be done which may prejudice the civil and religious rights of non-Jewish communities in Palestine, or the rights and political status enjoyed by Jews in any other country.' I should be grateful if you would being this declaration to the knowledge of the Zionist Federation. Yours sincerely, Arthur James Balfour

A Triumph for Zionism

Our London Correspondence: The Government's declaration of sympathy with the Zionist movement for a Jewish national home in Palestine is published to-night, but it is interesting to note that it was despatched to Lord Rothschild on 2 November, the day when the attack on Gaza was begun. The capture of Gaza goes a long way towards putting it within the power of Great Britain to give practical effects to its declaration. The document is interesting in another way. It is the first time, I believe, that the British Government has ever addressed the Jews as a nation.

10 November
A Week of the War

Mr. Balfour's statement that the establishment of the Jews in Palestine as their national home is one of the objects of our policy greatly simplifies the political issues. It is not an accident that the Eastern policy of Alexander the Great, Julius Caesar and Napoleon was markedly pro-Jewish. They all saw, in a strong Jewish State in Palestine, a bulwark of their position in the East. So does the British Government, and it is to be congratulated on having at last broken finally with Turkey and laid the foundations of a new and genuinely liberal Eastern policy.

In the wake of the declaration came a wave of optimism.

10 December
Meeting of Thanks in Manchester: Sir Mark Sykes's Warning

Last night a crowded meeting of Jews was held in the Manchester Hippodrome to thank the British Government for their declaration in favour of Zionism … Colonel Sir Mark Sykes MP and Mr. James de Rothschild were among the speakers … The meeting was a most enthusiastic one.

Sir Mark Sykes said that … although within the two thousand years past, Jewry had on occasion been moved in unison, it had always before been on some matter of grief and never of joy. The war had been fruitful in negatives, but here was a great positive. For centuries there had been something amiss with civilisation. Every nation and every continent had had its Jewish problem, oppressive laws, ghettos, pales; here Jews were proscribed and evicted, there tolerated and assimilated, and between the two one did not know whether the first was not better. The realisation of the Zionist ideal was the end of all that. Zionism would give the Jews of the world a higher position than they had ever held before. Although few might go to Palestine in proportion to those who remained without, the latter would not suffer. No British Jew would be less British because he could look at the cradle of his race with pride and at the religious centre of his faith with happiness and reverence. When the spiritual citizenship was clearly and nobly defined, the civic citizenship would be higher than ever before ...

He regarded it as vital for the success of the Zionist plan that it should rest upon a Jewish, Armenian and Arab entente. The Armenian was one of an oppressed people, and until he could live his life and realise his national aspiration the Jews could have no guarantee that the tyranny which fell upon him would not fall upon them ... Until they had liberated the Armenians they could not be secure; they must have between themselves and their possible aggressor a stable, progressive Armenian State.

When he spoke of Arabs he entered into no nice distinctions. He referred to those in Asia who were one in language and in blood. By environment they were called Syrians, Mesopotamians, Mosulis, Aleppines; by religion they were called Christians, Mussulmans, Druses, Mitawelis, Ansaries; in blood, there was on the male side a little infusion in Syria of Crusader, and in Mesopotamia of Turanian and Iranian, but scientists would call these only traces. Eighty-five per cent of the stock was Semitic. For 800 years the Arabs had been under Turkish dynasties. Their canals of Mesopotamia had been ruined, and when Vasco de Gama rounded the Cape he cut them off from European commerce. They were bound, impoverished, denied by policy and isolated by events. Were they dead? Never. 'You know the Semite sleeps but never dies.' Wherever there were men of Arab stock, whether in Nigeria or Chicago, Java or Manchester, one would find progressive people who took interest in art, in literature, in philosophy, and had a high place in commerce. [...]

There were seven or eight millions of them; they were prolific. There was a combination of manpower, virgin soil, petroleum, and brains. What was that going to produce in 1950? The inevitable result was that the seven or eight millions would turn to 20 millions; the Mesopotamian canal system would be reconstructed; Syria must become the granary of Europe; Bagdad, Damascus and Aleppo would be each as big as Manchester; universities and a great press must arise.

Arab civilisation was coming there ... It was the destiny of the Jews to be closely connected with the Arab revival, and co-operation and goodwill from the first were necessary, or ultimate disaster would overtake both Jew and Arab. Therefore he warned Jews to look through Arab glasses.

What did the Arab fear? He feared financial corporations, pivoted on Palestine, controlling Syria and Mesopotamia. He feared the soil of Palestine would be bought by companies, and that he would become a proletariat working on the soil. He feared the Palestinian colonists might drop their colonies and drift into Syria and Mesopotamia as middlemen and crush him out of existence. It was essential that Zionists should realise and face these dangers. The Arabs should understand that the Jews sought no land not willingly sold; that all land would only be developed through Jewish labour; that the colonists would be bona-fide colonists, and that the Jews were out to win Palestine not by financial manoeuvres, but by the sweat of their brow. The co-operation of the two races offered such prospects to mankind; hostility would mean such an unthinkable tragedy that he felt it his duty to give the warning.

... Zionists should remember that Jerusalem was a triple shrine, sacred to Christian, Jew and Moslem alike. Jerusalem throbbed with history; it was inflammable ground, and a careless word or gesture might set half a continent aflame. Jewish policy would not be realised by diplomacy, tact, delicacy, or the virtues of the drawing-room politician. Jerusalem called for more than that. It did not call for toleration, but for sympathy, understanding, compassion, sacrifice – 'sympathy with the Moslem, to whom the mosque of Omar is the most sacred spot on earth; understanding the Christian, who, like myself, feels that in helping Zionism he is doing something to make a great amend.' [...]

He believed that, approached in the right spirit, Zionism would be the cause of a great reconciliation, not of fusion, but good-fellowship between members of three faiths of common origin. Misused it would be the beginning of bitterer strife than ever the world had known. Timidity was the road to ruin; let them face facts boldly. In the realisation of their ideal he saw security for the world's peace. He saw them co-operating as the moral guarantors and protectors of small States, being perhaps the smallest and the greatest at the same time. He saw them healing the religious distractions which had severed the best from the best throughout the ages. In Jerusalem there would be a great vital heart, healing the scars of Europe and calling Asia once more back to life.

In 1916 Sir Mark Sykes and France's François Georges-Picot, with the acquiescence of imperial Russia, had secretly agreed on the dismemberment of sections of the Ottoman empire. France's sphere of influence was to be Syria, while Britain's was what was then Mesopotamia.

In November 1917 the Bolsheviks took power in Russia. On 23 November the Manchester Guardian *journalist M Philips Price visited the Russian Foreign Office – now occupied by the new Foreign Affairs Commissar Leon Trotsky – and was presented with copies of various*

'Secret Treaties', including details of the Sykes-Picot deal. Philips Price telegraphed the details to the Manchester Guardian. *Between 27 and 29 November, to the anger and embarrassment of the British and French governments, the paper published details of the secret treaties, including Sykes-Picot. CP Scott editorialised on the subject.*

28 November
The Secret Treaties

Secret diplomacy is morally and politically indefensible; neither before a war nor during a war have governments the right to do anything that might add to its sacrifices, unless they have very good reason to believe that the people whose interests they are protecting are willing, and this they have no means of knowing except by reasonable publicity, reasonable candour and reasonable discussion.

The British had driven the Turks out of Gaza at the end of October. Jerusalem was next.

11 December
The Capture of Jerusalem

The coming of the British to Palestine and to Jerusalem has long been desired and long been predicted. It is recognised that the English as wardens of the Holy City will do impartial justice to Christian, Moslem, and Jew, and one of General Allenby's first acts will symbolise this. He will confirm the Moslems in their office as doorkeepers of the Church of the Holy Sepulchre, an office which Moslems have held, save for the Crusades, uninterruptedly since the days of Caliph Omar. It is not in the spirit or with the aims of a Crusader that General Allenby enters Jerusalem, but to free the city from a Turkish tyranny which has weighed upon Moslem, Christian and Jew alike, not so much, in Jerusalem itself, as the tyranny of government which know no other way of ruling but by dividing and setting race against race and sect against sect. All that is now gone, and it will be as a deliverer that General Allenby will be welcomed to Jerusalem to-morrow.

'A LADY OF TITLE'

Some things do not change. The Manchester Guardian*'s 'Country Diary' provided a counterpoint to world events, but even here ladies of title were turning their hands to war work.*

9 October
A Country Diary

The barometer was falling at the weekend, and yet on Saturday the sun and wind combined to make an ideal day for fruit-getting. Many worked, as we did, from early morning till dusk. Since the storms of wind and rain have swept over the country … I find from very recent inquiries that farmers in Cumberland and Westmorland

Gong Soups provide a ready-to-hand substitute for fresh meat during the present restrictions. Three good portions of delicious Gong Soup can be made in 15 minutes for 2d.

With so many varieties of Gong Soups to select from, a different kind can be served every week-day for a fortnight.

TWELVE DIFFERENT VARIETIES.
ALL ONE PRICE, 2ᴅ.

GONG Soups
SUFFICIENT FOR 3 PORTIONS
2ᴅ
MADE BY OXO LTD LONDON

have come through their labour difficulties exceedingly well, owing to the ready help given them by their friends and neighbours in all ranks of society. To see a lady of title drive a milk cart and at a pinch shoe her own horse, and young and old take their share of the work, rough or smooth, as they have done now for months past, shows one that there is no degeneration in the race.

'TANKS IN LONDON'

The annual Lord Mayor's Show also adapted to the war.

10 November
The War Show

Our London Correspondence: In the old days everyone said that the Lord Mayor's Show was a nuisance, but nearly everyone seemed to see it and to enjoy it in a certain sub-acid way. It made everyone feel so superior. But since the war the Lord Mayor's Shows have gone on as usual, and whether you think it right or not you cannot feel superior about it. Very different feelings, indeed, were aroused in most people by seeing the march past of so many men in uniform with little gold lines on their sleeves [indicating a war wound], and the girl war-workers from the farms – a very sturdy and remarkably good-looking regiment – (I think the beauty chorus at our crackest theatre would look Class C beside them). Then there were Women's Auxiliary Corps, who suggested – like a man's regiment – a recruitment from all classes and from different parts; the munition girls among their shells and cartridges, and the parade of eager, hard-looking little Boy Scouts, the advance guard of the generation of war. And there were, of course, the tanks, and the sight of these monsters grinding along the sanded street to Temple Bar with a friendly hand protruding from the top waving a piece of oily waste over their black ugliness, and even the well-trained City constables' horses jibbing and rearing at them, was the strangest war sight the City has ever seen. The impression they left on the street will disappear long before the memory of it. The captured guns and aeroplane took one's mind back to ancient times when enemy trophies were dragged through the street, and here was the same pageant to-day. It was, as usual, a day for the children, and everywhere you saw them held up to see the coming of the new world in its grimmest form in the tanks and in its comeliest in the girl war-workers. What sort of world will those children be sitting in when they are old people and telling their descendants how they saw the tanks in London in 1917?

Talking with some of the women in the procession as they waited for it to re-form after the interval (writes a woman correspondent), I found that they had various views about their experiences. The members of the Women's Army Auxiliary Corps had looked on it as something of an ordeal to march past those miles of cheering, sympathetic crowds. They know by experience how critically soldiers watch their drill, but they held their heads up and marched gallantly. The munition girls thoroughly enjoyed themselves, and the yellow-faced 'canaries' [munitions workers with black hair and yellow faces] talked cheerfully about their work.

But it was the land workers who enjoyed themselves most. They were proud of the months or years they had already given to very hard work, and the public recognition of the way they had stuck to it was new to them. The new ones expected the winter would be trying, but they meant to stick it. 'If the men can stand winter in the trenches surely we can stand it on the land.'

'LEAPING RATHER THAN RUNNING'

Meanwhile, that autumn Italian troops were confronted by a new challenge. Throughout 1916 and into 1917 the Italian and Austro-Hungarian armies had suffered huge losses in their struggles in the Trentino mountains and on the Carso plateau above Trieste. The growing Russian military collapse from the summer of 1917 began to free up German military resources for deployment away from the eastern front. The Italian Commander Luigi Cadorna, having lost more than 200,000 men on the Carso, was faced with an Austro-Hungarian onslaught bolstered by seven German divisions on 25 October 1917. The battle of Caporetto (now Kobarid, Slovenia) ensued. August von Mackensen was a veteran of the eastern front.

27 October
The German Attack on Italy

The arrival of Mackensen on the front is sufficient proof of the importance of Germany's share in the offensive, and the German forces that are being used on the battlefield are already in due proportion with the renown of their commander. It now appears certain that the great attack which debouched into the Isonzo valley between Monte Nero and Polonnik ... was conducted by an entire German army corps. Favoured by the thickest mist, they came pouring through the pass at Caporetto at a terrific speed, the men almost leaping rather than running through the valley.

The German Headquarters Reported Yesterday: Pressing forward irresistibly the German and Austro-Hungarian regiments, outrivalling each other, have passed beyond their objectives and have thrown the enemy out of strong rearguard positions which he sought to hold. Under our pressure the Italians have also begun to evacuate the Bainsizza Plateau. We are already fighting at many places on Italian territory.

The disaster at Caporetto led to the transfer of French and British divisions to Italy in order to restore stability. At the Rapallo Conference on 5 November, Lloyd George and the new French Prime Minister Georges Clemenceau imposed their authority over the allied generals, and General Cadorna was replaced by Armando Diaz.

10 November

Our London Correspondence: Criticism of General Cadorna in Italy has been mainly directed to his relation with the civil population, particularly against the manner of his demands for a war spirit behind the front. His military reputation stands unaffected.

General Cadorna had no military reputation, having fled during Caporetto, and was singled out for criticism in a post-war inquiry. In 1924 Benito Mussolini promoted him to field marshal.

10 November

Our London Correspondence: The name of General Diaz is … new even to many Italians. He was born in Naples, and has commanded the Sardinian brigades with great success. He was a lieutenant colonel on the staff at the beginning of the war, and was largely concerned in the taking of Sabatino, by which the Gorizia victory was achieved. He held a command in the Second Army, and his action in command of Bersaglieri troops was the brightest spot in the history of that army after the breaking of the front. After the first success of the Austro-Germans he retook the key-hill of Globocak with great bravery.

'THE CRIMINAL LENIN'

In revolutionary Russia the slogan of Lenin's Bolsheviks, 'Land, Peace and Bread', was immediately appealing to peasants, soldiers and workers. On Tuesday 6 November 1917 (25 October in the Old Calendar), the Bolsheviks began their seizure of power.

8 November
Government Firm – Kerensky's Declaration in Parliament

Petrograd, Tuesday: In the Preliminary Parliament yesterday M. Kerensky, replying to a question as to what the Government intended to do to foil the attempt of the Nationalists to seize supreme power, made a speech, in the course of which he said that the nearer the date of the Constituent Assembly approaches the more intense were the efforts made to interfere with its summoning by the disorganisation of the defence forces of the country and by treason to the Fatherland. 'These efforts,' he said, 'are made from two sides – namely, by the Extreme Left and Right – urged on by articles by the criminal Lenin, who is a fugitive from justice. These efforts, whether conscious or unconscious, are useful, not to the German proletariat, but to the governing classes in Germany, for they contribute to the penetrating of our front by the troops of the Kaiser and those of his friends.'

Maximalist Rising in Petrograd – Parliament Building Seized

Petrograd, Wednesday 12pm: An armed naval detachment, acting under the order of the Maximalist Revolutionary Committee [effectively the Bolsheviks], had occupied the offices of the official Petrograd Telegraph Agency.

4.25pm: The Maximalists have also occupied the Central Telegraph Office, the State Bank and the Marie Palace, where the Preliminary Parliament, the proceedings of which have been suspended in view of the situation, has been holding its sittings.

As an elite part of the Imperial Russian Army, the role of the Cossacks – halfway between a caste and an ethnic community – was seen as significant to the fate of the Bolshevik revolution. During the ensuing civil war, while the majority were with the White armies, some fought alongside the Bolsheviks.

9 November
The Petrograd Coup d'Etat

Our London Correspondence: Russians of various shades of opinion whom I have seen to-day are agreed on one thing, and that is that the information about the situation in Petrograd is not sufficient at present to indicate the real position. It is agreed that the statements issued through the Maximalist party, who have control of the wires, are probably more accurate, and, indeed, that the careful mention of the number of Cossack regiments who have agreed not to fight against the Maximalists showed that they did not intend to overstate things. There are, however, gaps in their announcements.

The next point is about Moscow and how far that city is affected by the Maximalist propaganda. One well-known Russian journalist, who recently arrived here from Russia, declares very emphatically that the Maximalist party there is comparatively small, and that whether Kerensky reaches Moscow or not there will be a great rally there of the Government forces. He doubts the possibility of the Petrograd section influencing the army, and believes that if Petrograd becomes wholly Maximalist it will be cut off from the rest of Russia, and that would mean starvation.

10 November
The Soviets and Russian Democracy

Our London Correspondence: I had a talk to-day with a Russian in an official position here who was in Petrograd five weeks ago. His chief point was that the English and still more the French newspapers attach an altogether exaggerated importance not only to the Maximalists as a democratic power, but to the importance of the Soviets themselves. The Soviets of Petrograd, and he thought of Moscow also, are now predominantly Maximalist, and have been since the Korniloff rising. But it is forgotten here that there are many other democratic organisations in Russia besides the Soviets, of greater numbers and influence.

The Council of Peasants' Delegates, which had an equal representation at the Democratic Conference with the Soviets, supports the Provisional Government, and economically their influence is very important. The Central Committee of Co-operative Societies, with over 20,000,000 members, sent more delegates to the Democratic conference than the Soviets. With very few exceptions, town and country councils in Russia support Kerensky, and five weeks ago at any rate it was the case that the bulk of the army committees at the front followed Kerensky.

It has been true all along, he said, that the soldiers at the front have been much less affected by the Bolshevik propaganda than the garrisons in the towns. He was sure that the bulk of those who made the Revolution would refuse to follow Lenin – he mentioned Prince Kropotkin; in fact they would become revolutionaries again. He did not think that the promise of sharing the land with the peasants in the proclamations would make much difference, as a vague promise of this sort had always been part of the programme of the Maximalists.

It was quite possible that Lenin might desire to make a separate peace, but the vast majority of the Russian people would not accept as binding upon them anything that the Lenin clique might do. When he left Petrograd a collision between the Bolsheviks and the Government was fully expected to take place sooner or later, but it was though that any Maximalist rising would be quickly suppressed. It is thought that the Leninites must have acted so quickly that the Provisional Government had not time to employ the military force faithful to it.

In his opinion it would be found that the Cossacks, who were extremely powerfully organised, would prove to be the rallying point for the vast forces in Russia who were against the Maximalists. If the Lenin Government was suppressed by force it would be, he thought, by the Cossacks. The Union of Cossacks, while disagreeing politically with Kerensky, would certainly not acquiesce in the supremacy of Lenin.

The Cossacks were indeed an important part of anti-Bolshevik forces in the ensuing civil war. But the Manchester Guardian'*s M Philips Price provided a contrasting analysis.*

20 November
Causes of Kerensky's Fall

The government of Kerensky fell before the Bolshevik insurgents because it had no supporters in the country. The bourgeois parties and the generals and the staff disliked it because it would not establish a military dictatorship. The Revolutionary Democracy lost faith in it because after eight months it had neither given land to the peasants nor established state control of industries, nor advanced the cause of the Russian peace programme ... The Bolsheviks thus acquired great support all over the country. In my journey in the provinces in September and October I noticed that every local Soviet had been captured by them. The Executive Committee of the All-Russia Council of Workers' and Soldiers' Delegates elected last summer clearly did not represent the feelings of the revolutionary masses in October. The Bolsheviks therefore insisted on a re-election and the summoning of a second All-Russia Soviet Congress, [with] only the right-wing of the Socialist parties opposing this.

*The Foreign Office Minister Lord Robert Cecil announced on 24
November that there could be no question of any dealing with, or
recognition of, the 'Maximalist government in Petrograd'. The*
Manchester Guardian *responded editorially a few days later.*

27 November
Russia and Her Allies

Whatever we may think of the Leninist Government – and for
ourselves we think extremely ill – it is for the Russian people alone
to determine who shall govern them …

The Maximalist theory is that the Allied Governments are
tainted by Imperialism as well as the enemy Governments, that
they are a 'bourgeois,' or essentially middle-class and capitalistic
system, with all the vices which Socialist doctrine attributes to the
bourgeois order. They have no confidence that these Governments
want a speedy peace or a democratic peace. To justify this lack of
faith they point to the secret treaties they are now publishing and to
the interminable postponements of the Conference for the revision
of Allied war aims. The democracies alone, they conclude, can give
the world a quick and a democratic peace, and they recognise that
the key to the whole fabric is held by the German democracy. So,
while they write to the Allied Governments, they try to negotiate
direct with the German soldiers in the trenches. Their instinct is
right when it leads them to single out the German democracy as
the heart of the problem, for it is absolutely certain that if the
German democracy manifests the will to a democratic peace it
can get it. The democracies of the Allies will respond instantly
when the German democracy asserts itself and establishes itself.
We should like to think that the Maximalists will prove successful
in appealing straight to the German soldiers in the trenches, but
there is nothing to encourage such optimism. Still, the seed sown
now may perhaps later not be without its fruits. The Maximalists

are trying in their own way to win them to the cause of peace and democracy. Let us try to study them objectively. Our duty and our interest are to get at the facts and to understand them, and this duty rests with particular weight upon the Allied Governments, who have not always distinguished themselves by an intelligent understanding of Revolutionary Russia. But let the Maximalists also try to understand the Allied democracies, who know that they are in this war through Russia, and that the new Russia cannot simply reject responsibility for the acts, and the consequences to other peoples of the acts, of the old Russia.

Bolshevik strategy hinged on their infant revolution being joined by successful uprisings in western Europe, crucially in Germany with its vast productive capacity. Negotiations with imperial Germany for an armistice were continuing amidst the cataclysm, as M Philips Price reported.

27 November
The Armistice Proposals

I have just returned from a sitting of the Executive Committee of the All-Russia Congress. Lenin stated that the Revolutionary Government had sent out instructions to regimental committees at the front to make proposals to enemy soldiers for an armistice … Lenin stated that no armistice was possible unless it was signed by the Revolutionary Government in Petrograd … [In the] meantime, it is hoped to receive a reply from the Allies about the proposal for an armistice on their fronts. The armistice is regarded as the first step for carrying on revolutionary propaganda in the German army. For this reason proposals were made direct to German soldiers in the trenches, special newspapers printed in German being issued. In this way it is hoped to undermine the authority of the German Government and bring about the downfall of Prussian militarism. Lenin stated that there would be no demobilisation of the army, which remains at the front to carry on the revolutionary fight for peace ... Everything points to the gradual reduction of the army to provide labour for the collapsing industries of the country. The policy of the Bolsheviks proposing an armistice is undoubtedly connected with the elections for the Constituent Assembly, which are taking place all over Russia during the next fortnight. They feel they will thereby secure the army, the proletariat and the peasants' votes.

'WEARY AND SOAKED AND PARTLY NUMBED'

The battle of Passchendaele continued to grind on in appalling conditions throughout the autumn, with few gains on either side.

12 October
Where the Advance Sagged: Yorkshireman's Battle in Marsh and Fog

Yesterday I spent a large part of the day with certain Yorkshire troops. The story of their advance is typical of that part of the field where we did not wholly succeed. There is no need again to emphasise the dreadful climatic conditions under which the attack took place, with wild storms of rain which swept over the water-logged ground driven by bitter cold wind. No man started to attack that morning who was not already weary and soaked and partly numbed, covered with slime from falling into shell-holes and chilled with standing hip-high in icy water. It was only half-light, and a thick white mist enfolded the battlefield.

Floundering, wading, and helping each other along amid bursting shells and a storm of machine-gun bullets, it was more than an hour's hard work for our men to force their way across those four or five hundred yards to where they closed in on Peter Pan. Here begins the first gentle rise to the ridge on the top of which the village of Passchendaele was in full view some 2,500 yards away. Along the face of this ridge, towards which the Yorkshiremen were going, ran one of the main trench lines of the Germans, built in the days when the Germans still hoped to hold us with trenches and wire. Pill boxes and redoubts are built into the old trenches at carefully planned angles. Peter Pan itself was only an outlying post of such a series of defences along the old Zonnebeke trench line. To the right of it along the road was another position, the core of which was two large concrete redoubts. About it and behind it lay tier after tier of pill-boxes and redoubts among twisted wire and holes and hummocks of trench line. The place was full of Germans, with machine guns everywhere, and our men, dragging through the mud, had been unable to keep close to the barrage. Here, therefore, they were temporarily held up … Then news came from the right that Peter Pan was taken, then from the left that some of our men had crossed the road and were walking towards Wolf Farm about 1,000 yards from the start … Each concrete post, almost each group of shell holes, constitutes a separate minor operation. A battalion becomes a number of scattered little units of half platoons or a dozen men or single individuals each working doggedly towards a single end. […]

Then the night shut down and with it came more rain and storms. The Germans made no attempt to counter-attack. Twice heavy shell-fire descended on our forward positions, but no infantry came after it. Far worse than anything the enemy did was the night, with the conditions of storm and cold out in those water-logged shell-holes.

Troops who 'mopped up' later found innumerable minor positions unreduced … These were taken one by one. Neither artillery nor distant machine-gun fire ever stopped. Scattered fighting went on everywhere at isolated posts which were holding out. Such was the chaos and confusion that ... many of our wounded started to walk or crawl towards the German lines having lost all sense of direction. For a time no transport or carrying parties with supplies could get up to the advanced posts, the mere physical difficulty of making progress through ever deepening mire carrying burdens made it impossible. [...]

Here in the middle the Yorkshiremen and the troops on their right and left won only perhaps 1,000 yards. But I doubt if the winning of 1,000 yards ever called for, or found, finer and sterner qualities than these men showed. None did better than certain third-line Territorials in the face of difficulties which demanded the utmost degree of fortitude and endurance.

It was Canadian troops who captured the ridge at Passchendaele in early November, at the cost of 16,000 casualties. By the end of the battle there were more than 200,000 allied wounded and 70,000 dead. German casualties, dead and wounded, totalled around 200,000.

'OUT OF THE MIST'

The last battle in 1917 on the western front was Cambrai, and took place between 20 November and 5 December. It was not the first mass use of tanks – the French had deployed them earlier in the year – but in the initial surprise attack, 476 tanks helped a total of six British Commonwealth divisions punch a hole in the German lines.

22 November
New Tactics and a Staggering Surprise to the Germans
Wednesday, 12.15pm: Yesterday morning the Third Army, under the command of General the Hon. Sir Julian Byng, delivered a

number of attacks between St. Quentin without previous artillery preparations, and in each case the enemy was completely surprised. Our troops have broken into the enemy's positions to a depth of between four and five miles on a wide front, and have captured several thousand prisoners, with a number of guns.

The Best-Kept Secret of the War

Correspondents' Headquarters, Tuesday Night: The enemy this morning had, I am sure, the surprise of his life on the western front, when, without any warning by the ordinary preparations that are made before battle, without any sign of strength in men and guns behind our front, without a single shot fired before the attack, and with his great belts of hideously strong wire still intact, our troops, led forward by great numbers of tanks, suddenly assaulted him at dawn, smashed through his wire, passed beyond to his trenches, and penetrated in many places the main Hindenburg line and the Hindenburg support line beyond.

It was a surprise to the enemy, and, to be frank, it will be a surprise to all our officers and men in other parts of the line, and, to my mind, it is the most sensational and dramatic episode of this year's fighting, brilliantly imagined, and carried through with the greatest secrecy. Not a whisper of it had reached men like myself, who are always up and down the lines, and since the secret of the tanks themselves, which suddenly made their appearance on the Somme last year, this is, I believe, the best-kept secret of the war. [...]

How could the enemy guess in his wildest nightmare that a blow would be struck at him quite suddenly – at that Hindenberg line of his, enormously strong in wire and redoubts and tunnels and trenches – without any artillery preparation or any sign of gun power behind our front? ... The enemy did not know that during

recent nights great numbers of tanks were crawling along the roads towards Havrincourt and our lines below the Flesquières ridge, hiding by day in the copses of this wooded and rolling country beyond Péronne and Bapaume. Indeed, he knew little of all that was going on before him under cover of darkness. [...]

We caught the enemy 'on the hop,' as the men say, and in spite of uneasy moments in the night they had no proof of what was coming to them and no time to prepare against the blow. Most of the prisoners say that the first thing they knew of the attack was when out of the mist they saw the tanks advancing upon them, smashing down their wire, crawling over their trenches, and moving forward with gunfire and machine-gun fire slashing from their sides.

The Germans were aghast and dazed. Many hid down in their dug-outs and tunnels and then surrendered. Only the steadiest and bravest of them rushed to the machine-guns and got them into action and used their rifles to snipe our men. Out of the silences which had been behind our lines a great fire of guns came upon them. They knew they had been caught by an amazing stratagem, and they were full of terror. Behind the tanks, coming forward in platoons, the infantry swarmed, cheering and shouting, trudging through thistles, while the tanks made a scythe of a machine-gun fire in front of them, and thousands of shells came screaming over the Hindenburg lines.

The advantage was not sustained. As the year ended the French army was, at best, in recuperation, the Italian army had been routed at the battle of Caporetto in November, the Bolshevik revolution was taking Russia out of the war, the US army was yet to arrive, and the British were left wondering how victory could be achieved.

CHAPTER 6

1918

In 1906 Germany's retiring chief of general staff, Alfred von Schlieffen, had bequeathed his plan for winning a two-front war to his successor Helmuth von Moltke. The Schlieffen Plan belonged to a lost world of peace, emperors in plumed hats and war games. It entailed quickly knocking France out of the struggle before settling with Russia. But, with von Moltke's alterations, it failed in 1914.

By 1918, in a world turned upside down, von Schlieffen – dead for six years – appeared, just possibly, to be enjoying a last laugh. But it was Bolshevik Russia that had fallen out of the war, not France, and it had taken four years, not three months. It was true, also, that Austria-Hungary seemed close to collapse, but as 1918 dawned Germany was finally focusing on one main front – in the west. It would be months, or maybe longer, before any sizeable contingent of the US army would arrive in Europe, which left the western allies to plan for victory, optimistically, in summer 1919.

For President Hindenburg and General Ludendorff, 1918 had to be the year. Germany's economy was under military control, its people were hungry, and in many cities they were teetering on – or in – revolt. What was needed was a shattering victory against the western allies. And that was what very nearly happened.

'UNFORGIVABLE HORRORS'

In Britain, politicians, papers and publishers vied with each other to express anti-German sentiment.

6 February

Miscellany: It was a strange type of mind that produced the 'German Crimes Calendar,' which is now fighting with illustrated weeklies for the best site on station bookstalls. In each month one day is set apart from its brethren by an encircling red line, and a picture at the top of the sheet illustrates the dark deed perpetrated thereon. In one bleak January Cardinal Mercier was arrested; February brought the unrestricted submarine campaign, and so on, through the twelve records of unforgettable horrors. There is something peculiarly unpleasant in the idea of English people hanging this grisly almanac in their kitchens or nurseries, and marking the passage of their quiet days as preceding or following the anniversary of some act of malice and unchristian hatred.

'FRIZZLED IN ENGLISH KITCHENS'

The sometime Liberal MP and survivor of the Lusitania *sinking DA Thomas, Lord Rhondda, was appointed minister of food control in 1916. As such, he was celebrated in verse in the* Manchester Guardian.

6 February
To the Sausage on Its Threatened Extinction
(The sausage, since it absorbs both meat and grain and is difficult to control, is threatened with abolition.)

> Friend, I have loved you under many guises,
> Sampled you, hot and cold, from clime to clime,
> Sliced, and with pickles, as the Boche advises,
> Frizzled in English kitchens to your prime.
> Coloured, and plain, gristly and even bony,
> In café, cabaret, and marble hall,
> And whether pork or beef or eke Polony,

I've loved you all.
The Ham, the Egg, that joy the Blackpool tripper,
Though in my scheme of life they play a part,
Not they nor Kidney, Kedgeree nor Kipper,
Can loose the hold you have upon my heart;
I who myself have oft with timely puncture
Over the camp fire coaxed you not to burst,
Shall I desert you at this tragic juncture,
Suspect, accurst?
Nay, though officials be already numbered
Like to the grains of sand that fringe the sea,
Life with one more of them must be encumbered,
And that one more should certainly be me;
Sausage Control is surely not beyond a
Man who will bring affection to the task;
The chance (I hereby make it plain to Rhondda)
Is all I ask.

'SPORT IS VERY FAIR'

5 March

A Country Diary

The best news I have this week is perhaps of the lambing season in the southern and midland counties. There has been very little severe frost, and as the ewes have had an abundant supply of roots and in most districts pastures have afforded a nice nip of fresh grass, they are in good condition. Lambs are above the average in number. It was interesting to watch the pigeons, now very numerous in the centre of our city, flying about in a confused way high in the air during the passing of the aeroplane to-day above the Town Hall. As it came round and round they seemed to have no settled determination to clear off, but flew in various directions. No doubt they will soon get used to the sight and take little notice of it.

Lamp-time for cyclists today: 6.24pm

Lights down: 7.24pm

14 May
A Country Diary

The Isle of Wight disease seemed at one time to have nearly put an end to bee-keeping in our district. There never was a greater demand for honey; and a top price can be got in every part of the country. Surely, the inducement is sufficient to tempt many to go into this very useful form of food production.

I hope those who live in the country and can gather young nettles are making the best of their opportunity, as they will found a food equal to spinach. There will be many this year who will be spending a few days of Whit-week in the country. I would suggest to them to try angling, even if only pond-fishing is available. Taking it all round, sport is very fair this season. River, lake and pond fishing seems to be giving more than the average return, and the result will make a pleasant relief to the restricted choice of food supply we most of us get.

Lamp-time for cyclists today: 9.31pm

Lights down: 10.31pm

21 June
Nature Notes in Wartime

Our London Correspondence: A nature enthusiast in Bloomsbury sends me [the] following notes of his observations on fauna and flora in Judd Street. I give them as a contribution to the history of London in wartime. He writes: 'The high price of cats' meat in Bloomsbury has caused a shortage of cats; consequently mice have increased in an appalling way. A loaf of mine was made unfit for human food, so I obtained the permission of the police authorities across the road to give it to the horses. In one week I caught seven mice, six of them in one trap baited with the same piece of bacon rind. The pigeons round our way were greatly alarmed during the air raid of Wednesday last, and they were very queersome for the next day. Last week was a wonderful week for growing things. Two twopenny tomato plants that I bought in Farringdon Street market on Saturday week and had replanted grew wonderfully. In seven days one of them had grown about a foot in height, whilst the other last Saturday had two tomatoes as big as peas on it. By Sunday morning a starving sparrow or pigeon had eaten one of the tomatoes (there are no breadcrumbs at the windows nowadays), but to-day the other tomato is as big as a thimble. Just as my crop is looking promising there is a slump in the price of tomatoes to-day – eightpence per pound as compared with 1s.3d. per pound on Saturday,' I take it that these are the North St. Pancras charges.

'THE DAM BURSTS'

Nina Boyle broke with the Women's Social and Political Union before the outbreak of war, working instead with the Women's Freedom League, which rejected Emmeline and Christabel Pankhurst's more violent tactics. During the war Boyle pioneered women's police units, campaigned against sexual harassment and what would now be labelled institutional sexism, and worked in hospitals in the Balkans. A visit to revolutionary Russia accelerated her post-war move to the right.

22 March
A Woman Candidate for Keighley

Miss Nina Boyle, for many years one of the leaders of the Women's Freedom League, has announced her intention of contesting the

Keighley by-election. It is not clear whether women now have the right to stand for Parliament, but she wishes to settle the matter by a test case. It is probable that several other women will follow her example.

14 June
Women Students in Hospitals

It is only a few days since the London Hospital announced that henceforth positions on its staff were to be open alike to men and women. It added that this decision was due to the admirable work down in the hospital already by women surgeons and physicians temporarily attached to the staff. The hospital ... has now ... given a lead which all the other great general hospitals in London are bound to follow. It is removing the bar against which medical women have fought for so long and is opening its magnificent medical school to women students. I understand that at first only students in their final year will be admitted.

The voting system had not been reformed since 1885. The votes for women campaign, as well as the war, made reform inevitable. Forty per cent of men had been denied the vote, and all women. In 1917 a Speaker's conference effectively recommended votes for all men and most women, and a bill was passed at the end of that year. Women over the age of 30 won the vote. Desultory arguments about proportional representation and alternative votes helped drag the legislation on into the summer of 1918.

21 June
A Revolution in England

When the division on the principle of women's suffrage last night was won, seven to one in favour of the reform, it was clear that that great revolution had been carried in our easy British way, for it is indeed a revolution. The only doubt was whether any kind of counter-offensive could be successful on today's division ... It would have been very gratifying to carry the extension of the vote to women on the same terms as men with the assistance of the opponents of women's suffrage if that extension of the reform had had any real chance of becoming a law. But it had not, and in rejecting that and any other amendment the House of Commons has shown that it is steady and practical in its decision in favour of women's suffrage. It has not only voted in favour of the reform, but it has voted steadily in favour of that measure of the reform that is sure to be carried out. The fight is over, the victory is won. Supporters and opponents alike recognise, with joy or fear as the case may be, how great a battle has been decided and how changed is the future as the result of that decision. It must be a very great piece of news to telegraph to Russia.

Strange Times in the House

An incident typical of these strange times was the appearance of the Countess Markievicz with her sister, Miss Eva Gore-Booth, on the terrace of the House to-day eating strawberries and cream. The Countess Markievicz was one of the leaders of the Irish rebellion of Easter week, and was first condemned to death, the sentence being reduced to imprisonment. She had just been released under the amnesty.

Six months later, the Irish nationalist Countess Markievicz (née Gore-Booth) would be the first woman elected to the House of Commons. She refused to take her seat, sitting instead in the new Irish parliament, the Dáil Éireann.

'OUTBREAKS OF MISCONDUCT'

In June 1918 a letter from John W Graham of Manchester was published in the Manchester Guardian. *It concerned the imprisoned James Brightmore, a young solicitor's clerk from the City.*

30 June
The Case against Persecution

The letter written on the yellow covering of a cigarette packet was smuggled out to his family by a friendly soldier at considerable risk. Mr. Brightmore, adjudged to be a humbug and a shirker by local and appeal tribunals here, and similarly rejected by the Central Tribunal in its still more discriminating wisdom, has already proved his courage and honesty by eight months in prison. [...]

'The Pit, Shore Camp, Cleethorpes. Sunday, 24 June 1917. This is the best stuff I can find to write what may be my last letter. Everything has been taken off me, and I should not have this pencil but for chance. I was bullied horribly when I was tried, and sentenced to 28 days detention in solitary confinement – to be given raw rations and to cook my food for myself. This does not sound bad, but I have found the confinement was in a pit which started at the surface as three feet by two, and tapered off to two feet six inches by 15 inches. Water was struck, but they continued until it was ten feet. The bottom is full of water and I have to stand on two strips of wood all day long just above the water-line. There is no room to walk about, and sitting is impossible. The sun beats down, and through the long day there are only the walls of clay to look at. Already I am half mad.

'I have not heard from you since I came out of prison, but I know there are many letters waiting for me. I cannot therefore tell what may happen when I get to France, whether the death sentence is being exacted ... I hunger-struck for two days in the hole here, but found I was getting too weak to resist, and my brain, too, seemed to be giving under the strain.

'I wish I could only see your letters. I could be reassured, or know your wishes. As it is I feel sentenced to death, knowing that within a few days I shall be in France and shot. The fact that men are being sent to France at all is proof positive to me that the military authorities have captured the machine, and are able to do as they like with us.

'What have our friends been doing? It is nothing but cold-blooded murder to send men out into the trenches to be shot like dogs for disobedience. I am not afraid to die, but this suspense, this ignorance linked up with the torture of this pit have plunged me intro misery, despair, madness, almost insanity … The hardest thing is leaving you three dear ones behind, and the suffering and anxiety I am bringing upon you. All these weary months of imprisonment we have lived on hopefully. Now the cup is being dashed from our hands, and in liberty's name. (Here there follow other pathetic last words.) Goodbye.'

The friendly soldier adds: 'They would not listen to him. They cursed him and told him he was a soldier and they would do just as they wished. It is no use Brightmore making any complaints, because they have orders to take no notice. This torture is turning the man's brain.'

He estimates the depth of the hole as 12 feet. 'In fact, they were going deeper until they found water.' He adds: 'He had a blanket or two, and an oil sheet on the top,' which sounds as though he was kept there both night and day.

Have the military authorities captured the 'machine' of British citizenship? … This cruelty cannot promote loyalty in the army or win the war; and I think the England we have known cannot endure it for long.

WE Mashford from Hull also wrote on the subject of Brightmore.

5 July
The Case against Persecution

I visited James Brightmore in the detention camp at Cleethorpes, and I earnestly appeal to all lovers of fair play to demand an immediate, full and impartial inquiry. As a result of the treatment he has received he is physically and mentally broken, and ought to be in hospital, not detention. During the last five weeks I have visited various camps in this neighbourhood where conscientious objectors have been detained; I have personally seen the men who have been victimised ... and I have formed the opinion that the officers concerned are acting on instructions. The charges of brutality can be proved to the hilt, and in many more cases than have appeared in the press ... Surely the bitterest enemies of conscientious objectors cannot defend treatment of this kind.

The fate of James Brightmore is unknown.

On 2 July 1918 the Manchester Guardian *published a letter drawing attention to the plight of Clifford Allen, a pacifist who chaired the No-Conscription Fellowship during the war. He became Baron Allen in 1934 and died in 1939, having never fully recovered from his wartime imprisonment.*

10 July
Mr. Clifford Allen in Hospital

House of Commons: Mr. JH Whitehouse (L – Mid Lanark) called attention to the treatment of conscientious objectors, of whom he said there were hundreds in charge of the Home Secretary ... Amongst them was Mr. Clifford Allen who was in prison for the third time and was now undergoing a sentence of two years with hard labour. [...]

Lord H Cavendish-Bentinck (U – Nottingham) confessed he was not all easy in mind as regarded those conscientious objectors who had over and over again proved their sincerity and courage. [...]

Mr. CB Stanton (Lab. – Merthyr Tydfil) said the conscientious objectors were anti-British and pro-German to the hilt. He had no sympathy with them and would be glad if their advocates were treated similarly to the objectors themselves. [...]

Sir G Cave (Home Secretary) said ... with respect to conscientious objectors, the Act of Parliament provided machinery under which any man who had a conscientious objection to military service had a right to apply for exemption to the local tribunal. Many of the men referred to in the debate either made no such application, or, having made it, alleging that they had this conscientious objection, were not believed. [...]

He asked the House whether the Government had not shown great indulgence to these men who would not fight, whilst other men had to go to the front to defend the lives of these same objectors and their wives and relatives. If the Government went further in the direction of indulgence it would put a premium on similar offenders who were trying to make military and civic punishment alike impossible. Under the Home Office scheme they were asked to do work to which there could be no sort of conscientious objection, and the Government could not recede from their position. With the pleas put forward as to Allen ... he did not agree in the least. It was the invariable practice in our prisons to take care of the health of the prisoners. He was as reluctant as anyone could be that men should suffer in health because of their imprisonment. Every precaution was taken that there should be no want of humanity, and, as far as possible, to see that the health of prisoners did not suffer even from their own fault.

'NOTHING PECULIAR TO OURSELVES'

The transition from 1917 into 1918 had been accompanied by a flurry of declarations of war aims. The invitation to the western allies from the Bolsheviks in late November to enter into peace negotiations with all sides in the conflict was rejected amidst accusations of treachery. In Britain, in December 1917, the Labour party and the Trades Union

Congress (TUC) urged openness and reconciliation between the belligerents, a stance adopted by Prime Minister David Lloyd George on 5 January 1918 in a speech in London to the TUC. Three days later, President Woodrow Wilson spoke to the US Congress and offered a liberal vision, both to contrast with Russian socialism and in the vain hope of enticing revolutionary Russia back into the war. He outlined 14 points that spoke not just to his (discomforted) allies, but also to idealistic Americans and war-weary Europeans. The new French prime minister, Georges Clemenceau, noted that 'the Lord God only had ten'.

9 January
Mr. Wilson's Peace Programme

In his message to Congress yesterday President Wilson contrasted the war aims of the Entente and of the Central Empires and referred to the admirable candour with which Mr. Lloyd George had spoken for the people and Government of Great Britain. There was no confusion of counsel among the Allies, he said – no uncertainty of principle, no vagueness of detail. The only lack of fearless frankness, the only failure to make a definite statement of the objects of the war, lay with Germany and her allies.

After an eloquent reference to the 'thrilling and compelling voice of the Russian people,' who, prostrate and all but helpless, would yet yield neither in principle nor action, Mr. Wilson and the United States desired to assist them to attain their utmost hope of liberty and ordered peace. [...]

'The day of conquest and aggrandisement is gone,' [Mr. Wilson continued]. 'So is also the day of secret covenants entered into in the interest of particular governments, and likely at some unlooked-for moment to upset the peace of the world. It is this happy fact, now clear to the view of every public man whose thoughts do not still linger in an age that is dead and gone, which makes it possible for every nation whose purposes are consistent with justice and the peace of the world to avow now, or at any other time, the objects it has in view.

'We have entered this war because violations of rights had occurred which touched us to the quick and made the life of our own people impossible unless they were corrected and the world secured once for all against their recurrence. What we demand in this war, therefore, is nothing peculiar to ourselves. It is that the world may be made fit and safe to live in and particularly, that it be made safe for every peace-loving nation which, like our own, wishes to live its own life, determine its own institutions, and be assured of justice and fair dealing by other peoples of the world as against force and selfish aggression. All the peoples of the world are in effect partners in this interest, and, for our own part, we see very clearly that unless justice be done to others it will not be done to us.'

'BACKED BY GERMAN BAYONETS'

A German–Russian armistice had been signed on 15 December 1917, and negotiations for a peace settlement began at Brest-Litovsk, in what was then eastern Poland. The Bolsheviks, led by Leon Trotsky, were simultaneously attempting to make a deal with the German–Austro-Hungarian high command while stirring up revolution among rank-and-file soldiers. To the west a strike wave was sweeping Germany, and Austria-Hungary was teetering on collapse. With the talks deadlocked, Trotsky went back to Petrograd to consult his comrades. Some wanted to fight a revolutionary war against the Germans. Not Lenin, though: Russian soldiers, he said, had 'voted with their feet by running away'. Trotsky proclaimed, 'No war, no peace' – in other words, they could not agree a deal but there would be no renewal of hostilities. However, the Germans, calling the Bolsheviks' bluff, resumed their advance. On

3 March the Treaty of Brest-Litovsk was signed, marking Russia's exit from the war. The Russian civil war, meanwhile, had already begun.

18 March
Brest Peace Treaty Ratified, Ministerial Resignations

Petrograd, Saturday: The peace treaty with the Central Powers was ratified at midnight on 15 March after an open vote. M. Steinberg, the Commissary of Justice, announced that the Left Social Revolutionaries would refuse responsibility for the ratification, and would reserve the right to hinder the fulfilment of the terms of the treaty by all means in their power.

Moscow, Saturday Evening: It is expected that immediately after the final ratification of the peace treaty, a German committee of control will be set up here in Moscow and other large Russian cities to supervise the carrying out of the terms of the treaty, especially on its military and financial side.

Saturday Night: The Revolutionary Socialists of the Left have resigned from the Government, declaring that they will not lay down arms in spite of the ratification of the peace treaty. They declare, further, that they will organise an independent armed resistance.

The Bolshevik Resolution

Moscow, Saturday: The following resolution, proposed by the Bolshevik party, was adopted today by the Congress of Soviets: The Fourth Extraordinary Congress of Soviets sanctions the treaty of peace concluded by our representatives at Brest-Litovsk on 3 March 1918, and approves of the actions of the Central Committee and of the Council of the Peoples' Commissaries, who decided to sign a painful, forced and dishonouring peace. M. Lenin delivered a speech showing the necessity of signing the peace. He added: 'But history teaches us that after the dishonourable peace of Tilsit with Napoleon Germany rose again. We should accept this peace as a temporary respite and await the moment when the European proletariat will come to our assistance.'

The Bolsheviks, escaping the German advance, had moved the Russian capital back to Moscow. The Manchester Guardian's *M Philips Price – near starvation in Petrograd – arrived there in mid-April 1918 and resumed his reporting.*

1 June
Germans in Russia, Far-Reaching Schemes

Moscow, 16 May: The occupation by German troops of the Don coal basin is a sequel to the occupation of Ukraine, and in the plan of the Prussian military party. Thereby the industries of Muscovite Russia are doomed to starvation for lack of fuel, and a road opened across south-east Europe to the cotton stores of Central Asia and India. The realisation of this full economic annexation programme is clearly causing difficulties to the Central Powers. Not only has the internal conflict between the extreme military and the moderate bourgeois parties over eastern policy revived, but the material basis for the conquest of these vast territories is lacking.

The immense extension of the front is draining the reserves of manpower, for in the presence of hostile peasantry every provincial town must be garrisoned. The hopes built on the Ukrainian corn supplies have completely broken down: only three out of 60 million poods [an imperial Russian weight of 16.38 kilos] so far have been obtained for Germany and Austria. On the other hand, revolutionary disorders have occurred in the German fleet at Helsingfors and Reval. Several naval officers were murdered and forty sailors executed. There has also been trouble among the German prisoners of war at Kieff, who have been affected by Bolshevik propaganda. All this encouraged the Soviet Government in its superhuman task of opposing its external Imperialist enemies and at the same time creating a basis for the new structure of society at home.

Today's *Pravda* clearly hints that the Prussian military party, instead of finding a beehive full of honey in the east, has stirred a hornets' nest instead. [...]

In an interview the popular Commissioner of Foreign Affairs, M. Chitcherin, told me that the Soviet Government has overcome its internal enemies, and as the organ of millions of workers and peasants has become the sole authority capable of restoring order and putting down anarchy. 'For this reason alone,' he said, 'we should have expected the Allies to recognise us if they sincerely wish order to be established in Russia.'

Asked if the arrival of the German Ambassador Mirbach in Moscow meant that the Central Powers recognised the Soviet Government, M. Chitcherin said: 'Although Germany has taken formal steps to recognise us, in practice she shows no more inclination to establish sincere relations with us than the Allies. For instance, we expressed readiness to conclude peace with the Ukraine, and sent our representatives to Smolensk, but Germany prevents the Rada from sending their representatives to open negotiations.' (These negotiations have since begun.)

'Do you recognise the Rada as the sole authority in the Ukraine?' I asked.

M. Chitcherin replied: 'We recognise the Ukrainian Soviet as the true authority, expressing the will of the Ukrainian peasantry, and if we enter into negotiations with the Rada, that is because we are compelled, by *force majeure,* temporarily to have relations with a clique of intellectuals who are backed by German bayonets.'

Across Europe, the empires were crashing.

22 July
Ex-Tsar Shot, Local Soviet Decision

It is now announced by the Bolshevik Government that the ex-Tsar has been shot by the order of the Ural Regional Council, who state that they decided upon that course owing to the threat of the Czecho-Slovaks against the capital of the Red Ural, and their discovery of a counter-revolutionary plot in which the former monarch was involved. The following message has been transmitted through the wireless stations of the Russian Government:

'At the first session of the Central Executive Committee elected by the Fifth Congress of the Councils a message was made public received by direct wire from the Ural Regional Council concerning the shooting of the ex-Tsar Nicholas Romanoff. Recently Ekaterinburg, the capital of the Red Ural, was seriously threatened by the approach of the Czecho-Slovak bands. At the same time a counter-revolutionary conspiracy was discovered, having for its object the wresting of the tyrants from the hands of the Councils' authority by armed force. In view of this fact the Presidium of the Ural Regional Council decided to shoot the ex-Tsar Nicholas Romanoff. This decision was carried out on 16 June. The wife and son of Romanoff have been sent to a place of security. Documents concerning the conspiracy which we discovered have been forwarded to Moscow by a special messenger.

It had been recently decided to bring the ex-Tsar before a tribunal to be tried for his crimes against the people, and only later occurrences led to delay in adopting this course. The Presidency of the Central Executive Committee, after having discussed the circumstances which compelled the Ural Regional Council to take the decision to shoot Nicholas Romanoff, decided as follows:

'The Russian Executive Committee, in the persons of the Presidium, accept the decision of the Ural Regional Council as being regular. The Central Executive Committee has now at its disposal extremely important material and documents concerning the Nicholas Romanoff affair, his own diary which he kept almost to the last day, diaries of his wife and children, his correspondence, amongst which are letters by Gregory Rasputin to Romanoff and his family. All these materials will be examined and published in the near future.'

'DENSE MASSES WHICH NEVER FALTERED'

At the beginning of 1918 the allies were planning a western front offensive for 1919, when the French and British Commonwealth armies would be joined by the full power of the new American Expeditionary Force (AEF). In the east the Bolsheviks were being pressured into a harsh armistice with Germany, who had also shackled Romania into a humiliating peace. The allied war against the U-boats had been successful, thanks to the convoy system, and in the Arab world the Ottoman empire was falling – largely into the hands of the British.

Germany, meanwhile, was being torn apart by strikes, mutinies and confrontation. The country's military leadership and its political allies were effectively holding on for total victory and the humiliation of their enemies, while the Social Democrats sought to accommodate the vision of President Wilson.

Russia's defeat meant that many German troops were freed up to fight in the west, increasing the numbers on the western front from 3.25 million in late 1917 to more than 4 million by spring 1918. Hindenburg and Ludendorff aimed to shatter the western allies via a series of offensives. The first of these, 'Michael', began at 4.40am on Thursday 21 March. By the end of that day German artillery had fired more than 3 million rounds, of which more than 1 million were chemical, saturating the British trenches. The day was foggy, British forward communications collapsed and the General Gough's Fifth Army fell back, sustaining heavy losses, as German 'storm troops' broke through, heralding the beginning of a superbly organised, but ultimately doomed, campaign.

23 March
The Onslaught of Dense German Masses

Correspondents' Headquarters, Friday: The enemy made no infantry attack last night, but heavy fighting is now being resumed after the lifting of the fog this morning, and our troops are heavily engaged on the right of our line near St. Quentin. They were all German storm troops, among them the Guards, trained for many months past for this great assault. They were all, as our men tell me, in brand-new uniforms, as though they were entering the war zone for the first time, and they advanced over No Man's Land in dense masses which never faltered until they were shattered by our machine-gun fire, and they were followed by successive waves. 'They were like bees out of a hive,' said a young soldier who saw them crossing the open country within 400 yards of him. 'The more one shot down the more seemed come.'

It was a return to the old methods of the German army in the early days of the war at Mons and Le Cateau and afterwards at Verdun. Indeed, it is surprising that, so far as I can find for present reports, the enemy have introduced no novelty of attack, no new frightfulness, no tanks, no specially invented gas. He relied yesterday morning on the power of his artillery and the weight of his infantry assault. What wire was not cut by his guns was attacked by the snipers of his assault troops, standing in front of the wire, spaced by their officers and mown down by our fire. The supporting waves advanced over the bodies of their dead and wounded, and other masses came behind them, and the German commanders were ruthless in the way they sacrificed life in the hope of overwhelming our defence by sheer weight of numbers.

It was during the last hour of the bombardment that they poured out gas shells, and they continued to concentrate gas about our batteries and reserve trenches throughout the day, so that they filled the atmosphere with poisonous clouds. With this last weapon they failed to achieve the success for which they had hoped. Our men had been trained for many weeks, as I have described in other messages, to work for long stretches in their gas masks, and this was of priceless help to them yesterday, when they were put to a supreme test of endurance. Many of our men had their masks on for hours, and fought in them. One man told me that his battalion, on the left of the attack, wore them from four o'clock in the morning until midday.

The offensive punched faster and further into the allied lines – 40 miles by late March – than any since 1914. On 23 March, a Manchester Guardian *editorial suggested that, in the wake of their success in the east, the Germans could have put out serious peace feelers towards the western allies, but: 'The Germans have, for the present, come down in favour of a military decision of the war, and seek it, where they must, upon the west.'*

23 March
The Choice of Germany

We stand then at the opening of critical days where words avail little and all depends on the strength of lines, the supply of munitions and, above all, on the stout hearts of the multitudes who are greeting the glorious spring sunshine for the last time. Upon them our future is staked, and whatever might have been done in the past, we non-combatants can do nothing now but watch and wait the event. The best that we can do is constantly to bear in mind, when people use brave words about military triumph, that while we are talking they are fighting, suffering and dying, and that the time will someday come again when the manner of our talk may perhaps be the make-weight which decides whether still more of them are to suffer and to die. For the time being, however, what is said here matters little, what is done there everything. There are points in the progress of a war where discussion is possible and the attitude of Governments and civilians all-important. In this war there have been such points. Probably the last such point occurred at Christmas, when there was a momentary gleam of hope for a peace which would at least have discredited aggressive militarism. There was another and a better last July, before the final collapse of Russian military strength, and when the German Government, alarmed at the growth of internal discontent, was constrained to accept the Reichstag resolution about 'no annexations and no indemnities.' When such points are past and fighting begins again in grim earnest, what remains for non-combatants is, in the first place, to hold together and support the men who are bearing the brunt, and, in the second place, to prepare their minds for the next occasion which the turn of the wheel may bring, if perchance they may be able to make better use of the opportunity.

Between 23 and 25 March, 73 of the 127-kg shells from the Germans' new 238mm 'Paris Gun' flew into the stratosphere before plunging down on the French capital. The practical effects of the artillery weapon were limited, but the psychological effects were considerable.

25 March
Paris Bombarded – A Gun of 75-Miles Range
Paris, Saturday: The enemy has been firing on Paris with a long-range gun at intervals of a quarter of an hour since eight o'clock this morning. Some of the shells, which are of 240 millimetres (9.6 in.), have fallen in the capital and its suburbs. About ten people

have been killed and about fifteen wounded. Steps for counter-measures are being taken. According to the latest information, the long-range gun was firing at a range of 120 kilometres (about 75 miles). It has been located at a point about twelve kilometres beyond the French front.

Sunday: The following official report was issued at 10.30 this morning: 'The bombardment of Paris by a long-range gun firing from a distance of more than 120 kilometres against the capital began again at seven o'clock this morning. The explosions occurred at the same intervals as yesterday. Up to the present only a few casualties have been reported.'

Press Association War Special

Paris this morning has assumed the appearance of a city on the front. The bombardment is going on regularly every eight or nine minutes. By 10.30 seventeen shells were counted.

Later: The bombardment of Paris having ceased, the 'All Clear' was given at 3.35 this afternoon.

'A QUEER GOOD FRIDAY'

Easter was in March that year, and by Good Friday, 29 March, there was a fear that the last German offensives of the war would finally break the allies.

30 March

Our London Correspondence: One could feel the pulse of London clearly this afternoon at the great service of intercession in Hyde Park. The evening papers fluttering in the hands of people in the crowd contained something to lift the load of anxiety for a moment. Everyone who listened to the Bishop of London and the Nonconformist leaders felt that such a sentence as, 'the cause of liberty is even now trembling in the balance out in France' was no rhetoric ... Every kind of soldier was there, wounded and unwounded, but notably Dominion men, and the number of men with wound stripes on civilian sleeves was a thing significant of the fourth year of war. Unity in faith was expressed on the platform, where the Bishop with his crozier had for neighbours the chief men of many Free Churches and a contingent of the Salvation Army.

In the crowd there was unity of mood – that of quiet hopefulness in trial, and it contained all the social orders, from 'bus driver to Ministerial peers. There was none of that restless movement on the fringes so characteristic of the everyday Hyde Park gathering. The simplicity and optimistic pugnacity of the Bishop of London – he is in everything typical of London mentality at its best – was in keeping with the hour. Over the pale façades of Kensington lay a leaden sky with gleams of light in it, and spring was kindling the trees in the Park.

Good Friday in London

It has been a queer Good Friday in London. One does not remember ever before seeing the streets so full on a Good Friday as they were this afternoon, partly no doubt because travelling was restricted, but more because people liked to be near the centres of life and news. The kinemas and other places of amusement did not open till the evening. [...]

In the afternoon, numbers went to the many excellent sacred concerts, and the others roamed about the parks or main thoroughfares. Whitehall, where work was going on as usual in most Government offices, was full of leisurely groups, and so was the Strand, and everywhere one saw khaki or hospital blue. One noticed how many hundreds of girls went in groups unaccompanied by men, where in normal times couples would have been keeping holiday.

There was a good deal of traffic at some stations, but 'bus conductors commented on the fact that the usual 'long-riders' – people who ride from terminus to terminus and back again for the fun of it – were absent this year. It was not quite like Sunday. There was a holiday feeling in the air, and the girls who poured out of munition factories made sport during their lunch hour.

The Triumphant Wounded

The wounded men from the great battle arriving at Charing Cross this evening had a great reception from hundreds of holiday-makers who had gathered there at the sight of the waiting ambulance cars. As usual, there were many soldiers in the crowd, and parents with small, enthusiastic and very serious children, munition workers, young girls in holiday attire, and older women with anxious faces. They were all very quiet and subdued.

The first ambulance cars as they rolled out through the gates with their loads of stretcher cases were received in dead silence. Eager faces were thrust forward, handkerchiefs were waved, but there was no cheering and no flowers were thrown. 'Poor lads, poor lads; isn't it sad?' the women murmured. Then came the open cars filled with jolly soldiers, their arms or heads bandaged, but their eyes bright with pleasure as the crowd cheered and cheered and flung spring flowers at them. The 'poor lads' laughed outright as they bent their heads before the showers of daffodils, narcissus and violets. They waved their tea-cups at the people or put out their hands to be shaken. Most of them wore woollen caps – some few, straight from the battle, still wore their tin hats. It was odd to see a golden daffodil plucked this morning in an English field fall on a tin hat brown with the mud and dinted with the shrapnel of yesterday's fighting. An irresistible greeting of 'Old Bill, old Bill' came from all down the line as one car passed bearing a battered veteran whose walrus moustache bristled from the muffler wound all round his head and face.

Cheers from the Battlefield

The joviality of the heroes had altogether changed the attitude of the crowds, who now cheered the stretcher cases too. They were not to be checked even by the warning hand put up by one driver, who came down the lane at a snail's pace, evidently in charge of someone badly broken. The line broke and people ran after the car to throw their tribute of flowers into it. Many of the stretcher cases waved their hands in response, and the crowd cheered again as they peered into the depths of one car and saw a hand seize a bunch of yellow flowers and then wave them in response. The flower girls passing up and down the line were doing a roaring trade, but were flinging their wares at the soldiers as lavishly as any.

'THE SUPREME MOMENTS OF OUR DESTINY'

On 5 April the 'Michael' offensive was ended. The Germans had hoped to take Amiens, divide the French and British armies and – at the most optimistic – reach the Channel. They had not managed to do so, but General Ludendorff (and British politicians) viewed the operation as a German success.

Four days later the Germans, switching to the north, launched the 'Georgette' offensive in Flanders and by 12 April seemed poised to take the town of Hazebrouck and then break through to Dunkirk – and the Channel. On Thursday 11 April 1918, Sir Douglas Haig made a famous declaration.

13 April
A Critical Moment, Haig's Order – 'Fight to the Last Man'

A Special Order to Every British Soldier: The following special order of the day has been issued by Sir Douglas Haig: 'To all ranks of the British army in France and Flanders: Three weeks ago to-day the enemy began his terrific attacks against us on a fifty-mile front. His objects are to separate us from the French, to take the Channel ports, and destroy the British army. In spite of throwing already 106 divisions into the battle and enduring the most reckless sacrifice of human life, he had as yet made little progress towards his goals. We owe this to the determined fighting and self-sacrifice of our troops. Words fail me to express the admiration which I feel for the splendid resistance offered by all ranks of our army under the most trying circumstances.

'Many amongst us now are tired. To those I would say that the victory will belong to the side which holds out the longest. The French army is moving rapidly and in great force to our support. There is no other course open to us but to fight it out.

'Every position must be held to the last man. There must be no retirement. With our backs to the wall and believing in the justice of our cause each one of us must fight to the end. The safety of our homes and the freedom of mankind depend alike upon the conduct of each one of us at this critical moment.'

A Task for Heroes; The Battle Story

Correspondents' Headquarters, Friday Night: Our troops, fighting with supreme heroism, but weighted down at some points by greater numbers, have had to give some more ground on the northern battlefield between La Bassée and the plain of Flanders. No armies have ever been called on to endure more violent blows or attempt a more difficult task than those now supporting our altered but still unbroken front. They have fallen back doggedly, making the Sixth German Army pay dearly in lives for each mile of ground thus relinquished, and although, as I write this message, the situation we face is a difficult one, there is no faltering, no fear of defeat. There have been darker hours in the history of our troops in Flanders. They came again into the sunshine, and they know as they give battle against great odds on this beautiful spring day that they will not be vanquished. They are fighting steadily, coolly, unselfishly, with no other though as they lie in the stricken fields of France than of the honour of Britain. They are splendid, simply splendid.

Highlanders' Fine Stand: The Highlanders of the 51st had to fight a force nearly four times as strong. They broke down attacks behind Vielle Chapelle with grim resolution, counter-attacked on their own, took back lost posts, and kept the line intact through all the hammer blows of the German storm troops. The enemy tried vainly to split the division into the isolated groups of men. Some were cut off, but they managed to find their way back, fighting as they went. The flat ground gave the Highlanders little cover. They had to lie in ditches, sometimes half-filled with foul water, and to scramble through the beds of narrow streams to work their machine-guns from fragments of broken walls, even under cover of derelict barges lying against the grassy banks. All the while the German guns plastered their line with shells of every calibre. The heavies made themselves felt from early morning, and throughout the day fresh batteries came into action.

In the Lancashire Labyrinth: The English troops, hanging no less resolutely to their portion of the wide front, fought against as great odds, and I hope it will soon be possible to reveal their identity as well. The Lancashire battalions on the right have had one marked advantage over the enemy; they know every inch of the ground around Givenchy, and he does not. The labyrinth of trenches is as familiar to the garrison as are the back streets of Manchester or

Liverpool. They crept down alleyways and round corners, surprising groups of Germans and cutting them off. In one place alone they took 300 prisoners.

Our London Correspondence, Friday Night: Although events seemed to go on as usual – theatres and music-halls well filled and shops busy, and no gathering with any special bearing on the war except today's fateful meeting of Parliament – it did not require much scrutiny to observe the change that has come over the look of people. The grimness of the war has at last reflected itself in people's eyes in London, but not till they see to-morrow Sir D Haig's message to his troops will the nation understand that we are at one of the supreme moments of our destiny. The men at the front are doing their part, giving their lives without a stint. There is no fear that the people at home will fail to do their little part in giving easy things like confidence. The danger is rather that we will take all this bravery and suffering for granted, and not give our brains and our work to help them.

'Georgette' was shut down at the end of April. The Germans had made gains, but not a breakthrough. And the greater their losses – 86,000 casualties in the offensive, while the British suffered 82,000 and the French 30,000 – the more intense was the pressure on an army running out of time. On 27 May the third German offensive, 'Blücher', which was aimed at the French interior and towards Paris, met with early, stunning success. But it also meant an encounter with a new enemy.

29 May
Americans Storm a Village

To the west of Montdidier (on the Avre, south of the Somme) the American troops, supported by our tanks, captured brilliantly on a front of two kilometres the salient of Cantigny as well as the village, which had been strongly organised by the Germans. One hundred and seventy prisoners and some material remained in the hands of the Americans. In the afternoon, counter-attacks of the Germans made against Cantigny completely failed. The artillery fighting continues very actively on the east bank of the Meuse and at several points of the Lorraine front. Two strong enemy surprise attacks in the regions of Veilo and Embermesnil were repulsed after lively fighting.

The American Expeditionary Force emerged on the western front in late May and early June, notably in the bloody victory at Belleau Wood on 6 June. Their presence set the US off on the path to global super power.

The Manchester Guardian *soon commented on the AEF's performance in an editorial.*

5 June
The Battle

The ninth day of the offensive finds the Germans still making a little progress, but slowly and painfully, and only on restricted sections of the front between the Oise and the Marne. On the northern section between the Oise and the Aisne they have not gained ground, and the French have kept them both from penetrating the very important forest of Villers-Cotterets on its eastern side and from pushing farther their effort to get round it on the south by way of the valley of the Oureq. The areas in which the French have lost a little ground are to the south of the Oureq, where American troops seem to have distinguished themselves as finely as they did the other day at Cantigny in the Amiens region, and in the angle west of Soissons.

For 12 weeks from late May, the French and Germans battled across Champagne. On 15 July the Germans staged a new offensive, but General Philippe Pétain's 'defence in depth' left the Germans to advance into a void, and three days later French, Moroccan, Senegalese and American troops counter-attacked in what became the second battle of the Marne. The Germans were forced to fall back to the River Aisne. General Ludendorff, who had been planning 'Hagen', another offensive against the British in Flanders, instead turned his ire on his long-time ally and superior Field Marshal Hindenburg.

'UP TO MY NECK IN WATER'

The unrestricted U-boat campaign against allied shipping, which had commenced in February 1917, inflicted serious damage, but it failed in its aim of crippling Britain. In March 1918, James Bone, the London editor of the Manchester Guardian, *dug into the records.*

18 March
The Seaman and the Submarines

'Master's reason for abandoning his ship was that she sank under him.' After a strange, long day in the quiet place where the records of the submarine side of the war are kept, turning over folio after folio of these testaments, with all their accompanying documents of official confirmation and comment, from the stories of survivors to the acknowledgements of the shipping companies and the latest telegrams from hospitals or sailors' homes, this is the passage that writes itself hardest in one's mind, for it is typical of most of those histories and of the men who tell them.

The documents deal with all kinds of ships, from big liners down to little topsail schooners loaded with china clay; from masters that report, 'One of the boats with twenty-four men is still missing,' to the master that reports that half his crew is missing, as the deck hand and boy were washed overboard in the explosion. These records are short and very realistic, and so is the official comment on them. Here you see how the British merchant sailors really behave under the ugliest and strangest tests of German warfare. They come through the scrutiny according to established tradition. Old Hakluyt would recognise them today as the same men who sailed and dared in his 'Voyages.'

There are a few instances where the men lose heart. 'Seven men managed to reach the upturned lifeboat, but one of these, the third officer, took his lifebelt off, saying he was going to finish it and slid off the top of the boat, and was not seen again.' In nearly every case the master reports: 'All ship's company behaved with great coolness, there being no confusion,' or 'Ship's company behaved excellently.' The narratives bear out how inadequate these terms were. One ship, which went down in about three minutes, had this report: 'Seaman Langfear attempted to get aft to his gun after the ship was struck but only got the stern as the ship sank, and he was picked up by the master's boat.'

The landsman, looking into these reports of sinking ships, smashed lifeboats, with submarines still firing, boilers exploding, and high seas running, all related in unimpassioned language, usually as short and verbal as if men were shouting their words out of the waters, cannot re-create the scene, except in glimpse like this: 'I then tried to go on aft, but was stopped by the water, so returned and got light to enable crew who were aft to see the way. Found one of the crew who said his leg was broken, placed him on hatch on boat deck, telling him that he must look out for himself, as I could do no more, as by that time I was up to my neck in water.' The name of the seaman who wrote this was W Cummings. Later he says: 'Just managed to seize the davit guy and was carried down with the ship, and whilst under the water I heard the boilers explode.' [...]

In these reports the commanders and crews of the German submarines are seen face to face, and their actions and words are set down quite without prejudice, credit always being given them for any decent thing they did. Despite the confusion you expect from men at the moment their lives were in the balance, our seamen seem to have scrutinised them closely and were able to give particular details of them. Again and again the submarine crews are described as 'very depressed' or 'very nervous.' Here is one description: 'Master and crew all agree and were very much struck by the pallid appearance of the officers and crew of the submarine and by their nervous and excited manner. The captain of the submarine was continually urging haste, and the officer who was placing the bombs could hardly hold them from the condition of nervous tension in which he appeared to be.'

One of the crew who had lived long in England, speaking to the boat's crew, 'cursed the war and wished it was over. He said it was not their fault, and they had to do their duty, adding, "You won't believe it but it's true."' [...]

In the middle of a prosaic account of a Mediterranean torpedoing this glimpse of horror is given: 'The firemen went mad in the boat and jumped overboard after six days in boat, and one body died from exposure in [the] third officer's boat.' One submarine commander, after bringing the men alongside, told them that they could go, and he hoped that they would meet again.

'INTERN THEM ALL!'

On 16 July, Ludendorff launched what turned out to be his final offensive, near Reims in the Champagne country. It failed, and the French counter-attacked. Yet nine days later Sir Henry Wilson, chief of the imperial general staff, suggested that the key battle of the war was likely to be fought one year hence. He was not alone; few in the military believed that the allies could win the war in 1918. Domestically, this gloomy prospect inspired xenophobes at a time when Bolsheviks had joined 'slackers', 'conchies' and 'Huns' in right-wing demonology, and organisations like the British Workers League – originating in a right-wing breakaway from the British Socialist party – could attract support. Sir Edward Pryce-Jones was a Conservative MP, James Hogge a Liberal MP and George Cave was home secretary. Arthur Henderson led the wartime Labour party, while Ben Tillet, Will Thorne and James O'Grady were prominent socialists, trade unionists, sometime MPs – and supporters of the war.

15 July
Week-End Eloquence

Our London Correspondence: There had been a notable outpouring of war eloquence at open-air demonstrations this weekend. The bad weather thinned some of the audiences but did not damp the fiery patriotism which was the note of most of the speeches. The 'intern them all' demonstration in Trafalgar Square yesterday displayed the union of leaders so diverse as Mr. Rudyard Kipling, Mr. Harry Lauder and the Bishop of Birmingham in support of a drastic anti-alien policy. Nothing but the internment of all aliens, naturalised or unnaturalised, would satisfy the meeting. The Government scheme was 'futile and useless,' and Sir E Pryce Jones, who ventured the mild remark that Sir George Cave seemed to have met most of the demand, was shouted down. There is undoubtedly, as Mr. Lloyd George has said, a strong public feeling on this subject just now. It was expressed again at Hyde Park meeting of the silver-badge men – the discharged and the demobilised soldiers – who went to the Park carrying banners inscribed with the popular catch-words. Mr. Hogge earned the admiration of the gathering by his claim to have secured the internment of a German whom he found – of all places – in the smoking-room of the House of Commons.

To-day there were two big pro-war Labour demonstrations. The Zouave Band collected a big crowd in Hyde Park for the British Workers' League. A peace-by-negotiation meeting announced to take place in the Park was stopped by the authorities. There was a great deal of spirited denunciation of negotiation, and Mr. Arthur Henderson's announcement of the war aims of German and neutral Socialists was treated with contempt and suspicion. In the afternoon Mr. Ben Tillet, Mr. O'Grady and Mr. Will Thorne carried on the campaign in Trafalgar Square.

The week-end speeches were well-meaning and vigorous; but cannot be said to have helped the great controversy of the day or bring any fresh lights.

'THE ENDURANCE AND THE DASH'

By June various attempts at liberalisation by Emperor Karl of Austria, (last) ruler of the Austro-Hungarian empire, had failed, as had a disastrous peace feeler sent out to the allies. In an attempt to stave off moves for national self-determination within his empire he put forward plans for a confederation, but it was too late. Within his domains there had been strikes, mutinies, soviets, transport chaos and food shortages, and within the central powers alliance the tottering empire had been subordinated to Germany. Ironically, Austro-Hungary's objectives of 1914 appeared to have been achieved: Serbia, Romania and Russia were all apparently vanquished.

Now the Germans had launched their major western offensives, they insisted on solidarity from Austria-Hungary. The imperial army had numbers, but lacked food and logistics, and it was up against an Italian army that was far better led, equipped and fed. The Italians were also operating with French and British divisions, and had – thanks to the British – air superiority. The battle of the Piave began on 13 June 1918.

19 June
The Battle in Italy

Our London Correspondence, Tuesday Night: The view held in informed Italian quarters ... is, as it was put to me tonight, that 'things are not only going well – they are going better.' The counter-attacks are growing stronger and stronger, and today's news shows that the Austrians are contained in the shallow advances, and are already largely on the defensive. [...]

They have produced no surprises. Gas and smoke were used in the Montello attack, but gas was also used in some quantity by the Italians. There seem to have been no tanks and no new gun or methods. The Italian artillery is being warmly praised, and their artillery concentrations have been remarkably well placed, showing the excellence of the information from the Allied air service.

The attack on the Montello is led by the Archduke Joseph, who is in command of the Sixth Austrian Army. It has been the privilege of the Eleventh Austrian Army to fail on the Grappa. Eighteen divisions up to yesterday have been located in the fighting line on the mountainous sector, while on the Piave twelve have been actually fighting and seven held in reserve. [...]

The first Austrian contingents that tried to reach the Montello positions by crossing the Piave at the two narrowest points were thrown back into the stream. The following waves, protected by smoke-screens, succeeded in establishing themselves on the steep north-eastern corner of the ridge, where they are contained by the Italian counter-attacks, which are growing in intensity and are made in ever bigger scale. [...]

In the mountains the tactical initiative seems to have passed to the Allies, and new positions have been won on the Mount Spinoncia. The correspondents of Italian papers at the front warmly praise the endurance and the dash of the British and French contingents grouped with the Sixth Italian Armies.

Ten days after it started, the battle ended. It was the last attack that Austria-Hungary would launch. By late September, Bulgaria, the central powers' Balkan ally, had been defeated and so had the Turkish army in Palestine. In October Austria-Hungary was defeated by the Italians, as the empire dissolved and its disparate nationalities moved to set up their own states. The emperor did not abdicate but died, in exile in Madeira, in 1922.

'AN EXCEEDINGLY ABLE GENERAL'

In October 1917 British imperial soldiers – largely South Africans and Nigerians – confronted the far smaller force of the legendary General Paul von Lettow-Vorbeck, at the battle of Mahiwa in east Africa. As usual von Lettow-Vorbeck won, but his losses affected his military capacity. Yet he marched on, first taking his African and German soldiers into what is now Mozambique.

6 September
Chasing von Lettow

Von Lettow, an exceedingly able general, has done wonders in staving off disaster. He appears on this occasion to have put his head in a hornets' nest. His method has been to keep himself supplied by raiding Portuguese posts. A short time ago he attacked a post at Lioma, which turned out to be British. He was driven away, and, changing his course from northwards to southwards he soon ran into another of our columns, by which he was severely handled. He then returned to the west, where there was a third British force waiting for him, and once more he was turned back and heavily defeated. As the result of these encounters he has lost about twenty-five of his small white army and between 300 and 400 askaris and porters, and – what is even more important to him – many thousands of rounds in a north-easterly direction towards the Lurio River, with the Allies at his heels. His army is now reduced to something less than 200 Germans and 200 blacks, but we have by no means finished with him yet.

Indeed not. Between March 1916 and August 1918, the troops of von Lettow-Vorbeck marched in, and out, of German east Africa (Tanzania), Portuguese east Africa (Mozambique) and northern Rhodesia (Zambia). It was there that on 25 November 1918, a fortnight after the end of the European war, he and 154 other Germans surrendered at Abercorn (now Mbala). But the 'Hindenburg of Africa' had difficulty in believing the German empire had fallen, and the war was lost.

'THE DASH AND VIGOUR OF THEIR ATTACKS'

On 26 July, as the second battle of the Marne continued, Ferdinand Foch, the French generalissimo of allied forces, ordered a counter-offensive. The armies of the allies had finally perfected the art of mixing infantry, armour and artillery. On Thursday 8 August, General Sir Henry Rawlinson's Fourth Army commenced the attack. The allied force included the Canadian and Australian corps, an American division and, to the south, the French First Army. Thanks to the four-month-old Royal Air Force the allies had air superiority, and thanks to excellent planning they also had surprise on their side. The battle of Amiens was the pivot on which the war turned. The allies advanced four miles, and the initiative finally slipped from the Germans' hands.

9 August
Allies Surprise Blow – Big Advance on the Amiens Front, Cavalry Break through the German Lines

Under the command of Sir Douglas Haig, a British and a French army yesterday morning attacked on a front of about fifteen miles on both sides of the Somme. On the south side the allies broke through the German positions on a wide front, and by the latest official news had advanced from four to about seven miles, taking by three in the afternoon over 100 guns and 7,000 prisoners. The advance covers over sixty square miles and creates a salient in the direction of Péronne, threatening extensive German positions to the south.

Sir Douglas Haig's Reports

Thursday, 10.15am: At dawn this morning the British Fourth Army and the French First Army, under the command of Field Marshal Sir Douglas Haig, attacked on a wide front east and south-east of Amiens. First reports indicate that the attack is progressing satisfactorily.

Thursday, 8.35pm: The operations commenced this morning on the Amiens front by the French First Army, under the command of General Debeney, and the British Fourth Army, under the command of General Sir Henry Rawlinson, are proceeding successfully. The assembly of the Allied troops was completed under the cover of night unnoticed by the enemy. At the hour of the assault French, Canadian, Australian and English divisions, assisted by a large number of British tanks, stormed the Germans on a front of over 20 miles from the Avre River, at Braches, to the neighbourhood of Morlancourt. The enemy was taken by surprise, and at all points the Allied troops made rapid progress. At an early hour our first objectives had been reached on the whole front of attack.

During the morning the advance of the Allied infantry continued, actively assisted by British cavalry, light tanks, and motor machine-gun batteries. The resistance of the German divisions in line was overcome at certain points after sharp fighting, and many prisoners and a number of guns were captured by our troops.

French troops, attacking with great gallantry, crossed the Avre River, and despite the enemy's opposition carried the hostile defences.

North of the Somme the greater part of our final objectives were gained before noon, but in the neighbourhood of Chipilly and south of Morlancourt parties of the enemy observed a prolonged resistance. In both localities fighting was heavy, but ultimately our troops broke down the opposition of the German infantry and gained their objectives.

South of the Somme the gallantry of the Allied infantry and the dash and vigour of their attacks had gained during the afternoon the final objectives for the day practically the whole battlefront. Assisted by our light tanks and armoured cars, the cavalry passed through the infantry and beyond our objectives, riding down German transport and limbers in their retreat, surrounding the capturing villages, and taking many prisoners.

A Wonderful Rush, Surprise and Tanks

British Army, Thursday: At 4.20 this morning the British launched an offensive on a large scale for the first time this year ... The front of the British troops' attack extended from the region of Marlancourt, between the Ancre and the Somme, to where our extreme right rests on the French. Below this, the French continued the battle for some miles down their line. The French on our right started to advance simultaneously with ourselves, but halted after carrying the German front line, according to scheme, and went forward again about forty minutes later. They too have achieved great success. The attack will undoubtedly rank as a great campaign battle. I think I may say that it has exceeded our expectations in the rapidity and completeness with which everything we started to accomplish has been attained. The strategic advantage gained by this magnificent stroke is too great to be fully realised as yet, when the smoke is still rolling over the many square miles of recovered territory. The prisoners are for the most part of a good type, but are very depressed at the news of all that has been happening during the past three weeks. They had heard ominous rumours and feared that things were not all well, but were certainly not prepared for the startling truth.

The New Allied Offensive

Our London Correspondence, Thursday Night: The new great battle, which began this morning at dawn east of Amiens … has achieved splendid results on the first day.

An officer who knows this region intimately tells me that the advance of our front line in a few hours from east of Villers – Bretonneaux as far as Framerville, more than half way to Péronne – constitutes the most remarkable achievement of the day. This movement is a definite breakthrough, and … this flat region of the Santerre plateau is eminently adapted to a war of movement, and does not afford many advantages for an inferior force on the defensive.

It is true that the Germans were able to save their wings to some extent by their late withdrawals on the Ancre and the Avre. But their centre remained badly exposed, and there they seem to have been quite surprised, with the result that their Santerre defences have now completely gone to pieces.

The British had the honour to fight on the main part of the new battle-front and the good fortune to score the greatest success. Their deep penetration into the enemy centre, by which the German salient towards Amiens has been turned into a pocket in the direction of Péronne, will before long exert a great influence on those enemy positions which have held out better farther north and farther south. It is considered here that this highly successful thrust along the Amiens–Péronne road is likely to alter the aspect of the whole front in Picardy from Albert to Montdidier.

As at the Marne, the German army had lost ground, but what particularly concerned its command was a collapse in discipline, and the wave of surrenders among the exhausted and demoralised soldiers. It was, wrote Ludendorff in his diary, the 'black day of the German army'.

10 August
The German Flight

British Army, Friday Night: It is a great victory. The 2nd German Army has suffered a humiliating reverse, the extent of which, even yet, cannot be fully estimated, and much of its organisation which covered the open country before Amiens has been, for the moment at least, practically destroyed. I do not think that war has ever yielded such extraordinary stories of rout and the confusion of trained soldiers. General von der Marwitz no longer has Amiens by the throat. It is doubtful whether he has any kind of grip on his own bewildered men. [...]

The British flag was hoisted on the headquarters of the 11th Corps (commanded by General Kuhne) by noon, and the tanks carried their own flag to victory as well. Germans could be seen streaming east on all the roads, pressing across the Somme bridges. At Brie (a few miles south of Péronne) they burned depots, blew up dumps and tried to bombard others. Despite the unorganised attempts at destruction, an enormous amount of stores and a large number of guns of all kinds had to be left to us, and the tank crew, who came back looking like sweeps, steadily added to the tale of success. [...]

The prisoners varied, as usual, both in physique and attitude. I saw over 3,500 of them in one great corps cage this morning – the first sweepings from the tanks and armoured-car drive south of the Somme. There were old and young men, sullen men and contented boys, strangely dilapidated and shabby in their patched uniforms and down-at-heel boots. Some of them wore ill-fitting trousers of dirty brown sacking, evidence of shortage of cloth, and not a few were bareheaded or wearing only a bandana handkerchief knotted over their shaven skulls, for they had been snatched out of funk-holes or village-billets without time to pick up their headgear, and one man came into captivity in carpet slippers.

'YOU COULD NOT STEP THERE FOR DEAD MEN'

By September the British Expeditionary Force and, to the south, the French and the Americans were advancing, as the Germans fell back to the Hindenburg Line. By the end of the month the allies, searching for breakthroughs, had arrived on the St Quentin canal. Between 26 and 29 September, along a five-and-a-half mile front, some 1,600 guns fired 750,000 shells weighing more than 17,000 tons. On Sunday 29 September, the breach was made and the battle of St Quentin, which involved British, Australian and American troops, was won.

4 October
Looking down on Lille, Midlanders Dash over the Water Line
British Army, Thursday: The story of the 46th Division's first dash across the canal is so extraordinary that I must return to it. Before going into the line these Midlanders were practised in swimming in lifebelts in the Somme ... In some places the canal is

full of water; in others it is shallower, but waist-deep in thick mud. Farther along it disappears into a tunnel like, but smaller than, the more famous stretch to the north.

In the smoky mist the men, armed with these lifebelts, dashed for the banks and threw themselves in. One corporal saw before him an undestroyed bridge defended by a machine gun on the near side, as well as swept by machine guns from the opposite side. He vowed to cross that bridge or die, and as a preface threw himself on the two machine-gunners on the near side and destroyed them in a hand-to-hand duel. Then he ran the gauntlet of the bullets swishing across our side of the bridge, and met, standing across the far side, three engineers, modern Horatii, keeping the bridge and preparing to blow it up. They went down before him as had the two machine gunners, and, the guardians gone, this thoughtful corporal at once cut the mines, which fell harmlessly into the water. [...]

Once across the canal the men went forward on a succession of new and yet stranger adventures. The most precious prize was to be the tunnel, and it more than fulfilled hopes. Both ends were seized, and then came the question of how its inmates were to be ferreted out.

A German piece of ordnance ... was fired down one end. Before the intolerable detonation has ceased echoing the inhabitants began to bolt. The stream seemed unending, and its final total came to exactly a quarter of the final sum of prisoners taken by the division, and that was 4,000. [...]

Six or seven tanks had crossed the canal elsewhere, and, making a detour, were to come to the help of the infantry. But they came under the observation of three enemy guns well posted on a flanking hill, and were under direct fire, so the infantry came to the help of the tanks, and, taking the only alternative, rushed the guns face to face.

The gunners stuck to their work and fired point blank at the charging Midlanders, but nothing stopped their impetus.

The gunners were bayoneted at their guns, which are among our captures. […]

As the Midlanders went forward they came upon as terrible a picture as modern war can give of artillery fire under modern conditions of density. Our barrage had descended on a force of the enemy who were apparently being assembled for a counter-attack, and had virtually annihilated them. 'You could not step there for dead men.'

To the north the Canadians had crossed the Canal du Nord, and the British and Belgians were advancing across Flanders. The fighting continued, but, within Germany, society was in crisis.

'BOWING TO FATE'

In late October 1918 Prince Max of Baden, the Kaiser's cousin, headed a new, short-lived German government determined to make peace. Erich von Ludendorff was sacked, and Paul von Hindenburg explained that the war must end because 'every day's delay will cost thousands of brave soldiers their lives'. On 30 October Turkey signed an armistice, and the collapsing Austria-Hungary was also seeking a peace deal. On 9 November Max unilaterally announced the abdication of the Kaiser – Emperor Wilhelm II was in Spa, Belgium, at the time and was informed of this by phone. The alternative, Max explained, was revolution and anarchy.

9 November
Germany Must Give Up the Struggle; Prince Max's Address – Lost Belief in 'Right of Might'
The Imperial Chancellor has issued the following proclamation to Germans abroad:

'In these hard days many of you who, living outside the boundaries of the German Fatherland, are surrounded by hatred and malicious rejoicing, will be heavy-hearted. Do not abandon your trust in the German people. Our soldiers have fought heroically to the last as no other army has ever fought. The homeland has shown an unheard-of power of endurance of suffering.

'Forsaken in the fifth year by its allies, the German people could no longer carry on the struggle against the growing superiority of its enemies. The victory for which many hoped has not been granted to us, but the German people has won a greater victory, for it has conquered itself and its belief in the right of might.

'From this victory we will draw for the hard times which are before us new strength, on which you too can build. From those of you who, during the cruel years of war have struggled and suffered for your German Fatherland, the new Germany will not withhold its thanks. So far as it lies in the power of the German Government and German people to mitigate the sufferings of this war and its consequences, its care will be equally for the Germans abroad as for the Germans in the homeland.'

At noon on Thursday 7 November, the German delegation to negotiate the armistice had left Spa. Two of the five cars crashed in the pouring rain as the convoy sped past retreating troops. At almost midnight, the party passed into French-held territory.

9 November
The Armistice Meeting; Severity of the Terms

Paris, Friday: The German delegates arrived this morning at the Headquarters of Marshall Foch and formally requested an armistice. The text of the Allies' terms were read to them, after which it was handed to them. The delegates asked for a provisional suspension of hostilities which was refused. The enemy has been given seventy-two hours in which to reply.

The German delegates have established contact with Marshall Foch and Admiral Wemyss. They expressed astonishment at the severity of the terms of our armistice and although fully empowered to treat asked to be allowed to communicate with Berlin. The general attitude was that they would have to bow to fate.

The radical tide that had swept over Germany by autumn 1918 brought the right-wing Social Democrat Friedrich Ebert to power – alongside figures far to his left. Revolution was anathema to Ebert, who allied himself to conservative – and proto-fascist – forces. Two key revolutionary figures were Karl Liebknecht and Rosa Luxemburg, Marxist socialists who had opposed the war from the outset. They founded the revolutionary Spartacus League, which in 1919 became the Communist party of Germany. On 9 November 1918 Liebknecht declared the 'free socialist republic' in Berlin.

11 November
Red Flag over Royal Palace

Copenhagen, Sunday: A telegram from Berlin states that the Workmen's and Soldiers' Council has issued the following announcement: 'The president of the police as well as the chief command is in our hands' … [signed] Karl Liebknecht.

The red banner has been hoisted on the Royal Palace, and a red flag is waving from the Brandenburg Gate.

'PROMPT ISOLATION'

As a chaotic peace spread across Europe, so did the Spanish flu pandemic, which is thought to have killed between 50 and 100 million worldwide. It had been in England since October 1918. Indeed, post-armistice, David Lloyd George was confined to bed for 10 days at Manchester Town Hall. An unsung hero of the disaster was James Niven, the medical officer of health for Manchester.

11 November
The Influenza: Preventative Measures

Dr. Niven has issued a statement in which he reviews and comments upon the measures which have been advocated to prevent the spread of influenza. The general closure of schools in large towns he regards as of doubtful value, though there are many instances in which individual schools should be closed. He approves of the complete stoppage of kinema houses, and the frequent cleansing and flushing with air of other places of public entertainment; but he points out that the congregation of people in these places is a small factor in the spread of the disease when compared with the effects of the overcrowding of trains and trams and the propagation of the disease in factories, workshops and offices. Prompt isolation of persons attacked is valuable. As to prophylactic injections, Dr. Niven thinks they might be tried if advised by the medical attendant in the case of those nursing the sick but it is not wise to rely on them exclusively. He approves the recommendation of the Committee of the Académie de Médecine of Paris that persons nursing cases of influenza should wear face masks of gauze. With regard to the use of mouth and nose washes recommended by the Local Government Board, he sees no objection to it, provided it is carried out under medical advice. The mouth wash and gargle recommended by the French committee is made by adding about 20 drops of chlorinated soda to a glass of warm water. For the nose an ointment of 1 per cent of resorcin in vaseline is suggested.

'A GIFT TO ALL'

The 11th day of the 11th month brought the ceasefire, and the following day, this editorial. Herbert Hoover was head of the American relief administration – he would, of course, become president of the United States in 1929.

12 November
The Great Day

This is the great day – the great day of Peace, hoped for, longed for, at times appearing remote, almost unattainable, yet never despaired of, resolutely pursued, at last conquered. Now it is ours, and not ours only: it is the world's, it is for our enemies no less than for ourselves; it is like the rain from Heaven, it is a gift to all. In name it is not peace but only the cessation of arms, but the arms, once laid down, will not be taken up again; the fighting is over, the slaughter is over; the armies may still stand on guard, and some of them must continue so to stand till the peace itself is signed, but their work is done. Recruiting has stopped. The vast machine of military munitioning may continue to work for a little, as it were by force of habit, but with fast-diminishing energy and with no serious purpose before it except that of bringing itself, as soon as possible and with as little injury as possible to the interests of the millions of men and women it has absorbed, to a complete standstill. Soon – as soon as possible – the men of the armies will begin to return, not for the present in masses, but rather by industries in prearranged order, with preference, no doubt, at the same time for the war-worn men, for those who for three years or four years have borne the heat and burden of the day, who have been wounded and returned to the fighting line, who at length have earned, if any men have earned, relief from the burden and the weariness of the long-drawn strife. Thus will hope come to many homes, and one by one at first and in ever-growing stream the men who have saved England, who have saved the world, will return to the land which owes them so deep a debt, which they have ennobled by their valour and their steadfastness, which will ever honour them but can never adequately repay.

It is a great hour, a wonderful victory which we celebrate to-day – hard won, bitterly fought for, dearly paid. Yet if we are true to ourselves, worthy of an heroic destiny, it should yet be worth, and well worth, the price. It was by a fine inspiration that Mr. Lloyd George, after his brief statement in the House of Commons, called upon the House to adjourn for a service of thanksgiving at St. Margaret's Church, hard by. In so doing he struck at once the note of seriousness, of deep responsibility, of appeal to what is best in the mind and purpose of the nation. It was well and fitly done, and marks, we may believe, the temper in which the Prime Minister desired that the nation should approach, and in which he himself intends to approach, the great task of the resettlement of Europe and the permanent terms of peace. Events within the last few days have moved with breathless rapidity, and the whole conditions of the problem as regards the Central Powers are changed. We have no longer to deal with two great and highly organised military autocracies, but with a whole series of States not merely democratic in form but in which the democratic forces have definitely assumed the upper hand. The process of change was as rapid as it was sudden, and even to the most careful observers unexpected. It has given us an Austria resolved into its elements of diverse nationality, each now claiming complete independence of the rest, and all, including even the German districts, having renounced allegiance to the ancient ruling house; a Hungary freed from its powerful ruling caste and no longer claiming itself to exercise rule over the subject nationalities so long held down by force within the body of the State; a Germany – most wonderful of

all – freed from Prussian dominance no less than from the personal rule of the Imperial house which Prussia had imposed on the other German States, founded as it was on military victory, now ruined and discarded through military defeat. Even the most sceptical, the most wooden-minded, must at length see in this mighty evolution something more than the German cunning, the Teutonic tricks, for which they are ever on the watch and have hitherto never failed to discover. Facts are at length too strong even for such purblind spectators of great and transforming events, and Germany stands disclosed before us not merely as a great democratic State – or rather, we should say, as resolved or resolving itself into a series of such States, destined, we may believe, to form the United States of the Germany of the future – but as one which may easily pass to a position far more extreme. The inborn and acquired sense of discipline so strong in the German people will, we may well hope, save them from the excess, the disorder, and the bitter internal strife of which Russia has shown the world an example, but Bolshevism had its root in the mind of a German doctrinaire, and it remains yet to be seen whether Germany, in her deep humiliation and staggering under the load which is the legacy of four years of war, will resist the contagion. We have yet to see what her returning legions, suffering and bitterly disappointed, may have to say. Certainly if they should go back to find themselves workless and foodless, the result is not likely to be happy for the German State.

It is this possibility, too clearly staring them in the face, which no doubt has prompted the serious protest addressed by the new German Government to the President of the United States against certain conditions of the armistice. It is not the military terms, the surrender of territory to be occupied by the troops of the Allies in pledge or of ships of war or aeroplanes that is resented. Germany has at present no use for munitions of war, and the temporary occupation of some parts of German territory may be a blow to pride but is not a permanent injury. What she dreads is that the means of life may be denied to her, and her complaint is not of the loss of munitions but of the loss of railway material and the obligation to feed the army of occupation. There is, however, some obscurity on the latter point, for the text of the armistice as we have it says not that Germany must feed the army of occupation but that she must pay the cost of their upkeep, which is a different matter. On the other hand, if the surrender of her 5,000 railway engines and 150,000 railway trucks and 5,000 motor-lorries will indeed cripple and perhaps fatally impede German internal transport, it ought, at least temporarily, to be forgone. But we cannot believe that this was the desire or intention of the Allies, or that if such would be the consequence they would insist upon the letter of their bond. On the contrary, there is embedded in the lengthy document of armistice conditions a most salutary and perhaps not sufficiently considered clause in which the Allies recognise the danger which threatens Germany and propose to meet it. 'The Allies and the United States,' it is there said, 'contemplate the provisioning of Germany during the armistice should it be found necessary,' and as a matter of fact Mr. Hoover is, we believe, already on his way from America with that very object in view. Nothing could be better. In the interest of order, in the interest of humanity, we must see to it that the German people, whose fate is now largely in our hands, shall not starve. That is a first duty which we owe to a conquered enemy. Let it be handsomely performed.

Hour the News Came Up to Manchester; A Day of Rejoicing

For once in a way it was a fine morning. A yellow autumn sunshine was coining the wet streets into gold, and at ten o'clock in the morning Manchester was making some attempt to get going in the routine of the week. Then the news came out, finding its way like water through the chinks in the boards where the newspapers were published, gathering volume, and in a few minutes flooding the whole floor of the town. Shortly after ten o'clock the all-night vigil at the newspaper offices was broken by an intimation that the news was coming and the wires were cleared. It arrived between 10.15 and 10.30, and at 10.25 the flags were out over the office of the *Manchester Guardian* and the *Manchester Evening News* and newspaper carts, already flying colours, were carrying the tidings far and wide. The sirens of which Manchester has such a full chorus spread it farther still from Northenden on the south to Prestwich on the north.

The first impulse of Manchester seemed to be to throw open the windows. It was as though people had heard the news and wanted to breathe it. It seemed just what occurs after a long and heavy thunderstorm, when people may be seen opening their windows as though some welcome release had come. Meanwhile the news was spreading from hand to hand; newspapers were common property, and all over the city the flags began to break out, and float idly over the streets, for it was a still morning and the colours drooped. About eleven o'clock, when the war was just ending, the crowd in Albert Square, with a kind of momentary stillness, watched the two flags go up slow and sure at the Town Hall. It was the very dawn of peace over the town; its small hours still unsullied by the noise and gesticulation which broke out later on, just as the dawn of day is untarnished before man wakes up. And it was impossible not to notice how many people were taking the news solemnly, and how frequently between, say, Victoria Station and Albert Square one saw eyelids which were not without a suspicion of tears. But the dawn did not last long. The full day of jubilation was coming up fast. The frequency of blue linen overalls in the streets announced that the munitions works had broken loose, and by one o'clock the streets had formalised themselves into processions, which gathered numbers as a snowball gathers bulk. Those first thoughts which lay so near to tears were swept away in a rush of tramping feet and the choruses of songs.

The City Let Loose

As the afternoon wore on, the stream in the streets thickened. Along all the main roads into the city, along Ashton Old Road, along Stockport Road and Hyde Road, work girls poured in hundreds, gathering as they went flags and the other patriotic symbols which had been so suddenly rushed out from the obscurity of the hawker's warehouse. They clambered on town-going lorries. In Market Street one saw a cart, drawn by the tiniest of donkeys, with seven or eight sturdy girls in overalls, cheering and flag-waving. But it was a crowd that had its discipline – four years of war have not gone for nothing. It formed its orderly platoons and battalions. Anyone with a big enough flag, and the courage frankly to display it, could lead a shouting army. There marched into Albert Square a procession of 300 girls headed by a small man, solemnly holding a flag, and with the bearing of a triumphantly entering conqueror. The girls – for the first crowds were mainly girls – flocked in their workclothes, shawls over heads or in the light trousered overalls of the munition works. They shouted and cheered, breaking up now and then to do a few steps of a wild fox-trot.

Albert Square was the artery from which the people circulated. In the early afternoon it vibrated with the chimes of the Town Hall bells. It was here one saw at their best the eccentricities of the day – the brave spirits who bore gorgeous paper umbrellas or trimmed their hats with red and blue, the American soldiers who had little of the shamefacedness behind which most men sheltered their feelings, and the Belgians who came down to display their boldly coloured national costume.

The infectious gaiety spread from the streets into shops. By early afternoon very many had shut their doors. Works had ceased too, in the Town Hall and in the offices and warehouses, and a holiday was declared at the Grammar School. The military tribunals and the recruiting offices, dread symbol of what we have passed through, closed. The tram service gradually slackened. Women guards and trolley girls left their posts, and cars had to be run back to the depots. By early evening the Manchester tramway system was practically at a standstill, though Salford kept a service running.

Lights Up

When darkness fell Manchester found itself, after so long an age, with unobscured lights, though there had not been time for street lamps to be freed from their 'mufflers.' The feverish energy of the crowd showed no slackening. It was given point and direction by bugle bands and drums. In almost every main street at any time during the evening one could see such a band, with its flag-waving leader and its long straggling tail of men and girls linking arms across the street. They marched quickly and unimpeded through the crowded streets, for there were no tramcars to break their ranks. It was, indeed, a wonderful contrast with the days that are just behind us – streets with lights but no traffic, crowds that moved about as if they had no care and no thought beyond the burning joy of the moment. The noise and shouting, the bugle bands and the processions went on in the main streets until far into the night; long pent up reserves of nervous energy and high spirits took long to work themselves out.

'MISTY SILHOUETTES'

On 29 October 1918, the German High Seas Fleet, commanded by Admiral Franz von Hipper, sailed to the Schillig Roads off Wilhelmshaven. It had last ventured out for the battle of Jutland in 1916, and the plan was for a last onslaught on the Royal Navy's

Grand Fleet, preceded by the shelling of the Thames Estuary. Hipper underestimated his sailors. Mutinies broke out, the ships returned to port, while soviets were being set up along the German coast. Following the armistice the High Seas Fleet, which with the Grand Fleet symbolised the ultimate deterrent in the pre-war world, sailed off on Tuesday 19 November for internment, at Scapa Flow. On Thursday 21 November the two fleets – plus a US navy battleship squadron – met in the Firth of Forth in what historian and Guardian *journalist Dan van der Vat has described as 'the largest assemblage of seapower in the history of the world'.*

25 November
Diary Jottings of the Great Surrender

Edinburgh, Monday Night: The pulse of the city doesn't seem to beat much faster because one of the biggest events in the history of the world is due on Thursday in her waterway. Edinburgh has recovered her old brilliance and loveliness. The unshaded yellow lights march high in procession down the middle of Princes Street. The full moon hangs over the Castle like a festal lantern. All down the black façade of the High Street, as seen from Princes Street, lights shine through unshaded windows. Edinburgh was never more beautiful or more light-hearted than to-night under the radiant sky, white at the zenith, and deepening down to violet over the roofs. Edinburgh has waited for four years for great news from the sea. Now it is coming, but how different from what anyone ever dreamed. She only thinks tonight that it is peace, and waits happily for her boys back from the war.

Wardroom of HMS —, Tuesday Night: Here I am, the one landsman guest of a thousand sailormen on this great battleship of the line. The social difficulties in this situation, of which I thought so much before I came aboard, have vanished already. They have a happy knack in the navy of taking everything for granted, even a lonely writing man. All intercourse is casual, easy, and founded on unerring good feeling. We are sitting round the blazing fire tonight and I find in this isolated community of men an almost touching eagerness to reach out through me to the world of ordinary life. I am in the unwelcome position of an oracle on the political situation. I don't want to be an oracle. I want to learn just what these splendid fellows are thinking at the culminating moment of what some newspapers call 'the ceaseless vigil of the sea.' Well, they are not very articulate about it. The surrender of the German fleet staggers them as it does us all. Not an officer ever dreamt that the German fleet, the menace that was greatest to those who knew most about it, would ever throw up the sponge. But I heard no general reflections. An officer remarked as he flicked his cigarette ask into the fire, 'What price those VC's all round now?' One thing I did hear from everyone – regret that the great naval chief of yesterday was not with the fleet to see the triumph. 'The Huns themselves admit that Jutland did the job for them,' said the engineer commander. 'I wish Jellicoe was here to see it.' Through all this there is chivalry towards a broken foe, and professional fellow-feeling seems to prevent any crowing over the great humiliation. Some of my friends believed, and they argued from the general naval mentality, that even at the last moment the Germans would make a fight of it and go out in a blaze of heroism. Such was the mind of the fleet from the flagship downwards. 'Action stations' on Thursday morning was no idle parade.

The Ship's Kinema, Wednesday Night: I have climbed through a bewildering tangle of stairs and soles into the foremost 6 in. battery, which is used as the ship's kinema theatre. The place is crowded with cheerful sailormen, and the pictures are dim through tobacco smoke. Every big ship has a kinema now, run and, I believe, financed by the crew. Nothing so relieves the intolerable monotony and strain. In a day or two these men will be seeing their own private film shows of the great surrender. To-night they think and speak of it not at all. They roar with delight over Charlie Chaplin and over George Robey grinning through a lifebelt. A super-sentimental American love story is reverently followed. This is their escape from the life of clockwork discipline. If they talk of the surrender at all it is chiefly as it bears on the great question of home leave, the question of questions throughout the fleet. There is no hate here; the German fleet is too impersonal a thing, and to these sailors has only been revealed for a few minutes in four years as a series of dim shapes in the haze.

The Captain's Bridge, Thursday 6am: We are sweeping out to sea to take our place in the mighty cordon that is to surround the surrendered ships and bring them home. It is piercing cold. My first feeling about the biggest naval show in history is that I wish I had stayed in bed. The light over the chart in the navigating bridge seems to concentrate all the life of the ship. There is not a sound. Two hundred and forty battleships, all cleared for action, are ahead of us and behind. I can make out in the haze a few of the masthead lights, and occasionally the broad, winking eye of a signalling lamp. A quarter of a mile in front there is a dim squat shape on the water. When the moon looks out through a rift in the clouds that minatory phantom is seen to be a sister Dreadnought to our own.

The Bridge, 8am: Our company on the bridge has increased. All the chief officers of the ship are gathered round the chart following our course along the pencil line drawn to the point fifty miles at sea where we meet the Germans. The fleet is now ranged in two long lines six miles apart. The other line is invisible in the haze, but ours can be seen marching with heavy tread over leagues of sea. The lighthouse on May Island winks a farewell from the land. The whole scene would be sombre but for the bright array of white ensigns, three apiece on every ship. From this height the ship is silent and unpeopled, but when I go below for a few moments and climb into a gun-turret I find the whole wonderful mechanism is ready for pouring out a broadside within half a minute of a word. We are not taking any risks.

The Bridge, 9.30am: 'German fleet sighted two points off the starboard bow, sir,' comes the quiet message from the masthead. The moment has come. The bridge takes the news calmly. Three miles or so away come a procession of misty silhouettes. They look, in fact, just like the silhouettes in the identification books which the officers round me take out of their pockets.

They look all alike to me, but the officers know. 'There's the *Derfflinger*,' says the torpedo-lieutenant. 'When last I saw her, on Jutland night, she was blazing merrily fore and aft. Heavens, what a come down!' The German battleships push on until the points of the great British pincers can grip them well. The fleet swings round and marches them home in step. It is all too like a peaceful manoeuvre to be believed. The splendour and majesty of the sight spread over the sea is beyond expression. Words can do little, but maybe the great artist who is working at this moment high on the mast of the Admiral's flagship will seize something of it for coming times.

Noon: I am writing below when a middy appears. 'Commander says would you like to come up, as we are going to cheer the Commander-in-Chief.' I go up, and find we are back in sight of land. The sun is bright, the whole fleet has put on a festal air. The flagship has fallen out of the line, and we sweep past her, and many thousands of sailormen cheer the Admiral at the greatest moment of his life. Up to this time there has been no cheering at all, just the ordinary cheerful bustle aboard. The sailors seem to look on the whole thing as all in the day's work. They were sent out to escort some German ships in, and they have done it. I can see the Germans quite plainly, lined along the decks of the *Hindenburg*.

'And I'll bet they're feeling pretty sick, too,' said a sailor. 'Wouldn't be in their shoes for the world. Chucking it without firing a shot. My God, I'd rather drown!'

2pm: I have seen the German fleet safe in its prison. We shepherded it into a bay at Inchkeith. There it lies all huddled together with land behind, a shoal on either side, and its gaolers, the British fleet, holding the gate. I felt pity as I gazed. The contrast was too cruel between the joyous and overwhelming power of our fleet and the humiliation of the giant penned in here, incapable of a blow.

4pm: The bugles are blowing for sunset at the end of a perfect day. We are going, like everyone in the fleet at the same time, to thank Almighty God with quiet hearts for what has been done, and tonight we shall dance in a blaze of light on the quarterdeck.

The Germans had the last word. On 21 June 1919 at Scapa Flow, to the fury of the British, they scuttled the Kaiser's High Seas Fleet.

CHAPTER 7

AFTER

Out of the wreckage of war came fragility: new states that struggled to survive and hopes that struggled to become reality. The British empire, having sorted through the detritus of its German and Ottoman rivals, was larger than ever – and possessed a life expectancy of little more than a generation. 'We saved the world,' said President Wilson in 1918, 'and I do not intend to let those Europeans forget it.' Forget they did, if they had ever noticed; Wilson himself was laid low by a stroke within a year, while the US Senate refused to ratify membership of his dream, the League of Nations.

Out of the wreckage of war came monsters: the Futurism of pre-war artistic salons hinted at Mussolini's fascist Italy, Stalin unleashed his first five-year plan in 1929, and, four years later, the victim of a 1918 British gas attack took power in Germany. Twelve years of Hitler's leadership ensued.

'HINDENBURG STILL AT WORK'

In January 1919 an abortive Spartacist rebellion broke out in Berlin. The great German-Jewish socialist Rosa Luxemburg was critical, but felt bound to support the uprising. The Social Democrat chancellor Ebert deployed the proto-fascist Freikorps to put the Spartacists down. This proved to be a fateful choice. On 15 January 1919, Luxemburg was murdered and thrown into the Landwehr canal. Just as the assassination

of Jean Jaurès had been a straw in the wind four years earlier, so was the
murder of Luxemburg – and, at the same time, that of Karl Liebknecht.

22 January 1919
'White Terror' in Berlin, the Spartacist Leaders Clubbed to Death

The transformation which Berlin has undergone within a few days ought to be reckoned one of the great wonders of political history. What is happening here is something of far greater significance than that which meets the eye on the surface ... there is nothing that will more richly repay the trouble of assiduous scrutiny than the discussions of the Berlin Soldiers' Council at the Conference yesterday ... In this assembly, the large majority of which consists of delegates of the military units which helped to crush the Spartacist rebellion, was lifted a corner of the veil from the proceedings which reinstated Prussian militarism in all its glory and power, and established a reign of 'White' terror in Berlin. It is they ... that invoked and put new life and strength into what seemed the corpse of Prussian militarism, and now, too late, they stand aghast and terrified before their own handiwork.

Brutus Molkenbuhr, who from his office at Berlin Kommandantur lent the Government the most powerful moral and military support in putting down the Spartacists, uttered a crushing indictment of the work that has been accomplished. He said: 'What is happening in Berlin jeopardises the achievements of the revolution. The Government has troops no longer under control. Officers have set up a White Guard and disarmed all the forces of the revolution ... They have been raging like Huns in Berlin, and the destruction they wantonly worked is worse even than anything the German armies performed in Belgium or France. Nobody can accept responsibility for the armed troops who now terrorise Berlin.'

Sergeant Machols, a delegate of the Reinhardt Regiment, which has been established without a shadow of doubt today is responsible for the murder of Karl Liebknecht, and of Rosa Luxembourg ... said: 'We accept the name of White Guard as a title of honour. We are fully determined not to allow arms to be wrested from our hands.' And, letting a most particular cat out of the bag, this precious sergeant continued: 'We have no Soldiers' Council in our regiment; we have only a committee. We call it a committee because Hindenburg wishes to have committees. (Tremendous uproar.) We are delighted to see Hindenburg still at work in defiance of all open and secret opposition.'

'THREE FRIENDLESS MEN'

On Saturday 28 June 1919, five years after the assassination of Franz Ferdinand, the peace treaty between the allies and the new German Republic was signed. Two days later, the Manchester Guardian *editorialised on the subject.*

30 June 1919
The Signing of Peace

Peace with Germany was signed at a few minutes past three on Saturday, in the great Hall of Mirrors at Versailles ... It is the end of strife; it is the end of destruction; it is the beginning of the possibility of decent human intercourse among the nations, the dawn of new hopes, the window through which light begins to shine on a troubled world. Peace in the bare sense of cessation of war and of preparation and readiness for was had become the prime necessity ... It was necessary that this cause of ruin and unrest should cease, that life should at least begin to revert to its normal channels, that intercourse should be resumed, that information should no longer be perverted and hindered, that the springs of mistrust and of hate should be given a chance to dry up and those of charity to find their course. For Europe it was necessary, if complete ruin were not to overtake its industry and the existing organisation of society to be violently assailed and perhaps destroyed, that the restraints on commerce and the external and internal menace to stability should be removed. This at least the signing of the peace should do. For ourselves … it will hasten and facilitate the disbanding of our armies; it will give confidence to enterprise; it will release our statesmen from at least the most urgent of their preoccupations, and clear the way for the work of resettlement and reform at home. […]

Undoubtedly the peace is not the peace which President Wilson had hoped for and designed. Neither, so far as we are able to judge, is it the peace which Mr. Lloyd George in his heart would have desired or which, if free to take his own course, he would have given us. How it comes about that the mighty forces represented by these two men have suffered such a defeat is one of the mysteries of that secret diplomacy which both have at once accepted and abjured. They may be unwilling to recognise or admit the extent of their frustration, but history and events will sufficiently record it … What is wrong in the terms of the treaty must, by degrees and as opportunity offers, be set right. Not for ever will the militarists rule us who have snatched a hasty and unmerited electoral victory from the immense national effort of the war, and as they disappear so will a new spirit direct our policy. The same thing is likely to take place in the other great European nations, and the democratic forces which the necessities of war have restrained are bound to assert themselves. Other treaties remain to be concluded. But the war was always felt to be first and foremost a war with Germany. Now that peace with Germany has been concluded there is room for a more generous handling of the rest. The peace has established, amid many fruits of unwisdom, one great monument of good, and in the League of Nations, derided and decried though it may be, we have the possibility at least of the foundation of the world-peace which the other terms of the treaty have gone so far to deny. That too will depend for life and efficacy not on the written terms of the Covenant, which leave a good deal to be desired, but on the spirit which animates the peoples. It all comes back, as was indeed inevitable, to that, since the only vital and transforming things in the world are the spiritual things. One condition of advance is intercourse and knowledge, both with deadly effect denied us through the whole course of the war, but at least, we may hope, about to be released. Another is the international spirit. At present this is strong and vital mainly in the ranks of Labour in all the countries, largely no doubt because it is Labour which everywhere is the first to suffer and to pay. But the spirit grows. In some countries, as in Russia and now in Hungary, it threatens even to destroy the national spirit and to substitute for the war of arms between nations a universal class war. That is a disaster from which Europe can escape only by showing that the militant nationalism which has proved the destruction of Germany has not taken refuge among the rulers or peoples of other great States. This revival in a new form of the spirit of militarism is the real menace to all our hopes. With this enemy there must be no armistice and no peace.

Discomfort and a Drab Outlook

Versailles, Saturday 11.10pm: A day of heavy clouds and pale sunshine. A stream of English motors along the dusty roads lined with rather impassive sightseers. A blaze of flags of all nations in the grey streets of Versailles. An uncomfortable hour in a crowded hall. And at last peace; not a very perfect peace maybe, but peace. The great cobbled courtyard of the Palace was lined by troops, horse and foot, in their blue uniforms and steel helmets, presenting arms as car after car drove in with its load of Ministers, officials, and State guests. At various entrances in the gardens and in the streets were little squads of the Republican Guard, picturesque enough in their uniforms of fifty years ago.

The public that was allowed into the precincts of the Chateau was a very select one – the clergy, nobility and gentry, one might say, with their wives and daughters. Long before the appointed hour the Galeries des Glaces began to fill. Guests and journalists jostled for their places, photographers edged into position in their niches, whilst Conference officials, Plenipotentiaries and secretaries conversed together in the middle of the hall within a wall of gorgeously-dressed Guardsmen with drawn swords.

The Vast Hall Crowded

The Galerie de Glaces is a vast and splendid room, nearly eighty yards long and eleven yards across, ornate with pictures of Louis XIV, and gilded decorations, with seventeen huge windows giving on to the gardens, and as many huge mirrors on the other side. But for all its size it was none too large for the thousand or so persons it held this afternoon. One cannot honestly congratulate the organisers of the ceremony on the seating of the guests and press. It was, in fact, practically impossible to catch more than glimpses of what was going on.

In the centre a dais about six inches high had been erected, and here sat the Plenipotentiaries. The press and visitors were on rows of packed benches at either end. They were screened by tables immediately in front, which were occupied by numberless secretaries. Their backs were an interesting sight. If there was a little disorder on these lower benches it was due to the natural efforts of those wanted to see but unfortunately had not been gifted by providence with the faculty of looking through two or three rows of human bodies.

Entry of the Germans

Soon after three, all were seated except the German delegates. In a moment these appeared and took their places at the side of the horseshoe table to M. Clemenceau's left. M. Clemenceau, as president, then rose and briefly stated the purpose of the assembly. 'The signatures will be affixed now. They signify a solemn undertaking to abide loyally and faithfully by the conditions of peace.' He invited the German delegates to sign first.

Captain Mantoux, the official interpreter, translated the speech into German, and immediately the three German Plenipotentiaries Herren Müller, Bell and Von Haniel walked to the tables where the treaty and the protocol lay and signed their names. They looked grave and mournful, and no doubt they felt so.

Without any delay there followed a series of little processions beginning with the Great Powers in alphabetical order. First came the Americans, led by President Wilson; then the British, by Mr. Lloyd George, Mr. Bonar Law, Mr. Balfour, Lord Milner and Mr. Barnes; then the British Dominion representatives; then Italy and Japan. Afterwards the rest of the belligerent Powers in quick succession.

But the Chinese were absent. They had pressed for the right to sign with the reservation that the question of Shantung [a dispute with Japan about the sovereignty of the Shandong province] should be left open. This demand was renewed for the last time this morning, but the Council of Four would not accede to it, with the result that the Chinese Delegation decided not to go to Versailles.

The Fountains Again

At a quarter to four there was the sound of guns and another softer sound in the gardens below – the play of the fountains, which have been silent for nearly five years. Suddenly M. Clemenceau rose again and announced that all was finished, and without more ado the whole concourse moved out. It had not been an impressive ceremony. There was nothing dramatic in it, no 'incidents,' no oratory. There was not even, if one must tell the truth, any remarkable solemnity. As a picture it was sadly lacking in colour, the uniforms of General Castelnau and the Maharajah of Bikanir and the few other soldiers who were there were lost in the great sea of black frockcoats. A black frockcoat is a dreadful thing. One would have liked in that room a little more of the blue and the khaki covering the common men who won the war.

As the meeting broke up the German delegates disappeared quietly, going back to their hotel, I suppose, three friendless men. The rest made for the gardens, where a crowd, the same select crowd, was waiting for the heroes of the hour. M. Clemenceau, President Wilson and Mr. Lloyd George were soon in the hands of a large band of enthusiasts of both sexes and all ages, who hustled them round the terrace amid congratulations and cheers. Then more guns and a rush to see the great men get into cars and drive through Versailles, and so home to Paris.

For France, at any rate, it has been a proud day, which none will be ungenerous enough to grudge her. And if we have not yet got real democracy, we have at least seen this afternoon something more democratic than Bismarck's Empire that was proclaimed here forty-eight years ago.

'THE EXCITED AND MUDDLE-BRAINED BOHEMIAN'

In the east of Europe a new state had been born out of the war whose existence changed everything about Europe – and the world. Without the single-mindedness and driving force of Vladimir Lenin, the early Soviet Union would not have emerged in the form that it did. However, between March 1922 and May 1923 the Soviet leader suffered three debilitating strokes. The last stroke rendered him speechless, and he died on 21 January 1924. Two years before Lenin's death, in summer 1922, Arthur Ransome, sometime Manchester Guardian *correspondent in Moscow (and MI6 agent) – and future author of 'brat books' such as* Swallows and Amazons *– assessed who would replace him.*

13 June 1922
The Men Who Will Control Russia

It is not yet certain that Rykov will actually succeed Lenin. It is possible that, as Vice President, his elevation was merely mechanical and temporary. On the other hand, nearly two years ago I was told by one who had good opportunities of knowing, that Rykov would be Lenin's successor. The other men who are, so to speak, near the Presidential chair are Bucharin, Stalin, Krestinsky and Kamenev … I am not sure of Krestinsky's nationality and have small personal knowledge of him, and none of Stalin.

In fact, by the mid-1920s it was Stalin who was effectively in power. He had Bukharin, Kamenev, Krestinsky and Rykov executed in 1938, following the staged Moscow trials that eliminated the rest of the Bolshevik central committee.

Stalin was first mentioned in the Manchester Guardian *on 23 November 1917. Another progeny of the first world war was profiled five years later, eight months to the day before his abortive 'beer hall' putsch in Munich.*

8 February 1923
The German Mussolini

The dreaded gathering of National Socialists in Munch has come and gone without 'incidents' of any kind. This was a triumph for Hitler, the National Socialist leader – a success scored despite the fact that the town was placed under martial law, and despite the fevered expectations of a contingent of young hotheads, whom Hitler managed to keep in check. Hitler is not a man of action. The sweeping, expressive gesture is his at will, but not the deed. Like all demagogues, the intoxication of his own oratory may incite him to action, but at the eleventh hour he is likely to draw back. Hitler, fanatic preacher of ruthlessness, has been carried along by the current of events, swept onward by the wave of reaction. [...]

'The world's salvation depends on the destruction of the Jews.' The war-cry is taken up by the multitude: a leader presents himself, Adolf Hitler, the German Mussolini. This comparison is not entirely fair to the Italian leader. Mussolini is a reformed Socialist, primed with the doctrines of his former party, whereas Hitler, the excited and muddle-brained Bohemian, is devoid of solid convictions and incapable of a definite line of action. A certain similarity between Mussolini and Hitler, however, cannot be denied. Both are addicted to opera effects attuned to the mentality of their different countries. Mussolini, black-shirted and toying with a red carnation ... would appear disarmingly comic under a canopy less bright than the Italian sky and amongst a people less emotional than the Italians. Hitler's effects are obtained by different means. A decorative painter by trade, he has retained his talent for decorative display. The placards he has drawn are very effective, the staging always well chosen, and there is yet another advantage his early life has given him. Viennese by birth, surrounded by Bavarians heavy of speech and movement, his vivacious personality and ready dialectic, the fruit of many a Vienna coffee-house discussion, carry double weight.

'WORDS ARE MADE TO SERVE TRUTH'

At the end of January 1929, Erich Maria Remarque's All Quiet on the Western Front *was published in Germany. A year later it was an Oscar-winning Hollywood movie.*

17 April 1929
Visiting Trenches

Not until this year, in sudden and sombre efflorescence, has the written word communicated the direct, immediate experience of the war itself. *All Quiet on the Western Front* is surely the greatest of all war books. The author, Erich Maria Remarque, is otherwise quite unknown. Perhaps it was necessary for someone innocent of fine writing, of style, of the 'mot juste,' to convey this immediacy of experience in trenches, dug-outs, No Man's Land and field hospitals. Words are made to serve truth, not truth words. And yet the book is not formless, but plastic and architectural. What makes it all the more impressive is the simplicity, the integrity and the strength of character that are its foundation. There is horror and suffering greater than Poe or Dostoievski felt or imagined. Yet there is no morbidity, no sentiment, no hysteria. Perhaps no one who went through the war came out of it completely sane, but Remarque lost very little of his sanity and can look back into that inferno with unevasive eyes. And yet, for all the gloom and tragic horror, there is humour, good-fellowship, and delicious vengeance on brutal superiors in his book. But beneath it all is the sense of ultimate pity and the complete, incurable pessimism of those who have either been proletarians or common soldiers. [...]

Remarque says that he and his fellow-soldiers fought to avert the same doom that menaced both themselves and the Frenchmen and Englishmen in the opposite trenches. Now that international disarmament is a blind alley, now that the nations are preparing for war as they were before 1914, it would be well if all who were not in the Great War would read these books, and even those who were should read them so as to keep their hatred alive. These books are not partisan, they are not pacifist propaganda, they are not specifically German. They are the books of common soldiers and as true of one side as of the other. They show that the Great War was a fratricidal war. Perhaps they will help a little to deepen the determination that there shall not be another.

On 10 May 1933, All Quiet on the Western Front *was part of that selection of world literature consumed by the fire of Nazi book burnings.*

BIBLIOGRAPHY

Barnet, Corelli, *The Lords of War* (The Praetorian Press, 2012)

Carolan, Victoria, *WW1 at Sea* (Pocket Essentials, 2007)

Fountain, Nigel, *Lost Empires* (Cassell Illustrated, 2005)

Goldman, Lawrence, *The Life of RH Tawney* (Bloomsbury Academic, 2013)

Hammond, JL and Bell, G, *CP Scott of the* Manchester Guardian (G Bell and Sons, 1934)

Howard, Michael, *The First World War* (OUP, 2002)

Lindley-French, Julian and Boyer, Yves, *The Oxford Handbook of War* (OUP, 2012)

Nichols, HD and Hammond, JL, *CP Scott 1846–1932: The Making of the* Manchester Guardian (Frederick Muller, 1946)

Oxford Dictionary of National Biography (OUP, 2004)

Paice, Edward, *Tip & Run: The Untold Tragedy of the Great War in Africa* (Weidenfeld & Nicholson, 2007)

Philips-Price, M, *My Three Revolutions* (Allen & Unwin, 1969)

Rowbotham, Sheila, *A Century of Women; The History of Women in Britain & the United States* (Viking, 1997)

Sheffield, Gary and Gray, Peter (Eds), *Changing War* (Bloomsbury, 2013)

Stevenson, David, *With Our Backs to the Wall* (Allen Lane, 2011)

Strachan, Hew, *The First World War* (Simon & Schuster UK, 2003)

Taylor, AJP, *English History 1914–1945* (OUP, 1965)

Taylor, AJP, *Essays in English History* (Pelican Books, 1976)

Taylor, AJP, *The First World War* (Hamish Hamilton, 1963)

van der Vat, Dan, *The Grand Scuttle* (Hodder and Stoughton, 1982)

Weintraub, Stanley, *Stillness Heard Around the World* (Allen & Unwin, 1986)

Wilson, Trevor (Ed), *The Political Diaries of CP Scott 1911–1928* (Collins, 1970)

ACKNOWLEDGEMENTS

Compiling *When the Lamps Went Out* was a privilege. It also, vicariously, linked me to those writers, sub-editors and printers on the *Manchester Guardian*, and elsewhere, who put together good, great and superb journalism in the midst of a world of war. I have edited their words but not, I hope, distorted them. There are some anachronisms – and the 'England' of 1914 often stood in not just for Great Britain, but for all the pink parts of the globe.

My thanks to Stephanie Cross, Helen Kelleher and Amy Treppass for deciphering, and typing, their way out of a blotched, blurred and smudged past; to Richard Nelsson and the ever-cooperative Guardian Information Department; to Lisa Foreman for her picture research; to Lindsay Davies for her enthusiasm, editing and advice; to Laura Hassan of Guardian Faber for her encouragement, and to my partner, Monica Henriquez for her support – and forebearance. *When the Lamps Went Out* was researched and written largely at the London Library, a place where civilisation has flourished through war, boom and slump.

The promise of many in that wartime generation was dashed. I dedicate this book to some of my friends, around 30 or under, who, a century on and free to explore their talent and creativity have done just that: Anny Ash, youth worker; Fred Fordham, artist; Leo Fordham, musician; Lex Karlin, community worker; Anna Karlin, designer and art director; Julia King, architect; and Hannah Mander, theatre production manager.

PLATE SECTION CREDITS

Page 1, *top* Museum of London/Heritage Images/Getty Images; *bottom* Bettmann/Corbis. Page 2, *top* Central Press/Getty Images; *bottom across both pages* Hulton-Deutsch Collection/Corbis. Page 3, *top* Topical Press Agency/Getty Images; *middle* Roger Viollet/AFP. Page 4, *top* Italian Army/National Geographic Society/Corbis; *bottom* Rex Features. Page 5, *top* Bettmann/Corbis; *bottom* Hulton Archive/Getty Images. Page 6, *top and middle* Corbis; *bottom* Daily Herald Archive/SSPL/Getty Images. Page 7, *top* Hulton Archive/Getty Images; *middle* Universal History Archive/Un/Rex; *bottom* Corbis. Page 8, *top* Time Life Pictures/Getty Images; *bottom* Hulton-Deutsch Collection/Corbis.

INDEX